MW01202159

Mighty GIANTS

A healthy American chestnut tree in Jackson County, Tennessee, spring 2007. Pollen from this tree has been used in The American Chestnut Foundation's breeding program. (Photo by Joe Schibig.)

Mighty GIANTS

AN AMERICAN CHESTNUT ANTHOLOGY

With a Foreword by Bill McKibben

Chris Bolgiano, Editor

Glenn Novak, Contributing Editor

THE AMERICAN CHESTNUT FOUNDATION

Richard S. Will, Chairman
Marshal T. Case, President

IMAGES FROM THE PAST

Bennington, Vermont

Front cover: *Gathering Chestnuts* by J. W. Lauderbach, from the *Art Journal* of 1878

All pictures not specifically credited provided by The American Chestnut Foundation and numerous generous individuals. Uncredited text and captions by the editors.

ISBN 1-884592-49X 978-1-884592-49-2 hardcover
ISBN 1-884592-48-1 978-1-884592-48-5 paperback

Mighty giants : an American chestnut anthology / with a foreword by Bill McKibben;
Chris Bolgiano, editor. — 1st ed.

p. cm.

Includes bibliographical references and index.
ISBN 978-1-884592-49-2 (hardcover) — ISBN 978-1-884592-48-5 (pbk.)
1. American chestnut. I. Bolgiano, Chris. II. American Chestnut Foundation.
QK495.F14M535 2008
583'.46—dc22

2007035080

Published by The American Chestnut Foundation
PO Box 4044, Bennington, VT 05201
www.acf.org

and

Images from the Past, Inc.
PO Box 137, Bennington VT 05201
Tordis Ilg Isselhardt, Publisher
www.imagesfromthepast.com

Printed in Canada

Indexing by Helen Passey
Design and Production: Toelke Associates, Chatham, NY
Printer: RAAND Print Specialties, Menands, NY

Dedicated to Glenn C. Price,
Number One Chestnut Benefactor

The sweetness of all things are promises
That sing our souls a little further on
Toward that which may be found in what is lost,
Which may come back again of what is gone.

Trumbull Stickney, from "Chestnuts in November"

CONTENTS

Foreword

I spend most of my life dealing with catastrophes yet to come—especially with the onrushing specter of global warming. Hence there's something oddly comforting about contemplating a tragedy past, and in seeing how, slowly but surely, people have done the work to start recovering from that disaster. The story of the chestnut is a story of biology and of trade and of genetics, but at this point it's mostly a story of human love and human will, two commodities we need more than any other.

I've spent most of my life in the upland Adirondacks of New York, too high and too cold to be part of the chestnut's normal range. I'd always heard of the trees whose blossoms made the eastern forest snowy in the spring, but I'd never paid that much attention. Not until one day when I was in the Smoky Mountains National Park, working on a story about the possible reintroduction of the red wolf. I was hiking with a wildlife biologist through one of those dense rhododendron-tangled coves when I started noticing giant trunks on the ground around me. "What are those?" I asked her.

"Oh, those are the chestnuts," she said. Still lying there, rotting only slowly, stumps still sending up their doomed sprouts.

I was thunderstruck. Something that had seemed to me out of quite ancient history was actually there to be seen, there to be touched. I looked around the glade and tried to recalibrate it, imagine the skinny stems of other species replaced with a few of these obviously mammoth trees. For me it was as unsettling as the first time I went to Alaska, and saw the incredible productiveness and diversity of the forests and the rivers and the estuaries and then realized: this is what all of America once looked like. Chesapeake Bay was once this intact and fecund, and the mouth of the Hudson once swam with this much life.

To tally our losses on this continent would take too long and cut too deep. Better to tally what we're trying to bring back. Better to stand on the ridgeline above the Hayden Valley in Yellowstone and stare down with binoculars at the flourishing wolf packs, reintroduced in the 1990s. Better to wander with the biologists who have managed to fledge eagle chicks in every state in the union. And better still to read about the noble band who has carefully nurtured the dream of a resurgent chestnut forest, and done the endlessly patient work to make it happen.

This fine book provides the whole story: the glory of the chestnut, its swift and savage demise, and then the slow process, begun almost immediately, to nurture it back. Why do humans do these things? What in our nature allows us to work at tasks that return no material reward, and whose glory will fully shine, if at all, only in some future we may not witness? That's the subtext here: this movement is about the biology of chestnuts but also about the psychology of people, about the nobility of this forest giant but also about the nobility of the people who have devoted themselves to its recovery.

That's a kind of nobility we may need a lot of in the future. If the scientists are right, we're in for a new round of devastation on this continent and on this planet as temperatures start to soar. But people are beginning to rally, finally, to slow that crisis down, and to build the kind of human communities that may be able to adapt to that which we cannot prevent. As we do that work, the story of the chestnut echoes like a fable—a fable about carelessness, and about the hard work and hard love needed to make up for that carelessness. A fable we need to start telling more and more, for the hope it gives and the lesson it provides.

I hope I live long enough to see the chestnut spreading white across the eastern forest. But I'm glad I've already lived long enough to see the people dreaming that dream. ∾

Bill McKibben

Acknowledgments

Like a big old tree, this book has deep roots. The American Chestnut Foundation, established in 1983, grew out of the longing, regret, and determination that followed what many scientists consider to be the worst ecological catastrophe in American history. There are multitudes of people past and present dedicated to restoring the American chestnut tree. Their faith has been inspirational.

Most if not all the staff of TACF worked on various aspects of the book, including but not limited to Lou Bedor, Meghan Jordan, Jeanne Coleman, Daphne Van Schaick, Wendy Callaert, and Rachel Maher. I'm proud to say I tried the patience even of Paul Sisco, TACF's meticulous and indefatigable historian-scientist, in pursuing arcane chestnutiana. Sara Fitzsimmons's maps, Leila Pinchot's photographs, and Fred Hebard's quiet expertise helped me greatly. TACF directors and members Bill MacDonald, Hill Craddock, Fred Paillet, Doug Gillis, Leif Meadows, and Joe Schibig all contributed essential information, exquisite illustrations, or both. Members of various state chapters graciously responded to my requests for data. Marshal Case and Ray Hornback invited me to do this book, and by the time they recovered their senses, it was too late: I had accepted.

Each of the living contributors to the book's content has been generous beyond measure, and since the dead ones are mostly out of copyright, they have been, too. A multitude of librarians, archivists, copy editors, and permissions managers kindly facilitated the completion of the book, including librarians at Southern Vermont College, the Forest History Society, Lisa Pearson at Harvard University's Arnold Arboretum, and Conni the mildly amusing archivist at Concord Free Public Library.

A special debt of gratitude is owed to TACF member and longtime contributor Bill Lord, who has been unstinting in his assistance and in sharing his expertise on all things having to do with the American chestnut. Without his generous contributions of both time and knowledge, this anthology would have been a much lesser book.

Hope is the thing with burs, I mantraed to myself during dim hours in front of a computer. Internet data bases provided chestnut stories that otherwise would be buried in the duff of history. Who knew that an occupational hazard for young men in the chestnut era was falling out of the tree while chestnutting? Enough such stories retrieved from digital archives revealed a pattern. As always, my library colleagues at James Madison University guided my connections to the outside world from my mountain retreat. The Images from the Past team, publisher Tordis Ilg Isselhardt, project editor Glenn Novak, and designer Ron Toelke, courageously took on the task of unifying a many-branched project.

Most of all, I owe a debt to this great tree. I thought I knew something about American chestnuts, and about their fate and potential future. I know now the humbling fact that what I don't know would fill a book. And *that* is truly an old chestnut.

Chris Bolgiano, June 2007

Introduction

By Marshal T. Case

Marshal T. Case is president of The American Chestnut Foundation.

This anthology is being published as part of The American Chestnut Foundation's twenty-fifth anniversary celebration. The American chestnut tree, on the brink of extinction, now has a chance to be brought back to eastern forests because of the heroic work of a widespread network of scientists and individuals. Just within the past ten years, a state chapter network alone has grown from four to fifteen incorporated organizations, all under daily guidance of TACF.

Historically, the American chestnut was "king of the forest," the dominant hardwood tree in our eastern forests. Arrival of the lethal fungus from Asia during the late 1800s destroyed an estimated four billion trees in a mere fifty years. The actions of state blight commissions and other state and federal agencies, along with valiant private efforts, could not stop chestnut blight from killing everything in its path, from Maine to Georgia and west to the Ohio River Valley.

The collapse of the trees had a domino effect on wildlife that had been sustained by abundant annual nut crops. Appalachian communities were virtually eliminated as the disappearance of the "cradle-to-grave tree" left mountain people without the abundant game they depended on, without the food they fed to domestic animals for daily requirements, and without the holiday cash crop of nuts they exchanged for shoes and other basic requirements. They were faced with vanishing supplies of a wood they relied on not only for shelter and countless other uses, but also for local industry. Large tracts of mature forest died seemingly overnight, and watersheds were compromised as the vast root systems of these often giant trees were for the most part eliminated. The cooling effect for forests was also greatly diminished by the loss of such a vast network of canopy.

Yet the potential survives in the remaining root systems of these former giant trees, at least for the moment. Over the original range of American chestnut, the deadly fungus that is still harbored in the forests cannot attack the root systems. It attacks the shoots—the new life from old, growing from underneath the forest floor. Almost always, the fungus kills new life before the trees flower. Reforestation cannot occur.

Could these trees come back on their own, over a long period of time? Perhaps. But look at the challenges with forest health today: Our global economy is introducing new invasive species, capable of doing vast damage; our fuel-use habits continue to contribute to an imbalance in nature, as pH of soils change. Twenty years ago, the change appeared subtle. Now we know that the pressures on forest health are alarming. The American chestnut holds great hope for mitigating this ominous trend.

The American Chestnut Foundation is coming to the rescue, with a lot of networking and hard work on the part of many dedicated scientists, conservationists, and lay people, young and old, poor and wealthy, and everything in between. Social status doesn't matter. What matters is that a fast-growing network of caring people is working very hard to do everything possible to restore what was lost. And with the new pressures on forest health arising from our global economy, it is time to capture the moment and bring this tree from the brink of extinction and introduce it back into the ecosystem from which it was lost.

Hope is in the blight-tolerant tree that The American Chestnut Foundation is developing, through a classic plant-breeding program initiated by famed corn breeder and geneticist Dr. Charles Burnham of Minnesota. It takes time, and there are many bumps in the road, but strong gains have been made. A network of partners will make the difference, beginning with our research farms in Virginia and a fast-growing alliance of "backyard" orchards and plantation-type plantings with our extensive state chapter network. Add to that growing partnerships with colleges and universities, the Department of the Interior Office of Surface Mining (with a focus on reforestation of Appalachian coalfields), the USDA Forest Service, and the National Wild Turkey Federation, with their extensive programs and expert field biologists. The list of participants is impressive.

Abraham Lincoln split rails from chestnut. George Washington and Thomas Jefferson worked with plantings of American chestnut at Mount Vernon and Monticello. TACF now has plantings at both these historic places. President Franklin Roosevelt also had a special interest in American chestnuts. A *New York Times* article from 1938 was headlined, "Roosevelt Discovers Chestnut Saplings, First in His Forest Tract Since Blight."

> Hyde Park, N.Y., Oct. 3 —A chance discovery by President Roosevelt on his Dutchess Hill forestation project today may mean that the all but extinct chestnut tree, devastated by a mysterious blight several years ago, may be coming back. Mr. Roosevelt was inspecting new growth with Nelson C. Brown, head of the School of Forestry of Syracuse University, when he came across several saplings which he identified as chestnuts. He called to Mr. Brown, who made a closer examination and found that the President was correct. Unable to conceal his astonishment, Mr. Brown congratulated the Chief Executive on his find.

Although the article's optimism may have been premature, the interest of America's chief executives in the fate of the tree has become a welcome source of support for TACF. The foundation's honorary (and active) director, President Jimmy Carter, planted trees at the Carter Center in Atlanta, Georgia, in August 2005, and on Arbor Day 2005 President George W. Bush planted an American chestnut on the north lawn of the White House. Every president, from Washington to Bush, has planted a favorite tree, and now a blight-tolerant American chestnut is at the White House.

President Washington planted trees, including American chestnut, because he was an active man with many interests. Even in the eighteenth century, long before the fungus that eliminated some four billion trees from the eastern forests, the American chestnut was greatly valued. Besides providing valuable nut crops and timber, the trees were magnificent to look at and graced many public places, including Philadelphia's Fairmount Park, as shown on the cover of this book. In recent years, TACF's network has grown to the point where it has taken root at the White House. A tree for the future and health of the nation. Good for the economy, good for wildlife and people—and even great potential for carbon sequestration that will help cleanse the air and play a part in reversing some of the harm done to nature.

It is a matter of time. Bringing back the chestnut will continue to take vision, patience, and hard work. Careful, methodical science. Lots of people working together. And a bit of luck.

Making the restoration a success will require participation of thousands, if not tens of thousands, of people, generations working together to achieve something that has not been done before. In a world of uncertainty, the restoration of the American chestnut offers great hope—hope built on sound science and dedicated individuals. From tree "farmers" to presidents, the return of the chestnut to our land is an American dream that is close to becoming reality.

This anthology offers a wide view of the American chestnut, of its nature and history, as well as current happenings in the mission of restoration, up to the long-term outlook. The beauty of the essays and accompanying recollections, photographs, poems, and other fascinating material is that they illustrate both the real and symbolic significance of a tree that was once dominant and is now waiting for the opportunity to return. This tree played no favorites. It was available to all who chose to make use of its many remarkable qualities. This anthology plays no favorites, and it invites its readers and all who hear of American chestnut restoration efforts to join that effort and share the wonder of a tree that was—and with our help will again be—a keystone species that will help shape the future.

Philadelphia's Fairmount Park was the scene for Gathering Chestnuts, *by J. W. Lauderbach. This engraving appeared in the* Art Journal *of 1878.*

MIGHTY GIANTS

This majestic and useful tree.

—Jimmy Carter

The morning after the first real hard frost. . . . It makes me think of long ago when we used to put on a warm coat, grab a splint basket and, before breakfast, run up under the three big old chestnut trees in the pasture to get the chestnuts ahead of the chipmunks and red squirrels—there were no gray ones. It would be very, very still, the sky a clear blue, and the chestnuts all around would go plop, plop, plop down onto the fallen leaves, and suddenly the blue jays would screech to split the silence.

Ruby Hemenway of Leverett and Montague, Massachusetts. Hemenway, who lived to over 100 and was a prolific newspaper columnist, died in 1987.

My brother Charlie and I have vivid memories of the large American chestnut snag which was over three feet in diameter and ten feet tall, and stood as a gray-white monument on our family farm's boundary line with our uncle Pete's place in Mason County, Kentucky. While both my dad and uncle were very tidy farmers, throughout the 1930s and well into World War II they deliberately allowed that large pronounced tree trunk to stand. Even more mysterious to us as youths was that it was surrounded by the littered ashen gray branches and tree parts which simply didn't rot. As kids we would use these to build forts and even hurl some at each other. We were too young to comprehend what species "The Big Tree" was, only that our grieving relatives never cleaned up the littered pieces of wood, which seemed to never decay. Once we brought a piece into the tobacco-stripping room and Daddy spoke of the tree with reverence, as though it was a family heirloom. No other tree received such respect, and he was a man who liked trees and carved wood as an avocation.

Albert J. Fritsch, Mount Vernon, Kentucky, 2002

No other tree received such respect.

A lone chestnut snag stands in Big Meadows in Shenandoah National Park, Virginia. (Photo courtesy of Shenandoah National Park Archives.)

Chestnuts in My Life

By Jimmy Carter

Jimmy Carter, the thirty-ninth president of the United States (1976–80), is an honorary director of The American Chestnut Foundation.

I first heard of The American Chestnut Foundation several years after it was established in 1983. Chestnuts were dear to me in my youth, and as an adult I had long mourned the loss of this majestic and useful tree. Plains, Georgia, where I grew up, was at the southern limit of native chestnut range, and the three trees that existed on our farm were something of a curiosity. From my earliest recollections, chestnuts have embodied some of the most profound lessons that nature—including human nature—can offer.

Plains (its original name was "Plains of Dura," as in Daniel 3:1 in the Bible, where King Nebuchadnezzar built a great image of gold) is set on land as level as any you will ever see. As the local people have always said, "When it rains, the water don't know which way to run." The town was laid out in the middle of a large pecan orchard, and almost every house has a few trees still in the yard. During my boyhood, when the nuts became mature in November, people eagerly gathered enough to pay their taxes.

From these pecans, to the rare Brazil nuts we sometimes received for Christmas, to the peanuts (admittedly a legume instead of a real nut) that constituted one of the main crops on our farm, nuts of both domestic and wild species were an important feature of my early life. Chestnuts remain of enduring interest because they were the most valuable of all the eastern hardwood trees for both people and wildlife, and their tragic demise continues to reverberate. Many experts have called the loss of the chestnut tree, with its unmatched combination of beauty and bounty, the greatest disaster ever to befall forests in the eastern United States.

I joined TACF because, after reviewing the proceedings of a 1994 technical meeting on breeding blight-resistant chestnut trees, I became convinced that this group had a serious chance of defeating the imported fungus that killed some four billion trees by about 1950. The possibility of restoring chestnuts to the eastern woods is a very powerful and motivating prospect. When I was invited to become a TACF honorary director, I seized that opportunity to plant seedlings from some of the first generations of cross-bred chestnut trees on my farm near Plains, and more recently in a public demonstration grove at the Carter Center in Atlanta. I know that many of these trees will die, but some will show enough blight resistance to contribute further to TACF's genetic strategy for healing a most grievous wound that we humans have inflicted on nature.

Like music and art, love of nature is a common language that can transcend political or social boundaries. One of Rosalynn's and my most important priorities is to

Like music and art, love of nature is a common language that can transcend political or social boundaries.

Jimmy Carter and his younger sister Gloria. (Courtesy of Jimmy Carter Library.)

spend more and more time in interesting and beautiful natural places—places that are quiet, simple, and secluded. When I look at how fragile and lovely the natural world is, I can understand the feeling of Henry David Thoreau: "The earth was the most glorious instrument, and I was audience to its strains."

I was born in 1924 and grew up on an isolated farm of 350 acres that was primitive by modern standards. My most persistent impression as a farm boy was of the earth. There was a closeness, almost an immersion, in the sand, loam, and red clay that seemed natural, and constant. The soil caressed my bare feet, and the dust was always boiling up from the dirt road that passed fifty feet from our front door, so that inside our clapboard house the red clay particles, ranging in size from face powder to grits, were ever present, particularly in the summertime, when the wooden doors were kept open and the screen stopped only the trash and some of the less adventurous flies.

I've often wondered why we were so infatuated with the land, and I think there is a strong tie to the Civil War, or, as we called it, the War Between the States. Although I was born more than half a century after the war was over, it was a living reality in my life. I grew up in one of those families whose people could not forget that we had been conquered, while most of our neighbors were black people whose grandparents had been liberated in the same conflict.

The legacy of loss in the War reinforced a deep-seated belief that only the land had any real and lasting value. Folks never considered that the real tragedy of Reconstruction was its failure to establish social justice for the former slaves. Our two races, although inseparable in our daily lives, were kept apart by social custom, misinterpretation of Holy Scriptures, and the unchallenged law of the land as mandated by the U.S. Supreme Court. This was the central moral issue of my growing-up years. Only later did I come to realize, in part through learning about chestnuts and their history, that love of nature carries a moral imperative of its own.

From the time I was a small boy, Jack and Rachel Clark, the African American couple that worked for my father as farm managers, had nearly as much influence on me as my parents. Each of them taught me to love and respect God's beautiful world. My earliest introduction to nature came through learning to hunt and fish as a way to contribute to the household economy. My father and all my ancestors had hunted and fished before me, and these activities are part of my identity, like being a southerner or a Baptist. Hunting and fishing were what my father, most of the men in town, families on the farm, and all of us boys wanted most to be doing when we were not working.

Even before I had my first gun, Daddy made me a sling-shot, which we called a flip. With rubber bands, cut from an old inner tube, connecting a leather pouch to the two prongs of a forked stick, I could shoot small pebbles at various targets, including birds, with no effect except to shatter some of the green glass telephone-pole insulators around our house. A chance shot killed a robin sitting on a fence that surrounded the yard. I took it to my parents with tears running down my cheeks.

"We shouldn't ever kill anything that we don't need for food." Daddy said.

"We'll cook it for your supper tonight," Mama said in an effort to salvage my feelings.

Foraging for wild foods was also important and supplemented the food we derived from hunting and fishing. The ripening of wild fruits and nuts was a vital part of the cycle of life for rural people: in spring, plums, blueberries, blackberries, and wild cherries, then mayhaws, muscadines, and scuppernongs. By October we were looking for persimmons, chinkapins, walnuts, hickory nuts, and chestnuts.

My birthday is October 1, and it became our autumn family ritual to visit the largest of our three chestnut trees, growing on the edge of our forest, the only one that still bore fruit. The smaller trees seemed to be dying. We would gather the few chestnuts on the ground not already eaten by animals, and then throw short sticks into the tree to knock down fresh ones. Mama loved to have them, but sometimes I took a few chestnuts to school with me, where I could swap each one for a good marble. This impressed upon me the value of chestnuts, although at the time I had little idea of the incalculable worth of chestnut trees in the forest and in society.

My birthday is October 1, and it became our autumn family ritual to visit the largest of our three chestnut trees, growing on the edge of our forest, the only one that still bore fruit.

Because I worked with my father and observed his daily activities, he was the center of my life and the focus of my admiration when I was a child. He was a successful farmer who did much of his own carpentry and blacksmithing, and excelled at business, baseball, tennis, dancing, poker playing, and outdoor pursuits. He was also deeply involved in church work, the county school system, and other community affairs. He was a stern man and tough, but also fair, generous, fascinated with sports, and fun-loving when his work was done.

In front of us children or visitors, Daddy's word was law, and it was not until I was in high school that I realized how strong-willed my mother was and how much influence she had in our family affairs. She grew in spirit and influence all her life. She came to Plains to attend the nursing school at the Wise Sanitarium in Plains. Illnesses that are now easily prevented or treated were life-threatening factors for many people during my youth. Hookworm, dysentery, pellagra, malaria, diarrhea, tetanus, mumps, measles, whooping cough, and many others were constant threats, especially for poor people who could not afford care. Mama's profession helped to shape my life and caused me to make disease a major target of programs at the Carter Center today.

After she married my father, my mother continued to nurse as much as possible between bearing and nursing each of her four children, either in the operating room of our local hospital or on private duty at a patient's home. Sometimes the black people she nursed would pay her in chestnuts.

Gloria, Ruth, and Jimmy Carter, with their father, James Earl Carter, 1932. (Courtesy of Jimmy Carter Library.)

I grew to adulthood during the hard Depression years of the 1930s, when the traditional activities of hunting, fishing, and foraging became more important than ever. Looking back, it seems obvious that the excitement and challenge of hunting were closely related to the acquisition of food. There was never any question about the morality of hunting, but neither was there any acceptance of killing for the sake of a trophy. When farmers had no cash and could pay my father for supplies or services only in such currency as rabbits, squirrels, raccoons, and opossums, these foods were commonly on our tables. Due to this practice, I am sure that there are few living Georgians who, in their lifetimes, have eaten more possum meat than I have.

Some of my proudest moments were when I brought squirrels home for Mama's skillet. I still-hunted squirrels by sitting quietly by that one large chestnut tree where squirrels could invariably be found in fall. More and more, though, as the tree lost vigor, I had to rely on the acorns and nuts produced by several stands of oak or hickory trees. We read about a chestnut bark disease sweeping down from the north—a new and different kind of invasion, caused not by conflict or malice but by reckless negligence—but no one was able to stop it.

My father was an active participant in efforts to rectify land abuses of the past through the Chattahoochee Valley Wildlife Conservation program, and he directed my work as a child in this effort. Daddy was a good shot, and was always one of the first to bag his self-imposed limit of doves and leave the field. We planted feed patches, utilized controlled burning, and attempted to improve habitat in our woods and along fencerows and terraces. Had we known of any way to reduce the impact of the blight and increase the abundance of chestnut trees in our woodlots, I have no doubt that we would have tried.

Landowners, large and small, thought of wild game as one of the important products of the farm, and studied and applied good conservation practices to enhance the value of this harvest in the proper seasons. These measures were even confirmed by our religious beliefs. At least once a year in all the churches, the minister offered a sermon on stewardship, in which the responsibilities and joys of landownership were emphasized. Often, when I am in a particularly beautiful or isolated place, a vivid image comes to my mind of bowed heads, quiet prayers, and old-fashioned church hymns, as I remember the habits of my youth.

After hunting, fishing was our second great love, and the outdoor activity I came most to enjoy through the course of my life. During my boyhood, there were no large, deep wells sucking up enormous quantities of water to supply paper mills or to irrigate fields. At almost any point on our farm, there was a flowing spring nearby. The constantly flowing springs merged into small branches and then into large creeks. I never heard of a landowner who restricted access to the creeks on his land. Every stream large enough to produce fish had a clearly defined path along both sides of it.

Lillian Gordy Carter with her children Ruth and Jimmy, 1933. (Courtesy of Jimmy Carter Library.)

Rachel Clark, the wife of our farm manager Jack, taught me how to fish in the creeks that drained our land. Rachel was my hero and a special person in my life. She was light brown, small in stature, laughed a lot, and was acknowledged by all as the best cotton picker, peanut shaker, and above all, fisher in the neighborhood. She knew the best spots in all the creeks, and would always fish seven lines at once for redbreast sunfish, catfish, chain pickerel, largemouth bass, and, when the water was muddy or rising, eels. On our long walks together, sometimes as much as five miles from our home, she would tell me about the flora and fauna around us and let me know that God expected us to take good care of His creation. Her teachings and example gave me an understanding of our obligations to the natural world, which in turn led me to embrace the possibility of restoring chestnut trees to our forests.

When it was too wet to work in the fields and the creeks were rising, the other boys on the farm—all black—and I would often camp out overnight on the stream bank and fish for catfish and eels. Sometimes I fished with Mama in the boat on our small pond, but she had a habit of catching more fish than I did and teasing me about it, a habit she continued even after I had grown up to be president. Rosalynn also sometimes exhibits this same disturbing characteristic with a fly rod.

Sometimes, Daddy would take me with him to fish in Southeast Georgia. These were the times when I felt closest to my father, and I appreciated deeply the fact that I was the only child permitted to accompany the grown men on this annual trip. Once, late one afternoon at the Little Satilla River, Daddy asked me to keep his fish while he walked down the path to talk to some of his friends. I tied his stringer with mine on the belt loop on my downstream side while I continued fishing. After a few minutes my pole bent sharply, and I hooked the largest fish of the day. But when I looked for the stringers at my waist, they were gone! My belt loop had broken. I began to dive madly into the river below where I had been standing. Then I heard Daddy's voice calling me.

"I've lost the fish, Daddy," I had to tell him.

"All of them? Mine, too?"

"Yes, sir." I began to cry, even as I continued diving. Daddy was rarely patient with foolishness or mistakes, but, after a long silence, he said. "Let them go. There are a lot more fish in the river. We'll get them tomorrow." He did not tell the others what had happened. I worshipped him.

In 1941, I graduated from high school, the first in the Carter family to do so. Shortly afterwards I was accepted at the Naval Academy, and after that spent nearly seven years at sea. I still remember with nostalgia the feeling of liberation when we cleared the last channel buoy and headed for the open water. Hours on the bridge, in the conning tower, or in the sonar room allowed me to know the ocean and the heavens in a unique way. As a sonar officer, I was expected to be familiar with all the sounds of the depths and could identify shrimp, dolphin, and other fishes, and different species of whales as we recorded their chatter and songs on our extremely sensitive listening devices.

I was pursuing a career in the Navy when my father became ill with pancreatic cancer and died in 1953. I thought I knew my father well, but it was not until I visited him during his terminal illness that I really understood how valuable a man's life could be. In almost all facets of community life he was a respected leader, and had just been elected to the state legislature. A stream of visitors, black and white, came to the door to bring a small gift or a special food delicacy, or to inquire about his condition. A surprising number wanted to recount how my father's personal influence, community service, and many secret acts of generosity had affected their lives.

Jimmy Carter, top left, and friends with Annie Mae Hollis, center, who helped care for him while his mother was working. Carter's sisters Gloria and Ruth are in front. (Courtesy of Jimmy Carter Library.)

I felt besieged by an unwelcome comparison of the ultimate value of my life with his. On the long drive back to Schenectady, New York, where I was helping to prepare one of the two prototype nuclear-propulsion plants for submarines, I could not escape a startling and disturbing question: whether I wanted to resign my commission and try to follow in his footsteps in this tiny rural community. Rosalynn was shocked and furious a few days later when I told her that I had decided to do just that.

By the time I returned home from the Navy in 1953, our large chestnut tree had succumbed to the pervasive blight. I knew of no other chestnuts in the area that survived. While the loss of timber and nuts was a blow to everyone, for the mountain people it meant the loss of an entire way of life. Not only were the trees one of Appalachia's finest hardwoods, but sale of the nuts provided hard cash for families who grew or bartered for most of their household needs. Many of the magazines and newspapers we subscribed to carried articles on the seemingly unstoppable chestnut blight and the attempts, especially in the mountains, to harvest the standing "ghost" trees for wood or tannic extract wherever possible.

Today, I continue to immerse myself in books and magazines to broaden and deepen my understanding of nature and its complicated interrelationships. But reading is never enough. It must be supplemented continually by personal experiences. I have never been happier, more exhilarated, at peace, rested, inspired, and aware of the grandeur of the universe and the greatness of God than when I find myself in a natural setting not much changed from the way He made it.

Through all the busy years of my life, there has never been any significant amount of time when I have stayed away from the natural areas that mean so much to me. During the most critical moments of my life I have been renewed in spirit by the special feelings that come from the solitude and beauty of the out-of-doors. In forests, mountains, swamps, or waterways I gain a renewal of perspective and a sense of order, truth, patience, beauty, and justice (although nature's is harsh). These feelings seem to be independent of the physical beauty of a place, for I have experienced them almost equally within a dense thicket of alders or rhododendron alongside Turniptown Creek in North Georgia and in the high mountains of Nepal.

I have had the opportunity and the pleasure of experiencing nature from Alaska to New Zealand, from Quebec to Japan, but I find the same excitement ten minutes from my home in Plains. We still take our grandchildren to the family cemeteries where our ancestors, born in the 1700s, settled, farmed the land, and were buried with their wives and progeny. The landscape is deeply familiar, beloved for its own beauty as well as for its generations-long association with family. When I cross the fields or circle the ponds I recall the intimate feeling I had walking alongside my daddy behind a bird dog or sitting in a boat with Mama.

We are committed to doing what we can to preserve the land and restore where we can those parts that have been damaged by human use. I consider the breeding and restoration of blight-resistant chestnut trees in the United States to be one of the most interesting and important scientific projects of our time. Even more, it satisfies a spiritual longing to acknowledge our obligation to be better stewards of God's creation. ⁓

Chestnut giants, Great Smoky Mountains, western North Carolina. Some of the trees in background may be poplar. Photo was first published in the American Lumberman, *January 1910. (Courtesy of the Forest History Society, Durham, North Carolina.)*

Chestnut Trees from Days Gone By

By Don Barger

In the year 1910 my mother's family harvested a chestnut tree just a few miles from where I now live. Due to the diameter of the tree it was difficult to fell. It was also necessary to split the logs so they could be handled on the sawmill. This one tree sawed enough lumber to frame a one-story medium-size house.

When Father returned home from service during World War I (1918), the chestnut trees in this area were in the process of dying. In the early 1960s there was still a few trees in the woods that would saw usable lumber. This makes a period of approximately forty years in this area, from time of dying to no longer being of use as lumber.

My work with chestnut began in the 1930s. I am still involved in timber, lumber, and woodworking. [The foundation's] work brings peace to my mind and joy to my heart. It is good medicine!

Our home was in the woods with a road and stream in front of the house. Behind the house was a steep hill running parallel with the road and stream. The hill was timbered with mixed hardwoods and dead chestnut trees.

Brother Tommy and I had three chores to do daily: carry water for household use, fill the oil lamps with oil, and cut kindling wood for two cookstoves, also when needed firewood to start a fire in the fireplace. After the fires were started coal was added to keep the fire up. The chestnut on the hill was the best source of firewood.

We had everything needed to harvest the chestnut. A Shetland pony, Buck by name, wooden sled, crosscut saw, ax, sledge, wedges, cant hook, and strict orders to only cut wood from trees lying on the ground. Older members of the family handled standing trees.

Today we hear much about our dependence on fuel and goods from overseas. Buck ran on oats, bran, hay, and apples, all produced locally. His harness was made in Mount Pleasant, Pennsylvania. Brother Tommy and I ran on corn bread, corn cakes, cornmeal mush, homemade bread with chokecherry and elderberry jelly, maple syrup, soup beans cooked with ham, milk, vegetables, and lots of apples. The tools used were made in America. The oil in the lamps was produced and refined in Bradford, Pennsylvania. It sold at 17 cents a gallon. The chestnut trees were made in America. The only thing from overseas was the blight!

My main work in life has been with timber and the products derived from timber. After I returned home from four years' service in the navy, Father and I decided to go into the timber and woodworking business. We worked with local hardwoods, and much of Father's work was with chestnut. He built furniture, picture frames, including frames for Mother's paintings, and turned many, many bowls. He signed all of his work.

The family of James and Caroline Shelton pose by a large dead chestnut tree in Tremont Falls, Tennessee, circa 1920. The tree was found to be hollow. (Photo courtesy of the Great Smoky Mountains National Park Library.)

Hey, Buck is in the stable, watered, fed, and bedded down for the night. The water is carried, lamps filled, and the kindling wood box is full. It's Friday and we don't have to do our homework tonight. We can stay up till 10 on Friday nights. We are going to work on our airplane tonight. The plane is red and yellow. It's a two winger.

Hey, are you going to boil sugar water this spring? Grandma says, "You should have your sugar camp ready to boil by the first full moon in February." Uncle George makes our spiles out of elderberry stems. Uncle George saw Buffalo Bill's Wild West Show. Uncle George has a sawmill. When I grow up I am going to have a sawmill.

Hey, we gotta go. Mother just called "Tommy, Donnie, supper time."

The Beginning . . . ∾

"Majestic Sentinels to Bygone Years"

Winslow Homer's engraving Chestnutting *appeared in the magazine* Every Saturday *on October 29, 1870. (Copyright © Sterling and Francine Clark Art Institute, Williamstown, Massachusetts.)*

About four miles from Friendship, New York, was a large grove of chestnut trees. In the fall of the year, after a new frost had opened the burs, some of the young fellows in town would take their girlfriends and travel to the huge grove, taking with them picnic lunches and chestnut-gathering equipment. Picking up splinters and small pieces of dried wood, they built a large bonfire. Near the end of a fun-filled day when the fire had settled down to coals, they spread a large sheet or blanket underneath one of the trees. One of the fellows would climb the tree and shake the branches. A shower of nuts landed on the blanket. To split open the burs was a task in itself, but it was all in the fun. The nuts were then put in a wire-mesh popcorn popper (I doubt if the modern generation even knows what that is) and roasted over the still-hot coals. This was repeated year after year, and several times during the year.

Many years later my brother bought a farm about a mile from this grove, long after the trees died. I can remember very well, some of those trees were thirty inches in diameter and still standing. Time and weather stripped them of their small branches, and they were gray from no bark, but they stood as majestic sentinels to bygone years. There were those who realized the value of the lumber in them, as they were cut down one by one until they were all gone. Today that same area is all second-growth heavy woods. One would never know the area was once an American chestnut grove. I still live on this farm.

Keith W. Rumsey, of Friendship, New York, 2003; as related to him by his brother

Chestnut split-rail fences are still a common sight.

When I was growing up on our 180-acre farm, the chestnut trees all along the lower elevations had already been taken for split rails, building beams, and furniture; however, the ridge on our farm was one of the highest points in Smith County [Tennessee], and along the summit was a thin stand of the mighty chestnuts. Although there were probably only twenty or so trees, they were all thirty to forty inches in diameter. On Sunday afternoons during the fall, my friends and I would gather at my home and climb the hill. There we would collect the beautiful polished chestnuts, dividing them among ourselves in relation to our efforts in collecting them. . . . I do recall that our ridgetop chestnut trees were hit by the blight in the late 1920s or early 1930s. Today the only remnants of that stand can be found in rail fences, some of which are still standing along our country hollows. ∾

Fred Gordon Key, as interviewed by Richard F. LaRoche Jr. Although Key, who was born in 1915, remembers storing chestnuts for the harsh winters of north-central Tennessee in his family's hand-dug basement, along with the annual cache of four hundred or so cans of fruit and vegetables, his best recollections of the uses of the chestnuts were as gifts or prizes for his many friends in the county who did not have access to or perhaps had never seen a chestnut.

1985, V

How long does it take to make the woods?
As long as it takes to make the world.
The woods is present as the world is, the presence
Of all its past, and of all its time to come.
It is always finished, it is always being made, the act
of its making forever greater than the act of its destruction.
It is a part of eternity, for its end and beginning
belong to the end and beginning of all things,
The beginning lost in the end, the end in the beginning.

Excerpted from *A Timbered Choir: The Sabbath Poems 1979-1997*, by Wendell Berry. Reprinted by permission of the author.

You could see them sticking up out of the woods, and it was just like big potted flowers standing up all over the mountains. It was really a sight to see.

—Noel Moore, Rabun County, Georgia

American chestnut trees in the forest grew straight and tall before the blight. The astonishing size of this tree in North Carolina can be gauged from the man barely visible to the left of the trunk. (Copyright © President and Fellows of Harvard College, Archives of the Arnold Arboretum.)

THE TREE

A very grandfather among trees.

—Henry Ward Beecher

In the youth of a man not yet old, native Chestnut was still to be seen in glorious array, from the upper slopes of Mount Mitchell [North Carolina], the great forest below waving with creamy white Chestnut blossoms in the crowns of the ancient trees, so that it looked like a sea with white combers plowing across its surface.

Donald Culross Peattie, *A Natural History of Trees of Eastern and Central North America*

American chestnut in full blossom. (Photo by Joe Schibig.)

Where there be Mountaines, there be chestnuts: they are somewhat smaller than the chestnuts of Spaine.

Believed to be the first recorded mention of American chestnut trees, by a member of Hernando de Soto's 1540 expedition into the southern United States

There also are chestnuts here, like those of the Netherlands, which are spread over the woods. Chestnuts would be plentier if it were not for the Indians, who destroy the trees by stripping off the bark for covering for their houses. They, and the Netherlanders also, cut down the trees in the chestnut season, and cut off the limbs to gather the nuts, which also lessens the trees.

Adriaen van der Donck, *Description of the New Netherlands,* 1640

Chestnut Trees grow very tall and thick, mostly, however, in mountainous regions and high land. Its wood is very lasting, and its fruit exceptionally sweet.

William Byrd, in *William Byrd's Natural History of Virginia, or the Newly Discovered Eden*, 1737

The [Cherokee] town of Cowe [in present-day Pickens County, Georgia] consists of about one hundred dwellings, near the banks of the Tanase, on both sides of the river.

The Cherokees construct their habitations on a different plan from the Creeks; that is but one oblong four square building, of one story high; the materials consisting of logs or trunks of trees, stripped of their bark, notched at their ends, fixed one upon another, and afterwards plaistered well, both inside and out, with clay well tempered with dry grass, and the whole covered or roofed with the bark of the chestnut tree or long broad shingles.

Botanist William Bartram, *Travels through North & South Carolina, Georgia, East & West Florida. . . .* Bartram arrived at Cowe, in what is now Pickens County, Georgia, in May 1775.

Eastern woodland Indians of various tribes lived in lodges, wigwams, or (after contact with white settlers) cabins covered with slabs of bark. References can be found to such dwellings covered with elm bark, birch bark, spruce bark, or chestnut bark. No doubt whatever bark was abundant locally and suitable to the purpose was employed.

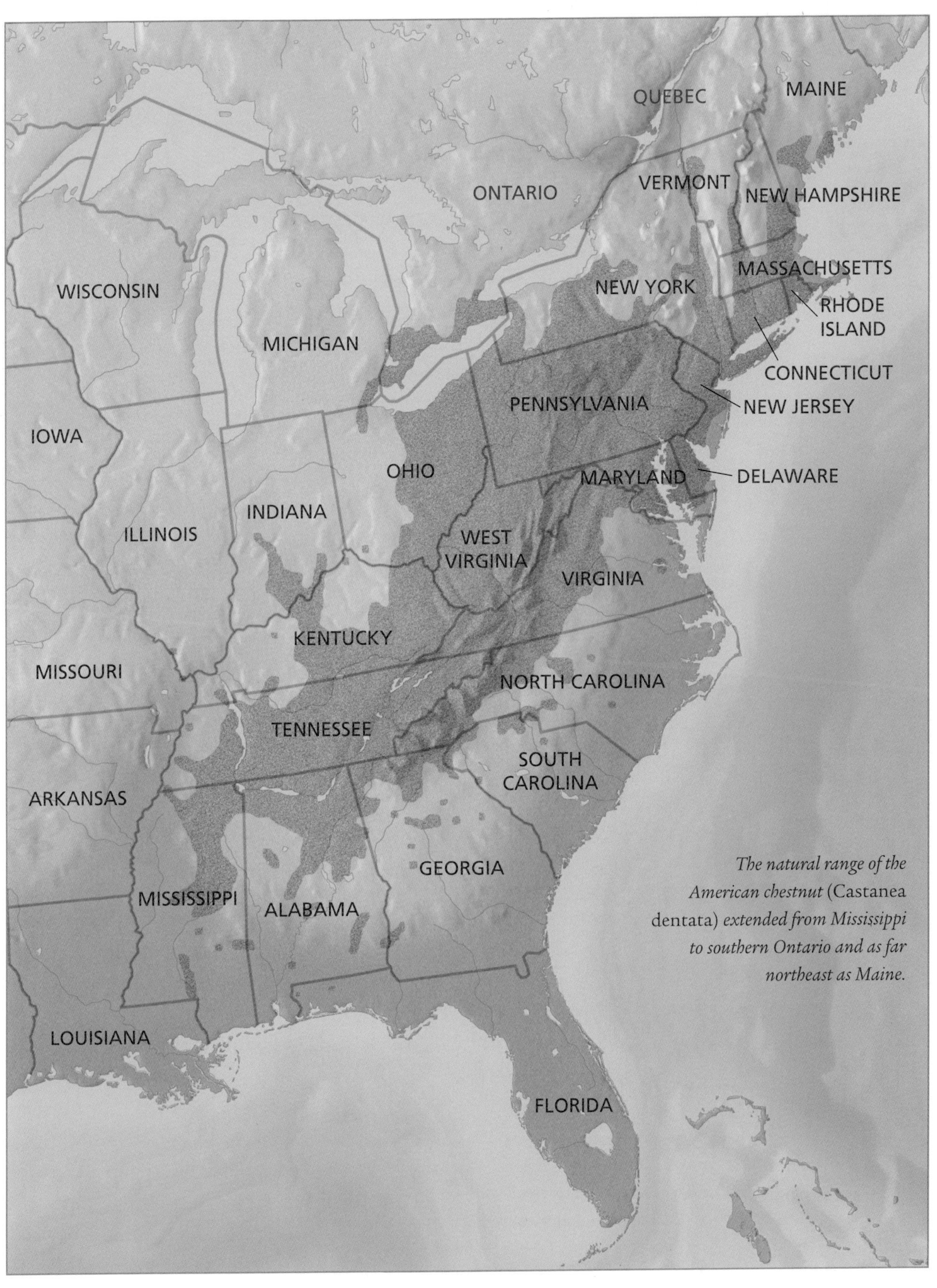

The natural range of the American chestnut (Castanea dentata) *extended from Mississippi to southern Ontario and as far northeast as Maine.*

A Country Perfectly Adapted

The North American Sylva *of François André Michaux was published in Paris in 1810, with an English translation following in 1818. This illustration and excerpt are from the 1865 edition, published in Philadelphia. The American chestnut was classified at the time as* Castanea vesca, *later changed to* Castanea dentata.

The Chestnut does not venture beyond the 44th degree of latitude. It is found in New Hampshire between the 43rd and the 44th degrees; but such is the severity of the winter, that it is less common than in Connecticut, New Jersey, and Pennsylvania. It is most multiplied in the mountainous districts of the Carolinas and of Georgia, and abounds on the Cumberland Mountains and in East Tennessee.

The beautifully illustrated North American Sylva *by François André Michaux was the first comprehensive survey of American forest trees. The engraving here was by Pancrace Bessa. (Courtesy of University of Delaware Library, Newark.)*

The coolness of the summer and the mildness of the winter in these regions are favorable to the Chestnut; the face of the country, also, is perfectly adapted to a tree which prefers the sides of mountains or their immediate vicinity, where the soil in general is gravelly, though deep enough to sustain its perfect development. . . . I have measured several stocks which, at six feet from the ground, were fifteen or sixteen feet in circumference, and which equaled the loftiest trees in stature.

Its leaves are six or seven inches long, one and a half inch broad, coarsely toothed, of an elongated oval form, of a fine brilliant color and of a firm texture, with prominent parallel nerves beneath. . . . [The nuts] are smaller and sweeter than the wild chestnuts of Europe, and are sold in the markets of New York, Philadelphia, and Baltimore.

The wood is strong, elastic,

and capable of enduring the succession of dryness and moisture. Its durability renders it especially valuable for posts. . . . In Connecticut, Pennsylvania, and a part of Virginia, it is also preferred for rails, and is said to last more than fifty years. For shingles, this wood is superior to any species of Oak, though it has the same defect of warping. . . . The Chestnut is little esteemed for fuel, and is not used in the cities of the United States; like the kindred species in Europe, it is filled with air and snaps as it burns. The [char]coal is excellent, and, on some of the mountains of Pennsylvania where the Chestnut abounds, the woods in the neighborhood of the forges have been transformed into copses, which are cut every sixteen years for the furnaces. This period is sufficient to renew them. ∾

It is certainly fair to consider chestnut as one of the leading hardwoods of America. . . . It is most numerous and important in the Southern Appalachian Mountains, where in the State of North Carolina it forms 27 percent of the total stand, and is the most numerous tree in the forest, occasionally forming almost pure stands, although generally growing in mixture with other hardwoods such as oaks and tulip poplars. Conditions are much the same in eastern Tennessee and southwestern Virginia. In these States most of the stand is composed of virgin timber, but outside of the Appalachians, most of the chestnut is second growth and is apt to be composed of sprouts from old stumps, often several generations having grown up and been cut from the original seedling's stump.

P. L. Buttrick, "Commercial Uses of Chestnut," 1915

Cherokees and Chestnuts

Tea of year old leaves for heart trouble; leaves from young sprouts cure old sores; cold bark tea with buckeye to stop bleeding after birth; apply warmed galls to make infant's navel recede; boil leaves with mullein and brown sugar for cough syrup; dip leaves in hot water and put on sores; tea for typhoid; for stomach; bark makes brown dye; firewood (pops badly); lumber (wormy or good); rails for fences; acid wood; coffee substitute (parched).

From *Cherokee Plants and their Uses, a 400 Year History,* by Paul B. Hamel and Mary U. Chiltoskey

"This Darling Old Fellow"

By Henry Ward Beecher

Henry Ward Beecher (1813–87) of Litchfield, Connecticut, was a leading thinker, writer, and abolitionist of his day, although his sister, Harriet Beecher Stowe, author of Uncle Tom's Cabin, *is more widely remembered today. This article, originally titled* "Chestnuts," *is from the* Pittsfield (Mass.) Sun, *Sept. 22, 1870.*

I fancy that trees have dispositions. At any rate they have those qualities which suggest dispositions to all who are in sympathy with nature, and who look upon facts as letters of an alphabet, by which one may spell out the hidden meaning of things. Some trees, like the apple, suggest goodness and humility. —They put on no airs. They do not exalt themselves. They are patient of climate, full of beauty in blossom, and in autumn beautiful in fruit.

The oak, when full grown, has the beauty of rugged strength, and sometimes it has grandeur. . . . An American elm is the tree of grace and beauty. . . . And yet, one never has with it the feeling of interest or personal intercourse. One may sit under its branches, but no one ever sat on or among them. We admire, but do not sympathize.

Still less did any one ever love a hickory-tree. They are beautiful, stately, but self-contained. When young, they are dandies; when old, aristocrats. Not so the chestnut tree. —This darling old fellow is a very grandfather among trees. What a great open bosom it has! Its boughs are arranged with express reference to ease in climbing.

Nature was in a good mood when the chestnut tree came forth. It is, when well grown, a stately tree, wide-spreading, and of great size. Even in the forest the chestnut is a noble tree. But one never sees its full development except when it has grown in the open fields. It then assumes immense proportions. Having a tendency when cut down to send up many shoots from the stump, old trees are often found with four or five trunks springing from the same root. In such cases no other American tree covers so wide a space of ground. Not even the oak attains to greater size or longevity. . . .

Still Life with Apples and Chestnuts, *1859, by John F. Francis (1808–86). (Photograph © 2007, Museum of Fine Arts, Boston.)*

A chestnut tree in full bloom is a fine sight. It blossoms about the first of July, in clusters of long, yellowish white filaments, like a tuft of coarse wool rolls. The whole top of the tree is silvered over. We have never seen them so finely in blossom as this

Reading under an American chestnut at Oak Dale, Dedham, Massachusetts. The circumference of this tree at three feet from the ground was twenty-one and a half feet. (Copyright © President and Fellows of Harvard College, Archives of the Arnold Arboretum.)

year, and we foresee a grand harvest for the boys. Oh, those golden days of October! The thought of them brings back the day of boyhood, the brilliant foliage of the forest now putting on its regal garments. The merry sport of squirrels racing on the ground, if one lies dead-still to watch, or scamper[ing] up the trunks, and leaping from tree to tree with chirp and bark, if disturbed!

It was a great day when, with bag and basket, the whole family was summoned to go "a chestnutting!" There was frolic enough, and climbing enough, and shaking enough, and rattling nuts enough, and a sly kiss or two, but never enough, and lunch enough, and appetite enough. The silver brook on the hillside carried down on its murmuring current the golden leaves which the trees, with every puff of wind, sent shimmering through the air. . . .

Long live the chestnut tree; and the chestnut woods on the mountain side! Long live the boys and girls who frolic under their boughs, and long live the winter nights, with the homely fare of apples and nuts, and no stronger drink than cider, and a merry crowd of boys and girls, with here and there the spectacled old folks, all before a roaring hickory fire, in an old fashioned fire-place, big as the Western horizon with the sun going down in it, which opens such a fusilade of snaps and cracks as sets the girls to screaming, and throws out such mischievous coals upon the calico dresses, as obliges every human boy to run to the relief of his sweetheart all on fire!

No doubt many an old gentleman will read this article with a face growing more and more full of smiles, and take off his spectacles at the end, and looking kindly over at his aged dame, will say, "Do you remember, Polly, when we were at Squire Judson's —" "Well, well, father, you are too old to be talking about such youthful follies." Nevertheless she smiles and looks kindly over at the old rogue, who kissed her that night, proposed on the way home, and was married before Christmas. ❧

And long live the winter nights, with the homely fare of apples and nuts, and no stronger drink than cider, and a merry crowd of boys and girls, with here and there the spectacled old folks, all before a roaring hickory fire.

"Like a Great Globe"

How few of us know how majestic and grand is a chestnut, grown on a lawn where there is "ample room and verge enough;" where it can form a gigantic and massy head, like a great globe. Certainly, the American chestnut is a more beautiful large tree than the oak; since, to equal grandeur of proportions, it adds greater variety of tint. Few things are finer than a group of chestnuts, in full tassel; and few trees afford a finer shade, or attain a large size more rapidly.

From the *Horticulturist and Journal of Rural Art and Rural Taste,* November 1850

The specimen chestnut trees on this page and opposite display a spreading habit markedly different from that of forest-grown trees. (Photo on this page copyright © President and Fellows of Harvard College, Archives of the Arnold Arboretum.)

The anatomy of an American chestnut tree. Illustration by Bruce Lyndon Cunningham, 2001.

Life and Death in a Pollen Garden

By William Lord

Soldier beetle, or leatherwing

Wheel bug

Tumbling beetle

A great variety of insects visit the American chestnut pollen gardens: butterflies, bees, beetles, flies, and an occasional marauder looking for insect prey. Two of the most common pollen seekers are the soldier beetle and the tumbling beetle.

The soldier beetle, about a half-inch long (13 mm), is smartly colored in bright and dark colors, calling to mind a soldier's dress uniform. It is also known as a leatherwing beetle, for the leathery aspect of its coat. There are many species. Those that feed on pollen and nectar have specially adapted mouthparts.

Tumbling beetles, at about one-eighth-inch long (1–3 mm) are small, typically black insects with a prominent pointed tail at the end of their abdomen. They position themselves among the stamens and feed with great concentration, but if disturbed they quickly tumble evasively or may take wing and fly away.

The wheel bug, about an inch long (25 mm), is named for a notched crest atop its back. It is a deadly assassin, waiting for an occupied pollen feeder to come within reach. Then it grasps it in its strong front legs and injects a solution that kills and softens its prey. Its hypodermic beak contains a tube for injection and a tube for ingestion. The red and black wheel bug in the photo is an immature that will soon molt and become a gray adult. (Photos by Timothy Eck)

Hairstreak butterfly on budding American chestnut. Illustration by Susan Bull Riley.

Squirrels and Porcupine Eggs

The fascination of Henry David Thoreau (1817–62) with all things having to do with chestnuts extended to the tree's dependence upon and benefits to wildlife. His meticulous journal observations of how mice and squirrels gathered the nuts, and how the trees benefited from this, extend to pages. Indeed, it could be said that Thoreau gathered observations of the chestnut as assiduously as the forest rodents gathered the nutritious nuts. The following is from The Writings of Henry David Thoreau, *edited by F. B. Sanborn and Bradford Torrey, Houghton Mifflin, 1906.*

October 17, 1860:

I was surprised at the sight of these chestnuts [seedlings], for there are not *to my knowledge* any chestnut trees—none, at least, nearly large enough to bear nuts—within about half a mile of that spot, and I should about as soon have expected to find chestnuts in the artificial pine grove in my yard. The chestnut trees old enough to bear fruit are near the Lincoln line about half a mile east of this through the woods and over hill and dale. No one acquainted with these woods—not the proprietor—would have believed that a chestnut lay under the leaves in that wood or within a quarter of a mile of it, and yet from what I saw then and afterward I have no doubt that there were hundreds, which were placed there by quadrupeds and birds. This wood lies on the south of the village, separated from it by a mile of open fields and meadows. . . . It is well known that the chestnut timber of this vicinity has rapidly disappeared within fifteen years, having been used for railroad sleepers, for rails, and for planks, so that there is danger that this part of our forest will become extinct.

Chestnut seedlings

The last chestnut tracts of any size were on the side of Lincoln. As I advanced further through the woods toward Lincoln, I was surprised to see how many little chestnuts there were, mostly two or three years old and some even ten feet high, scattered through them and also under the dense pines, as oaks are. I should say there was one every half-dozen rods, made more distinct by their yellow leaves on the brown ground, which surprised me because I had not attended to the spread of the chestnut, and it is certain that every one of these came from a chestnut placed there by a quadruped or bird which had brought it from further east, where alone it grew.

You would say that the squirrels, etc., went further for chestnuts than for acorns in proportion as they were a greater rarity. I suspect that a squirrel may convey them sometimes a quarter or a half a mile even, and no doubt as soon as a young chestnut fifteen or twenty feet high, far advanced beyond the chestnut woods, bears a single bur, which no man discovers, a squirrel or bird is almost sure to gather it and plant it in that neighborhood or still further forward. A squirrel goes a-chestnutting perhaps as far as the boys do, and when he gets there he does not have to shake or club the tree or wait for frost to open the burs; he walks [?] up to the bur and cuts it off, and strews the ground with them before they have opened. And the fewer they are in the wood the more certain it is that he will appropriate every one, for it is no transient afternoon's picnic with him, but the pursuit of his life, a harvest that he gets as surely as the farmer his corn.

A squirrel goes a-chestnutting perhaps as far as the boys do.

Now it is important that the owners of these wood-lots should know what is going on here and treat them and the squirrels accordingly. They little dream of what the squirrels are about; know only that they get their seed-corn in the adjacent fields, and encourage their boys to shoot them every day, supplying them with powder and shot for this purpose. In newer parts of the country they have squirrel-hunts on a large scale and kill many thousands in a few hours, and all the neighborhood rejoices.

Thus it appears that by a judicious letting Nature alone merely we might recover our chestnut wood in the course of a century. ❧

Born Naturalists:

Two small boys were walking in the woods, seeking for adventure and what they might find. One picked up a chestnut burr. "Tommy!" he called excitedly. "Come here quick! I've found a porcupine egg!"

Newspaper clipping from the early 1900s, found by ninety-six-year-old Evelyn Glazier of Mansfield, Connecticut, in her mother's scrapbook. The newspaper humorist might have read Thoreau's journal entry of October 22, 1857, which observed of the chestnut bur: "It bristles all over with sharp green prickles, some nearly half an inch long, like a hedgehog rolled into a ball."

Neither chestnut burs nor porcupine eggs, these three are hedgehog babies. (Photo © 2007, Sean Sosik-Hamor, HamorHollow.com.)

Bountiful Giants

Memories of the American Chestnut

Originally published in 1980 in Foxfire 6, *the following oral histories tell in a way no scientific paper can the meaning of chestnut trees to people in the southern Appalachians. The speakers were residents of Rabun County, Georgia, in the state's far northeastern corner.*

Marie Mellinger (a naturalist in Rabun County):

In 1859 an American chestnut tree somewhere on the western slope of the Great Smoky Mountains in Tennessee was reported as being thirty-three feet in circumference four feet from the ground. That's about ten or eleven feet in diameter. I was informed that in Greenbriar, North Carolina, in 1934 a large chestnut stump was found that measured thirteen feet the long way across. Wilbur Savage, a forester in the Great Smoky Mountain National Park, reported he measured a fallen, dead chestnut [that was] nine feet, six inches in diameter, and at sixty-five feet from the ground it measured four feet, eight inches [in diameter]. Those were some giant trees. And the nuts were a tremendous source of food for people, [their] animals, and wild animals, such as turkey and deer.

An American chestnut in blossom, place and date unknown. (National Archives.)

Noel Moore:

In the spring when the chestnuts first came out (they would bloom a little later than any other tree), they had a light, cream-colored blossom, and a big tree that grew up a hundred feet high would have a spread at the top of it a hundred feet wide, maybe. You could see them sticking up out of the woods, and it was just like big potted flowers standing up all over the mountains. It was

"Nothin' else tastes like them." Illustration by Susan Bull Riley.

really a sight to see. I was just a boy then. They all died by the time I was eighteen years old, and I can remember them just as well now. We'd talk about what a good chestnut crop we were going to have. The blooms were a creamy white, big long fuzzy things, six to eight inches long. There were from one to three nuts in each burr.

The nuts were real sweet, especially if they were roasted or boiled. Didn't taste like a walnut or a pecan; nothin' else tastes like them. And the blossoms gave up one of the best honey crops we ever had. We've never had a honey crop like we did since the chestnuts died, because there's not that much nectar in the wild now. Whenever chestnuts bloomed, in the morning, early, the trees looked like just the whole tops were alive with honeybees working on getting the nectar. They'd really go for it.

Chestnut trees, Bedford County, Pennsylvania. (Pennsylvania Chestnut Blight Commission.)

Mrs. M. C. Speed:

"We used to make medicine out of the leaves, for swelling. Boil the leaves in a pot and get the juice out of them and set [the pot] off the heat and let it cool. Then bathe [the swelled area] with it. People back then had swelled feet and they'd put that on them to get rid of the swelling. ~

My memories of the American chestnut date back to my childhood years on a farm in Morgan County, Kentucky. I especially remember three large chestnut trees that stood in a meadow near our home. They were nearly three feet in diameter, tall and straight, with well-developed crowns. Each fall, in order to obtain some chestnuts to enjoy, we had to compete with a neighboring youth who usually showed up shortly after sunrise. We also had to compete with squirrels, birds, and almost every other critter that happened to pass by. I can remember picking up chestnuts as a barefoot lad of seven or eight years, and I also remember the painful experience of stepping on a prickly chestnut bur. An even more painful experience took place a time or two when a large bur fell from the tree and landed on my bare foot.

I'm not sure just when the chestnut trees died, but it must have been sometime during the early 1930s. Chestnut logs were still cut and sawed into lumber for several years after the trees had died. Many beautiful items of early American furniture were crafted from chestnut wood. The wood grain closely resembles that of ash or oak, and in antique furniture, dark with age, it is often not recognized as chestnut. The wood is strong, straight grained, and highly resistant to decay. It had many uses in construction, and especially so where resistance to decay was needed, as in fence posts and rails. During an earlier era, it was a preferred material for building log houses.

But in the fall—oh, in the fall—the whole area burst forth in blazing golden color.

Like most rural Americans during the 1930s, we had no electricity or natural gas. A wood-burning fireplace provided winter heat, while cooking was done with a wood-burning stove. . . . As youngsters, my brother and I preferred to provide stove wood from chestnut, because it was clean, straight grained, and easy to split. We couldn't use it in the open fireplace, however, because it "popped" quite forcibly and scattered sparks, and thus constituted a fire hazard when burned in an unconfined space. My mother sometimes objected to its use even in a stove, because of the annoying mini-explosions. Despite that objection, chestnut wood made excellent fuel, igniting readily and burning with a clear and hot flame.

Harold L. Barber, West Liberty, Kentucky, 2002

In late spring, their fuzzy bloom added a tinge of color to the green background that reminded one a bit of fall. But in the fall—oh, in the fall—the whole area burst forth in blazing golden color, with tan burs opening wide to reveal those delicious brown nuts that began to drop to the ground. . . . after chestnuts had fallen to the ground and "sweetened" for a while, we would go up the ridge behind the house and gather the nuts in these [twenty-five-pound cloth flour] sacks. It was not uncommon to come home with more than one sack full each time we made a trip.

William A. Banks, 2002; Banks was born in 1924 in Burnsville, North Carolina

Opposite: *Chestnut leaves beginning to turn.*

The chestnut trees will soon be ready to be clubbed.

—*Wheeling (W.Va.) Register*, September 23, 1874

Gathering Chestnuts, *painting by Ernest Smith (1907–75), a Tonawanda Seneca artist and craftsman. From the collections of Rochester Museum & Science Center, Rochester, New York.*

THE NUT

Chestnuts! Real chestnuts that were so very wonderful to enjoy! How anxiously we waited for the first fall frost to drop those prickly burs to where they split open and ejected their brown jewels.

—Lester H. Harris, Marion, Connecticut

The Moon of the Chestnuts

Food was getting scarce in the mountains, and the [bear] council was to decide what to do about it. They had sent out messengers all over, and while they were talking two bears came in and reported that they had found a country in the low grounds where there were so many chestnuts and acorns that mast was knee deep. Then they were all pleased, and got ready for a dance. . . .

. . . By this time the hunter [who had been befriended by a bear] was very hungry and was wondering how he could get something to eat. The [bear] knew his thoughts, and sitting up on his hind legs he rubbed his stomach with his forepaws–so–and at once he had both paws full of chestnuts and gave them to the man.

"The Bear Man" myth, from *James Mooney's History, Myths, and Sacred Formulas of the Cherokees.*

We judg'd by the great Number of Chestnut-Trees that we approach't the Mountains, which several of our Men discover'd very plainly. The Bears are great Lovers of Chestnut, and are so discreet as not to Venture their unwieldly Bodys upon the smaller Branches of the Trees, which will not bear their Weight. But after walking upon the Limbs as far as is safe, they bite off the Limbs which falling down, they finish their Meal upon the Ground.

William Byrd, *The History of the Dividing Line Between Virginia and N. Carolina Run in the Year of Our Lord 1728*

This nation [the Natchez] begins its year in the month of March . . . and divides it into 13 moons. . . . The twelfth moon [January–February] is that of the Chestnuts. This fruit has already been collected a long time ago, but nevertheless this month bears the name. Finally the thirteenth moon is that of the Nuts. It is added to complete the year. It is then that the nuts are broken in order to make bread, mingling it with corn meal.

Le Page Du Pratz, *Histoire de La Louisiane,* 1758. This mention of chestnuts used by Gulf Coast Indians probably reflects the range of American chestnut trees before ink disease, a foreign fungus, was introduced in the 1800s and killed most trees south and west of Georgia. Unlike the chestnut blight fungus, ink disease cannot survive the winters farther north.

Boyd Lyles, a bear hunter of the early 1900s, told years ago of seeing a bear gathering nuts and eating his fill: "The b'ar corkscrews up a chestnut and rakes down a bunch of burs, then gather 'em up and set beside 'em. He takes a rock in each paw and mashes the burs open and eats the nuts. The first time I seen one of them piles I thought it was some kids up in the mountain."

As recounted in 1951 to William Lord

Old-growth forests dominated by chestnuts offered prime foraging territory for black bears. Illustration by Frederick Paillet.

Castanea dentata. *Note the number of nuts in each bur. (Copyright © President and Fellows of Harvard College, Archives of the Arnold Arboretum.)*

"Fell from a Chestnut Tree . . ."

For the agile and the daring (or the foolhardy), the lure of ripened chestnuts could be irresistible, as the following headlines and news stories attest.

Fell From a Chestnut tree—

John L. Kelly, living at No. 2020 Christian street, went out into the suburbs yesterday after chestnuts, and in order to assist his companions in obtaining that delicacy climbed one of the trees. Missing his hold upon a branch he fell to the ground, a distance somewhat less than twenty feet, and but for the branches which partially intercepted his fall, might have been fatally injured. As it was, he was taken to the University Hospital with a compound fracture of the left wrist, which it is feared by the physicians will necessitate the amputation of the hand.

Philadelphia Inquirer, October 11, 1880

Unfortunate Chestnut Hunters.

William Righley, of Second and South streets, and Joseph Reichert, of 1309 North Fourth street, both boys, fell from chestnut trees in the western portion of West Philadelphia and were seriously injured, the first-named having both arms broken and the last receiving internal injuries and a fracture of the shoulder blade.

Philadelphia Inquirer, October 6, 1890

A CONTORTIONIST KILLED.

Frank Geary Falls from a Chestnut Tree and Breaks His Neck.

Frank Geary, of Lancaster avenue, fell from a limb of a chestnut tree in Smith's woods, opposite the old Schuetzen Park, yesterday morning and broke his neck. He only lived about five minutes. The unfortunate man was 25 years old and was well-known as an acrobat of much merit. He had lately been giving daily exhibitions at the Bijou Theatre under the name of the Zulu contortionist. He was also connected years ago with Forepaugh's Circus as a tumbler.

Philadelphia Inquirer, October 5, 1890

Dangerous Fall From a Chestnut Tree

Little Willie Casteel, son of Mr. S. Casteel, corner of Crooked and Middle street, while out with a number of companions, fell from a chestnut tree to the ground, a distance of sixteen feet. He was carried home and Dr. Fisher was called in who examined Willie and found him pretty badly injured; but it is hoped that there is nothing serious.

Daily Journal and Journal and Tribune, Knoxville, Tennessee, September 23, 1893

Chestnut Clubbers Will Be Prosecuted
Special to The Inquirer.

READING, Sept. 3.—A meeting of persons owning land on Mounts Penn and Neversink was held in this city, for the purpose of taking steps to prevent the clubbing of chestnut trees. It was agreed to give the school children permission to gather chestnuts on certain days, but anyone found clubbing the trees before that time will be proceeded against as trespassers.

Philadelphia Inquirer, September 4, 1899

ANGRY FARMER SHOOTS THREE BOYS
Mad Because His Orchard and Chestnut Trees Had Been Robbed
Special to The Inquirer.

ATHENS, Pa., Oct. 10—Three sons of Charles Bowman, of Waverly, were standing on the Erie bridge, just across the State line, last evening, when an excited farmer ran towards them. Taking aim at the boys he fired a load of birdshot from a gun. All three of the boys were slightly wounded. It is thought that the farmer had been angered by boys robbing his orchard and chestnut trees.

Philadelphia Evening Post, October 11, 1899

Fall From Chestnut Tree Fatal
Special to The Inquirer.

CHESTER, Pa., Oct. 9.—Albert C. Peters, 21 years old, of Bethel township, fell from a chestnut tree this afternoon and was killed. His neck was broken. Peters had been married but a few weeks.

Philadelphia Inquirer, October 10, 1904

The object of autumn desire. Illustration by Susan Bull Riley.

Maidenly Gathering

Rough rural images of barefoot boys braving burs, clubbing branches, tossing rocks, and clambering out on limbs to gather nuts had its high-Victorian counterpart for the fairer sex. The following sentimental portrayal of a chestnut-gathering idyll was originally published as "Nutting-Parties," from The American Girls Handy Book, *Charles Scribner's Sons, 1887.*

Off they go with bright, laughing eyes and glowing cheeks, each one carrying a light little basket or fancy bag slung carelessly on her arm. The girls are full of life and spirits as they walk briskly along toward the woods in the delightful fall weather, talking and laughing in a happy, thoughtless fashion, now telling where the best nuts are to be found, the shortest route to take, or where the prettiest walks lead, and again lingering or stopping to admire the many wonderful beauties of autumn. Leaving the road they enter the woods, where the dry leaves rustle pleasantly beneath their feet, and in some places the gold and brown leaves through which they walk lie ankle-deep.

All this is fully enjoyed by the party as they proceed on their way discussing the best place for lunch, which consideration is quite important, as it is necessary, if possible, to be near a clear, cool spring; otherwise the water must be transported.

Arriving at the selected spot about noon, all bring forward their baskets and bags to contribute the contents to their "nutting-dinner." Soon the white cloth

The "Little Brown Squirrel": nut gathering at its most refined.

is laid and the tempting feast spread, when the hungry but merry maidens gather around to relish their repast in the forest, where, all about, are seen sure signs of coming winter.

The airy dining-hall is carpeted with the softest moss, and the gorgeous coloring of the surrounding foliage is far more beautiful than the most costly tapestry, while the sky forming the roof is of the serenest blue.

Now and then the sound of falling nuts is heard as they drop from the trees. This is music in the ears of the girls, and they hurry through their lunch, collect the empty baskets, and are soon busy gathering the glossy brown chestnuts, which are thrashed down from the branches by some of the party, who use long poles for the purpose. Down comes the shower of nuts and burs, and away the party scamper to patiently wait until it is over, as the prickly burs are things to be avoided. Some wise girls have brought tweezers to use in pulling open these thorny coverings. Others have their hands well protected by heavy gloves which cannot easily be penetrated with the bristling spikes.

It does not take long to fill their bags, and the one who first succeeds in the feat receives the title of "Little Brown Squirrel." Then all the others, for the rest of the day, obey her wishes. Nor is this difficult, for their Little Brown Squirrel is blithe and gay, generous and kind, and does all in her power to render her subjects happy.

As they turn their faces homeward the girls plan for another nutting-party to come off soon, for they wish to make the most of the glorious Indian summer, which belongs, we claim, exclusively to our country, and which may last a week or only a few days.

The chestnuts are brought home, where in the evening some are eaten raw, others have the shells slit and are then roasted or boiled, making a sort of chestnut festival, as in the North of Italy, only of course on a very much smaller scale, for there the peasants gather chestnuts all day long and have a merry-making when the sun goes down. This harvest lasts over three weeks and is a very important one to the dark-eyed Italians, who dry the nuts and grind them to flour, which is used for bread and cakes during the barren season. The harvest in the Apennines is quite an event, as the trees are plentiful, the fruit is good, and the people gladly celebrate the season. ~

Chestnut images from The American Girls Handy Book, *1887.*

Daring Girls

Not all Victorian-era young women heeded the strictures of the "Little Brown Squirrel." The following, gently subversive episode, which appeared as "Chestnuting" in the New York Times, *was reprinted November 22, 1877, in the (Keene)* New Hampshire Sentinel.

To the youthful mind there is a rare fascination in gathering chestnuts. This is due partly to the meritorious qualities of the chestnut itself, and partly to the fact that there is a spice of danger in the act of gathering it. . . . The boy who has climbed to the topmost branch of a chestnut tree, and sees approaching in the distance the angry owner, accompanied by a large club and a savage dog, will hastily fill the front of his jacket with unopened burrs, and grind them against his body as he slides down the tree, with a fortitude surpassing that of the historical Spartan small boy, who stole an anise-seed bag from the master of the Argos County Hunt, and allowed it to blister the entire surface of his stomach in preference to admitting his guilt and undergoing the inevitable thrashing. It is a curious provision of nature that chestnuts must always be stolen. The trees always belong to another man, and there is no small boy living whose father ever had a chestnut tree on his own land. Why this should be so is a mystery which it is the province of moralists to solve, and which therefore needs no discussion here.

Nevertheless, there are exceptionally daring girls who indulge in the hazardous amusement of secret chestnuting.

It is the opinion of Miss Anthony that the tyrant man has committed one of his worst outrages in monopolizing the sport of chestnut gathering. It cannot be denied that the female sex is virtually shut out from that delightful pursuit. To gather chestnuts successfully involves climbing trees, and the mature woman or the full-grown girl rarely cares to incur the risks which are inseparable from climbing in the present fashion of female dress. . . . Nevertheless, there are exceptionally daring girls who indulge in the hazardous amusement of secret chestnuting, and the experience of a Massachusetts young lady who recently climbed a chestnut tree in Berkshire county is worth narrating.

The young lady in question . . . was remarkably beautiful, and was the object of the devoted attachment of two local young men, one of whom was a model of all possible virtues, while the other was a bold, bad youth, who was known to be in the habit of smoking, and who was currently believed to have more than once visited a circus. Early in October this estimable young lady suborned her younger brother, aged ten, to accompany her on a clandestine chestnuting expedition. A chestnut tree, separated from the road by a narrow but dense belt of trees and bushes, was soon found, and the pair zealously searched the ground for fallen nuts. The young lady . . . soon grew weary of this occupation, and determined to climb the tree. With the aid of a fence-rail and the zealous "boosting" of her brother, she succeeded in reaching the lowest branch, from which her progress was easy. Pleased with her success, she soon grew careless, and finally ventured out upon a limb until it bent under her weight. Becoming frightened, she lost her presence of mind and her hold, and suddenly fell. Fortunately, she did not fall far, for her skirts caught in a fork of the limb, and suspended her between heaven and earth in the attitude of an umbrella which has struggled with a violent gust of wind and experienced a reverse.

Her voice, though somewhat smothered by the peculiarities of her situation, could be easily heard by her astonished brother, and in accordance with her calm directions that devoted small boy instantly fled for help. Now, it so happened that each of the young lady's lovers had noticed her as she started from home in company with her brother, and each had independently determined to meet her as if by accident. Thus it fell out that the first person the small boy met as he rushed along the road was the mild young man, who listened to his incoherent tale and hastened to the rescue. No sooner, however, did he come within sight of the tree than he promptly paused, turned his back upon the object of his adoration, and in a faltering voice explained to the small boy that he thought his sister would not care to have him help her, but would prefer the assistance of a vague servant girl, in search of whom he professed himself ready to start. The small boy, having no sense of delicacy whatever, called the good young man names, and said he was afraid to climb a tree, but failed to shake his resolution. So the latter started on a run to find his hypothetic servant girl, and unlike Lot's wife, refused to look back, though the indignant small boy sent a shower of stones after him. Meanwhile, the bold, bad young man was approaching the scene of action, "cross-lots," at the top of his speed. His iron nerves did not falter even when he reached the tree that temporarily bore such marvelous fruit. Requesting the young lady to calm herself and trust him to rescue her, he armed her brother with a knife, and instructed him to climb the tree and cut his sister loose. The small boy, hailing with delight the opportunity to cut something, did as he was bid, and in a few moments, amid the noise of rending garments, the young lady dropped safely into the bold, bad lover's extended arms. Half an hour afterward, eleven women, bearing five step-ladders, approached the tree, while the good young man waited behind the bushes to receive his rescued mistress. It is needless to say he was disappointed, and his disappointment was still greater when he was subsequently told that she was to be married at an early day to his bold and bad rival. Thus we see that, as Solomon might have said, there is a time for step-ladders and a time for decided action, and that the bold young man gathers his bride from a chestnut tree, while the simple-minded man flees afar off and howls for servant girls, who are useless, and for the step-ladder which satisfieth not. ∾

His iron nerves did not falter even when he reached the tree that temporarily bore such marvelous fruit.

"The Dealers are Crying Chestnuts"

A failure of the chestnut crop had repercussions even in the cities, while a normal, plentiful crop was hardly matter for comment, as the following pair of news articles attests.

NO CHESTNUTS. This Year's Crop a Complete Failure and The Dealers Correspondingly Unhappy.

The dealers are crying chestnuts, but there are no chestnuts, or, at least, very few of the eating kind this year. The men who other seasons stood behind their charcoal fires and pans to deal out "roasteds" to the fattening of their pocketbooks are disconsolate, for 1886 shows them no profits. What nuts are sold generally come up eighty rotten to the hundred. In short, the crop this autumn is an entire failure. "Wots the reason they're skeerce?" said a Montgomery county farmer, "they're skeerce because there hain't none on the trees. Them trees always take a rest once in ten years and this here's their restin' year, that's all. How much a bushel? I'd like to know where you'd get a bushel in this market. The chestnut men's glad when they kin buy ten quarts."

Andrew Wyeth (born 1917), Roasted Chestnuts, *1956. Tempera on panel. Collection of Brandywine River Museum, gift of Mary Carey Haskell, 1971. © Andrew Wyeth.*

The venders of fruit and nuts on the street corners, a dozen, at least, of whom were talked to upon the subject, agreed that as far as this year is concerned chestnut selling is a losing business. Last autumn, and since the short crop about the time of the Centennial, the nuts could be purchased at prices ranging from one dollar and a half to three dollars per bushel, according to size and quality. At present they cost from five to nine dollars, and are scarcely worth purchasing at that. They are mostly small, half-shriveled looking affairs, with very little flavor and that of a somewhat rank character.

"We did sometimes pick out the worst of the rotten ones before roasting, when the nuts were cheap," said one honest Italian, as he sadly made an incision across the face of a diminutive specimen and tossed it into the pan, "but we can't do it this season. If we were to throw away the bad fellows we'd be paying people to eat our good ones. No, sir, this time you've got to take 'em as they come, and be satisfied to get any at all." The only hope of the sidewalk merchant for profit in the chestnut line at present is the advent of the "jumbos." These big nuts are comparatively cheap, and it takes very few to fill up a five cent cup. If these prove bad or dear when in market, the chestnut selling season will be designated by a black mark all around.

It is probable that within a week or two the roasting-pan will be laid sorrowfully away until next year, a full month sooner than usual. One little trick of the venders they will not be able to practice. It has generally been their custom to lay away one or two bushels before the nuts become scarce and higher in price, in order to sell them later on in the season. When required for roasting purposes these nuts were soaked in water until sufficiently freshened and swollen, permitted to dry a little and then roasted and sold. This year it isn't probable any such course has been pursued. It is said that the year following one of scarcity the crop during the autumn is generally a large one and the nuts of excellent quality. The dealers must therefore wait until 1887 to make up for the losses incurred or small profits of 1886.

It is probable that within a week or two the roasting-pan will be laid sorrowfully away until next year.

Philadelphia Inquirer, November 8, 1886

Chestnuts Are Plentiful.

Chestnuts ought to be cheap this year, for they are abundant, and never were finer or larger. At present they cost seven dollars a bushel in New York. The chestnut tree thrives best by the roadside or at the edge of clearings—not so well in thick woods—and its fruit is therefore easy to find. In Sussex county, N.J., the trees are hardly seen, except on a narrow slate ridge, half a mile wide, that runs for some miles nearly east and west.—New York Letter.

The State, Columbia, S.C., October 23, 1892

There are no statistics to show how many bushels of chestnuts are marketed every fall, but one has only to visit the produce houses in our large cities at the proper season—or, better still, the country stores and express offices in the small towns in the Appalachian Mountains—to realize that it is large indeed, for the bulk of the nuts on the market come from these mountains. With the first frost, the women and children seek the woods to collect the freshly fallen nuts, taking them to the country stores, where they are sold or exchanged for other commodities. . . . Realizing the value of the nuts, some of the mountaineer farmers have selected suitable tracts of chestnut growth . . . and thinned out the trees so as to develop specimens with large crowns, which results in increased nut production. These places are locally called chestnut orchards.

P. L. Buttrick, "Commercial Uses of Chestnut," 1915

"Went a-chestnutting": Thoreau the Gatherer

Henry David Thoreau (1817–62), philosopher, naturalist, and the author of Walden *and "Civil Disobedience," is closely identified with the transcendentalist philosophy of Ralph Waldo Emerson, who taught the unity of nature and God, but Thoreau went on to live far more deeply immersed than Emerson in the natural world. Chestnutting in autumn was among Thoreau's favorite occupations. Following are only a few of the numerous references to chestnuts in his voluminous journals. From* The Writings of Henry David Thoreau, *edited by F. B. Sanborn and Bradford Torrey, Houghton Mifflin, 1906.*

January 10, 1853:

Went a-chestnutting this afternoon to Smith's wood-lot near the Turnpike. Carried four ladies. I raked. We got six and a half quarts, the ground being bare and the leaves not frozen. The fourth remarkably mild day. I found thirty-five chestnuts in a little pile under the end of a stick under the leaves, near—within a foot of—what I should call a gallery of a meadow mouse. These galleries were quite common as I raked. There was no nest nor apparent cavity about this store. Aunt M. found another with sixteen in it. Many chestnuts are still in the burs on the ground.

October 23, 1855:

Now is the time for chestnuts. A stone cast against the trees shakes them down in showers upon one's head and shoulders. But I cannot excuse myself for using the stone. It is not innocent, it is not just, so to maltreat the tree that feeds us. I am not disturbed by considering that if I thus shorten its life I shall not enjoy its fruit so long, but am prompted to a more innocent course by motives purely of humanity. I sympathize with the tree, yet I heaved a big stone against the trunks like a robber,—not too good to commit murder. I trust that I shall never do it again. These gifts should be accepted, not merely with gentleness, but with a certain humble gratitude. The tree whose fruit we would obtain should not be too rudely shaken even. It is not a time of distress, when a little haste and violence even might be pardoned. It is worse than boorish, it is criminal, to inflict an unnecessary injury on the tree that feeds or shadows us. Old trees are our parents, and our parents' parents, perchance. If you would learn the secrets of Nature, you must practice more humanity than others. The thought that I was robbing myself by injuring the tree did not occur to me, but I was affected as if I had cast a rock at a sentient being,—with a duller sense than my own, it is true, but yet a distant relation. Behold a man cutting down a tree to come at the fruit! What is the moral of such an act?"

Now is the time for chestnuts. A stone cast against the trees shakes them down in showers upon one's head and shoulders. But I cannot excuse myself for using the stone.

October 18, 1856:

"A-chestnutting down Turnpike and across to Britton's, thinking that the rain now added to the frosts would relax the burs which were open and let the nuts drop. . . . The chestnuts are not so ready to fall as I expected. Perhaps the burs require to be dried now after the rain. In a day or two they will nearly all come down. They are a pretty fruit, thus compactly stowed away in this bristly chest,—three is the regular number, and there is no room to spare,—the two outside nuts having each one convex side without and a flat side within; the middle nut has two flat sides. Sometimes there are several more nuts in a bur, but this year the burs are small, and there are not commonly more than two good nuts, very often only one, the middle one, both sides of which will then be convex, each way bulging out into a thin abortive mere reminiscence of a nut, all shell, beyond it. It is a rich sight, that of a large chestnut tree with a dome-shaped top, where the yellowing leaves have become thin,—for most now strew the ground evenly as a carpet throughout the chestnut woods and so save some seed,—all richly rough with great brown burs, which are opened into several segments so as to show the wholesome-colored nuts peeping forth, ready to fall on the slightest jar. The individual nuts are very interesting, of various forms, according to the season and the number in a bur. The base of each where it was joined to the bur is marked with an irregular dark figure on a light ground, oblong or crescent-shaped commonly, like a spider or other insect with a dozen legs, while the upper or small end tapers into a little white, woolly spire crowned with a star, and the whole upper slopes of the nuts are covered with the same hoary wool, which reminds you of the frosts on whose advent they peep forth. Each nut stretches forth a little starry hand at the end of a slender arm—and by this, when mature, you may pull it out without fear of prickles. Within this thick prickly bur the

Henry David Thoreau was fascinated by chestnuts.

December 1, 1856:

I have seen more chestnuts in the streets of New York than anywhere else this year, large and plump ones, roasting in the street, roasting and popping on the steps of banks and exchanges. Was surprised to see that the citizens made as much of the nuts of the wild-wood as the squirrels. Not only the country boys, all New York goes a-nutting. Chestnuts for cabmen and newsboys, for not only are squirrels to be fed.

Chestnut vendor, New York City, circa 1903. (Courtesy of the Museum of New York, Byron Company Collection.)

nuts are about as safe until they are quite mature, as a porcupine behind its spines. Yet I see where the squirrels have gnawed through many closed burs and left the pieces on the stumps. . . . I forgot to say that there are sometimes two meats within one chestnut shell, divided transversely, and each covered by its separate brown-ribbed skin.

December 12, 1856:
At the wall between Saw Mill Brook Falls and Red Choke-berry Path, I see where a great many chestnut burs have been recently chewed up fine by the squirrels, to come at the nuts. The wall for half a dozen rods and the snow are covered with them. You can see where they have dug the burs out of the snow, and then sat on a rock or the wall and gnawed them in pieces. I, too, dig many burs out of the snow with my foot, and though many of these nuts are softened and discolored they have a peculiarly sweet and agreeable taste.

October 22, 1857:
What a perfect chest the chestnut is packed in! I now hold a green bur in my hand which, round, must have been two and a quarter inches in diameter, from which three plump nuts have been extracted. It has a straight, stout stem three sixteenths of an inch in diameter, set on strongly and abruptly. It has gaped in four segments or quarters, revealing the thickness of its walls, from five eighths to three quarters of an inch. With such wonderful care Nature has secluded and defended these nuts, as if they were her most precious fruits, while diamonds are left to take care of themselves. First it bristles all over with sharp green prickles, some nearly half an inch long, like a hedgehog rolled into a ball; these rest on a thick, stiff, bark-like rind, one sixteenth to one eighth of an inch thick, which, again, is most daintily lined with a kind of silvery fur or velvet plush one sixteenth of an inch thick, even rising in a ridge between the nuts, like the lining of a casket in which the most precious commodities are kept. I see the brown-spotted white cavities where the bases of the nuts have rested and sucked up nourishment from the stem. The little stars on the top of the nuts are but shorter and feebler spines which mingle with the rest. They stand up close together, three or more, erecting their tiny weapons, as an infant in the brawny arms of its nurse might put out its own tiny hands, to fend off the aggressor. There is no waste room. The chest is packed quite full; half-developed nuts are the waste paper used in the packing, to fill the vacancies. At last Frost comes to unlock this chest; it alone holds the true key. Its lids straightway gape open, and the October air rushes in, dries the ripe nuts, and then with a ruder gust shakes them all out in a rattling shower down upon the withered leaves.

What a perfect chest the chestnut is packed in!

Such is the cradle, thus daintily lined, in which they have been rocked in their infancy. . . . The chestnut, with its tough shell, looks as if it were able to protect itself, but see how tenderly it has been reared in its cradle before its green and tender skin hardened into a shell. The October air comes in, as I have said, and the light too, and proceed to paint the nuts that clear, handsome reddish (?) brown which we call chestnut. Nowadays the brush that paints chestnuts is very active. It is entering into every open bur over the stretching forests' tops for hundreds of miles, without horse or ladder, and putting on rapid coats of this wholesome color. Otherwise the boys would not think they had got perfect nuts. And that this may be further protected, perchance, both within the bur and afterward, the nuts themselves are partly covered toward the top, where they are first exposed, with that same soft velvety down. And then Nature drops it on the rustling leaves, a *done* nut, prepared to begin a chestnut's course again. Within itself, again, each individual nut is lined with a reddish velvet, as if to preserve the seed from jar and injury in falling and, perchance, from sudden damp and cold, and, within that, a thin white skin enwraps the germ. Thus it is lining within lining and unwearied care,—not to count closely, six coverings at least before you reach the contents! ∾

"They are a pretty fruit, thus compactly stowed away in this bristly chest,— three is the regular number, and there is no room to spare." (U.S. Department of Agriculture.)

Chestnut Orchards

By Ralph H. Lutts

The following is excerpted from the author's "Manna from God: The American chestnut trade in southwestern Virginia," in the journal Environmental History, *July 2004.*

Chestnut orchards provide an interesting case that has not been studied. These orchards, sometimes called groves, were common and are often mentioned in interviews and memoirs. "The chestnut groves were about as valuable to us in those days as other orchards," wrote Pedro Sloan of Franklin County. One Great Smoky Mountains informant recalled that, "Just about every farm on Fines Creek and Crabtree had a chestnut orchard even though chestnut trees grew wild everywhere." Yet little is known about the orchards. In many cases they were natural forest stands that were managed to favor chestnuts. Louise McNeill, who served as West Virginia's poet laureate, recalled one example: "We had always called Uncle Dan'l's trees 'the chestnut orchard,' just across our line fence on the flat knoll of his part of Old Tom's farm. Forty or fifty big American chestnut trees stood there together, as the old men had saved them from the first clearing back in the Indian times, and for generations they had been the neighborhood nutting ground."

One Patrick County resident explained that chestnut orchards were natural stands cleared of underbrush. Farmers kept the ground within the orchards clean to make it easier to find and gather the nuts. Early Hopkins, who lived in the county's Blue Ridge foothills, told an interviewer: "I believe there was more people on top of the mountain had the chestnut orchards, cleaned out all of the undergrowth, than they did down here. But some of them down here you know, they'd go through and cut all their undergrowth, and there was little fine grass come up under that, made it easy to get the chestnuts." Max Thomas, a respected Floyd County elder, local folklorist, and former biology teacher, reported that "people years ago had cleared the woods of everything except chestnut trees, which they lined up in rows about fifty feet apart."

Other tree species were weeded out, which opened the grove's canopy and promoted chestnut growth.

These chestnut orchards began as natural forest stands. Other tree species were weeded out, which opened the grove's canopy and promoted chestnut growth. Hogs and other farm animals foraging in the woods also had a great impact upon the undergrowth and forest regeneration. Perhaps fire also was used to manage the undergrowth, though only one bit of evidence suggests that: A newspaper article, circa 1900, recorded that "Wilber Phipps, a farmer of Freeling, had his barn destroyed by catching fire from some burning leaves about his chestnut orchard." Perhaps Phipps was burning the undergrowth in his orchard.

If fire was used as a management tool, did European colonists learn this method from the natives? Native Americans used fire to manage vegetation near their villages, and some scholars speculate that they also managed forests to encourage nut-bearing trees, including chestnut. In any event, it appears that at least some chestnut orchards were natural stands of trees that, through the labor of individual farmers and their families, were culturally redefined as objects of agriculture. Given the effort that farmers must have devoted to maintaining the orchards, it is reasonable to assume that they tried to control access to them. If so, the chestnut orchards were removed, to some extent, from the foraging commons.

The West Virginia chestnut orchard that Louise McNeill described was used by the neighborhood, so it still was a communal resource to some extent. However, there is an intriguing tale from Cumberland County, Kentucky, that suggests that some people were very possessive of their orchards. According to folklorist William Lynwood Montell, the African American community of Coe Ridge had "a large chestnut orchard," which became contested ground: "Friction between the races was intensified by some of the white boys who made it a habit to go to the ridge and freely partake of the abundant chestnut supply. The Negro boys and girls, who picked up the chestnuts and sold them for cash, resented the intrusion on their personal property. On one occasion, a fight over chestnuts broke out between the races. 'That's what started all of the killing,' claimed Tim Coe."

In this incident and the ensuing feud, issues of racial conflict overshadowed those related to the resource commons. Nevertheless, the incident raises questions about the right of access to the resource, individually and communally. It also introduces race as a framework within which the chestnut commons and trade need to be studied. ~

Farmer with a thirty-five-year-old tree from seed, Crawford County, Pennsylvania. (Pennsylvania Chestnut Blight Commission.)

"A Sight on Earth"

The following oral histories, recorded in Rabun County, Georgia, were originally published in 1980 in Foxfire 6. *Gathering, eating, storing, cooking, and peddling the nuts of the American chestnut were recurring subjects of interest.*

Jake Waldroop:

The nuts grow inside a burr, and it's a big thing, as big as your fist, and 'long about the fall of the year when it starts frosting they'll open. Then the chestnuts fall out, and later the burr itself will drop off. I've seen them a time or two in the fall, it's come a dry spell of weather and the [burrs] would open, but there wouldn't be enough moisture, and [the nuts] wouldn't get loose of the burr, and it'd stay in there. I've seen hundreds of bushels hanging up, and you couldn't pick one to eat. Then it'd start to cloud up, rain some, and it was a sight on earth—just in an hour or two the whole earth would be covered with chestnuts. The moisture would hit them, and they'd all drop out. They'd generally start falling along the latter part of September up till the middle of October. October was the main chestnut month.

We'd pick them up in the fall of the year, and whenever they went to falling a wagoner would [come through] and buy 'em and go South with 'em. Down around Toccoa and Lavonia and Athens, all the way to Atlanta, Georgia. Everywhere, selling them chestnuts.

A small little kid could pick up chestnuts. We'd get up before breakfast and go to these trees where a lot of chestnuts had fallen overnight, beat the hogs there, and pick them up. Take them to market, sell them, and get our shoes, clothes, or other things with them. We'd take 'em and boil 'em or roast 'em or just hang them out and let them dry. Now a good way to keep them through the winter—keep you something to eat all winter—was to get a big box and put [in] a layer of chestnuts, then sprinkle some salt on that, another layer of chestnuts, and sprinkle salt, and keep going. If you didn't do something like that the worms would get inside the shell.

I've seen the ground when there were just hundreds and hundreds of bushels of chestnuts on it, just laying on the ground everywhere. They were good for the squirrel, turkey, bear, hogs, and mice. The squirrels and little mice [would] put them up for their winter feed. I've chopped into a mouse den and got a peck to half a bushel. Be a little bit of a hole in the tree where they went down and started to fill it up with chestnuts. They'd put in a layer of chestnuts, a layer of mud, a layer of chestnuts, a layer of mud, and the chestnuts would stay there right like they grew, all winter. Now the chestnuts supported everything. There wasn't no kind of game that roamed these mountains that didn't eat chestnuts. Everything.

Noel Moore:

We put the nuts out in the sunshine and let 'em dry and that would sweeten 'em. The sunshine would do something to the sugar, sweetened 'em. We'd always gather several bags and put 'em out on a rack and let 'em dry in the sunshine. You'd have to pour boiling water over 'em, though, to kill the eggs that were laid in 'em by some kind of insect. If you didn't, the worms would eat 'em up, and you'd have a sack full of worms. [In cooking, people] used chestnuts principally for making stuffing and they made a bread out of it, too, called nut bread. They'd beat it up [couldn't grind it in the mill because it was too soft and would gum up the mill], beat it up with a wooden mallet and mix it with meal and flour.

There were people who made their living picking up chestnuts and carrying them to the store. I've seen 'em coming out of the mountains [behind] where we lived over where Burton Lake is now. There was a big mountain back of our house with just a tremendous amount of chestnut trees on it. We'd hardly ever see these people at all, except when they came out to go to the store, and in the fall we could see 'em coming, maybe the parents and three or four kids coming down the trail. The old man would have a big coffee sack full of chestnuts on his back, and the little fellers would have smaller sacks, and even the mother would have a small sack of chestnuts caught up on her hip. They'd all trek to the store and they'd swap that for coffee and sugar and flour and things that they had to buy to live on through the winter. That's the way they made their living. You could go in the woods in the fall, and where a log had fallen across the side of the hill, and the chestnuts had rolled down against it, you could reach down and pick 'em up by the double handful.

We had what you call a free range here then and you had to fence your farm and fields to keep out the stock that was turned loose in the mountains.

The hogs and deer and turkeys and squirrels thrived on the nuts. . . . We had what you call a free range here then and you had to fence your farm and fields to keep out the stock that was turned loose in the mountains. People would let their breeding stock run free in the woods, and the hogs would live on the chestnuts and acorns that they could pick up off the ground. In the fall, after [the hogs] got fat on the mast (they'd get as fat as they could and still walk), the farmers would catch 'em with dogs. That's the way they got their meat. If they wanted to cure the meat and keep it through the winter, they'd put the hogs up and feed 'em on corn for a few weeks, then butcher 'em. But the ones that was killed in the mountains, right off the mast, you had to eat 'em then, [because] you couldn't cure [the meat]. It wouldn't keep—wouldn't take salt and cure like grain-fed meat would. It was better-flavored meat, sweet and tender. You could eat all you wanted and it wouldn't hurt you. Didn't have so much grease, and what it had was mild. . . .

There's a man in Mountain City who has an orchard of Chinese chestnuts [which are resistant to the blight]. He has a terrible crop of them each summer, more than he can sell. But they're not as good as the wild chestnuts. They don't have a sweet nutty taste. But you can boil those or roast 'em, and that enhances the flavor. But the wild chestnuts you could eat raw, right after they fell, especially when they were green. Before they dried, they were soft and tender and you could chew 'em easy.

Mrs. M. C. Speed:

Now my daddy used to—we called it peddling. [He'd] take a mule and a wagon and go to South Carolina with a load of stuff every week or two. When the chestnuts were in, I'd pick 'em up and get the money for 'em, and I was glad to get to pick 'em up 'cause I'd get the money for 'em. And I was stingy with 'em as I could be, I'll just tell you the truth! When I was little I thought every chestnut I picked up had to be sold. I did that starting when I was just a little girl, just big enough to pick 'em up. I'd go in the morning to get the ones that fell overnight. They were [usually] easy to gather, but sometimes you'd stick your finger [on the burr] and it'd hurt. You see, if the nut hadn't fallen out of the burr you could stomp on them, or sometimes you could take your fingers and pick 'em out.

From Appalachia to New England, chestnut season is still fondly remembered, as evident in this selection of reminiscences gathered over the years by The American Chestnut Foundation.

"They were easy to gather, but sometimes you'd stick your finger and it'd hurt."

I grew up in rural southern Kentucky in the late 1920s and 1930s. We looked forward to fall when the chestnuts would get ripe. As was common back then, I walked to school barefooted. My feet were really tough and I could stomp chestnut burs open with my heel (you had to be careful to use your heel and not the softer parts of the foot). There was a huge chestnut tree in the churchyard that I passed as I walked to school each day. It was too big to climb so we would throw rocks up into it to knock the chestnuts down.

My grandfather had a huge tree in his yard that I could climb and crawl out on a limb to get the nuts right from the tree. When my grandparents cleared "new ground," they always left the chestnut trees.

Arles Weaver, in the fall 2005 issue of TACF's newsletter, *The Bark*

I am 95 years old and can remember picking up native chestnuts. In the fall of the year, after a frost, the burs would fall on the frozen ground and burst open and we would pick up three or four nice large nuts from each bur. I can remember filling my pockets with the nuts on the way to school. During class, I would make believe I was reading a book and I would be peeling a chestnut and eating it. One time the teacher caught me and she made me put my chestnuts on her desk. After class, I waited until the kids had all left the room, and I went up to the teacher's desk to get my chestnuts. The class was gone, the teacher was gone, and so were my chestnuts! I guess my teacher liked chestnuts too.

Carl A. Anderson, Upton, Massachusetts, 2002

I was born 1916 at Slatyfork, West Virginia, and chestnuts were a part of rural life. When anyone went squirrel hunting their choice location was where there was a group of chestnut trees. One sat down near a chestnut tree loaded with ripe chestnuts and wait[ed] quietly for the squirrels to come to get nuts to hide underground for winter use. Sometimes the squirrels were already in the big tree and you didn't know it.

Dave Sharp, Cincinnati, Ohio, 2002

I grew up in the small college town of Farmville in mid-state Virginia. I don't remember that I ever knew what a chestnut tree looked like. But, my father was a hunter and when he would return from a hunting trip with a squirrel, quail, rabbit, or turkey, he often emptied chestnuts from the pockets of his hunting jacket. They were wonderful roasted and often enhanced the stuffing for the turkey.

Marguerite Y. Rupp, Wellesley, Massachusetts, 2002

Chestnuts! Real chestnuts that were so very wonderful to enjoy! How anxiously we waited for the first fall frost to drop those prickly burs to where they split open and ejected their brown jewels. We would rush to the woodland spots to find carpets of those nuts and fill our caps within minutes. We were too young to pay much attention to those great trees that gave us their sweet bits but I do remember how we roasted our find on the old iron range top and tasted the unique flavor.

Lester H. Harris (nonagenarian), Marion, Connecticut, 2003

"A Painful Experience": Bare Feet and Hungry Hogs

Lola Cook Miller's earliest memories of chestnuts go way back to when she was about five years old in the early 1930s. She walked with her father up behind the house to a huge, spreading chestnut tree. She remembers that you never walked barefoot under a chestnut tree! They picked up sackfuls of the nuts, carefully plucking them out of the opened prickly burs. The nuts were smaller than the Oriental chestnuts, but had much better flavor. They were roasted or boiled and sometimes were the whole meal. With a smile, Lola said that when many were eaten, they were pretty gassy!

As told to Barbara Whitener of Greensboro, North Carolina, 2002

My earliest memory of the old chestnut tree was when I was very young and the whole family would go chestnut hunting in the fall. Since the trees were very tall, taller than the other ones around, they were easily located. The fruit grew within a bur about the size of a baseball. Those of you who have never attacked a bur have missed a painful experience. Burs were very unforgiving and a porcupine didn't have anything on the chestnut bur when it came to pricks. The fruit was gathered and put into buckets or bags to dry. During the winter months the fruit was boiled, roasted on the fire, or just eaten raw like eating a walnut or hickory nut. The fruit had a sweet taste.

Forrest Stafford, Liberty, Kentucky, 2002

The year was 1929 or 1930. The place was Henry County, [a] Tennessee River County in Northwest Tennessee. I was 7 or 8 years old. I remember distinctly that there were three or four large chestnut trees on that particular wooded slope where we went to gather chestnuts during those bright October days. And I remember quite vividly too that one of the trees had a portion of its bole that was bare of bark, showing grayish white wood. Of course we knew nothing of the chestnut blight. . . . The large chestnut trees were loaded with burs. My father screwed a large metal nut on the end of a two- or three-foot long broom handle. We called this a flailing stick. We threw the stick into the tree, dislodging the nuts or bringing down the entire bur. The burs that were not open we opened with our feet, usually clad in canvas tennis shoes. I remember well the distinct discomfort from the spines sticking through the canvas. I remember best however the pocketfuls of sweet chestnuts. We carried the pocketfuls to school and for some reason the teacher permitted nibbling on chestnuts, but definitely not on a Milky Way candy bar.

Robert W. McGowan, Somerville, Tennessee, 2002. McGowan is professor emeritus of biology at the University of Memphis.

Wild chestnuts were a favorite fall forage for hogs.

Chestnut trees were found all over the valley of the Elk [River, West Virginia]. Any barefoot boy who was still trying to get a few more miles from his unshod feet before the severe chill of autumn quickly learned that life under the spreading chestnut tree could be hazardous. . . . Chestnuts were eaten in the home, at school, on trips to the mailbox, and on any excursion more than 100 yards from the house. No boy would even consider going to a pie supper, protracted meeting, or any other night event without a pint of chestnuts in his pockets. Some chestnuts, particularly those which had been stored for several days, were inhabited by small white worms, and many a tiny creature met death in the darkness of night somewhere along the road to or from church.

Raymond Mace of Slatyfork, West Virginia, courtesy of Dave Sharp, Cincinnati, Ohio, 2002

In the spring, as you got away from the mountain [Massanutten Mountain, Rockingham County, Virginia], you could see spring coming as the bloom moved up the mountain. The forest was so thick with chestnuts that at a distance Massanutten seemed to be nothing but a band of creamy white that got larger as it crept up the mountain. . . . In the fall, because people didn't raise corn to feed their hogs, farmers would let them run in the mountain where they fattened up on chestnuts. The hogs would have to eat through the big burs on the outside to get the nut out. The burs were rough to the hands, even with a pair of gloves on, but the hogs must have liked the nuts so much they would chew through them until their mouths were bleeding.

William A. Good, interviewed by Charles A. Miller

"A Noticeable Decrease in the Game"

Wildlife Food: The Pre-blight Chestnut and the Post-blight Acorn

By William Lord

This article first appeared in a different form in the spring 2005 Journal of The American Chestnut Foundation.

By two paramount standards, the American chestnut, prior to the blight, was the most important wildlife food throughout its range in the forests of eastern America. It was the single most abundant tree, and its plentiful, reliable nut crop provided more nourishment than any other member of the plant kingdom.

The trees that replaced the chestnut varied north to south. In New England the sugar maple and the northern red and the chestnut oaks benefited from the chestnut's demise; in Pennsylvania, it was the red maple, black cherry, chestnut oak, and hickories. Oaks and hickories dominated in the South. Of these trees only oak acorns provide nourishment to sustain wildlife through the scarcity of winter.

Wildlife biology did not become a university trained profession until the 1930s. Therefore our knowledge of how wildlife fared before the chestnut blight lacks hard data. However, we have the apt and timeless observations of writers like Henry David Thoreau, who, describing "chestnutting in mid-winter," recounts finding "thirty or forty nuts in a pile left in its gallery just under the leaves by the common wood mouse," and "one February, as much as a peck of chestnuts in different parcels within a short distance of one another, under the leaves, placed there . . . by the striped squirrel."

Moist and protected beneath a cover of dead leaves, chestnuts remained fresh and viable until they germinated in spring. As such they provided winter sustenance for deer, rabbit, bear, raccoon, wild boar, squirrels and chipmunks, mice, wood rats, turkey, grouse, crows and jays.

Fallen chestnuts covered with leaves would remain fresh through the winter. (Photo by Joe Schibig.)

How well has the acorn crop sustained wildlife since the demise of the chestnut? Obviously not as well. The chestnut was noted for the abundance and reliability of its fall harvest. Oaks flower in spring, and killing frosts may null an acorn crop. The chestnut flowers in June to early July, when killing frosts seldom occur.

Oaks of the white oak group, including the post and chestnut oaks, produce acorns annually. The acorns of the red oak group, including the black, pin, and scarlet oaks, require two years to mature. A killing frost in one year would deplete the white oak crop; a killing frost in two successive years could eliminate the entire acorn crop.

But even in the absence of killing frosts, acorn production is much less reliable than the well-recorded bounty of the chestnut. Recent studies show that acorn production is a complex of cycles with highs and lows regardless of the weather. Thus, frost or no frost, acorn abundance is hard to predict.

Wildlife biologists use the term "mast" to describe food produced by plants available to wildlife. Soft mast includes berries, grapes, and apples. Hard mast refers primarily to nuts like the acorn, chestnut, hickory, beech, and walnut. Only hard mast provides food during winter. Now with no chestnut bounty, acorns are the principal winter food.

Studies on black bear during poor mast years have shown that starvation is a real threat. In Minnesota a female black bear with three cubs was monitored by a radio device contained in a collar. Acorns were in short supply. A research team located the bears the following spring, and the yearlings were so weak they could not climb a tree.

In West Virginia wildlife biologists observed bears that were "skin and bones" in the spring following a mast failure. Reports were common of weakened bears unable to walk along steep trails or stream banks.

How did bear and other wildlife fare in the pre-blight forest? Folk tales expand the bounty described by Thoreau. Even with allowance for exuberant exaggeration, doubt is not possible. "The chestnut mast is knee deep. . . . A man fell waist deep in the mast and had to be pulled out. . . . Did game fatten on chestnut? Lord have mercy, yes. Rabbits were so fat and lazy a child could fetch one with a chucking stone."

The most abundant acorn crop seen today is seldom more than a sprinkle among the fallen leaves. It must be admitted that cold, rainy weather during chestnut bloom could depress the nut crop, but such events had less effect than killing frosts on acorns.

The return of a chestnut blended forest will result in more wildlife maneuvering among its branches and foraging beneath its shade. ~

I remember a tree in New Jersey whose trunk was so large that three persons by taking hold of hands and stretching their arms could barely reach around it. In bearing years it produced bushels of nuts. One day some young friends shook off more than a bushel. The dinner bell rang before all were gathered and about half a bushel were left on the ground. When the young people returned after dinner for the nuts not one could be found. A flock of turkeys had just finished the last of them.

The Congregationalist, October 1896

Wild turkeys foraging for chestnuts in a New England hardwood forest. Illustration by Frederick Paillet.

Illustration by Susan Bull Riley.

After I'd been at Emory for eighteen years, I moved back up here, and I do notice a lot of difference in the presence [then], and the absence [now], of the chestnut. First in the game. We used to be able to get turkeys and squirrels everywhere. I'm not certain that we had as many deer then as we do now, as you know deer forage on other things as well. But there were a lot more squirrels, and a lot more of other types of game. Turkeys in particular. I remember getting five turkeys on one hunt. You just don't see that these days. There has been a noticeable decrease in the game.

Dr. John Brown, from "Memories of the American Chestnut," in *Foxfire 6*

About 100,000 long cords of chestnut wood per annum are used in this [tannin] industry in North Carolina alone.

—P. L. Buttrick

Fifteen thousand cords of American chestnut are piled outside the Champion Fibre mill in Canton, North Carolina, in 1937. The plant used 275 cords a day. (Courtesy of Great Smoky Mountains National Park Library.)

THE WOOD

At last when the tree can serve us no longer in any other way it forms the basic wood onto which oak and other woods are veneered to make our coffins.

—P. L. Buttrick

"It Touches Almost Every Phase of Our Existence"

By P. L. Buttrick

Philip Laurence Buttrick, born in 1886, was the author of Forest Economics and Finance *(1943). Based in New England, he led an active career in forestry in the first half of the twentieth century. The following is from "Commercial Uses of Chestnut," which appeared in the October 1915 issue of* American Forestry.

Chestnut is neither a very strong nor very hard wood, not nearly so strong or hard as oak, but it is very even grained and durable. It will outlast almost all the oaks and most other hardwoods, its durability being due to the high percentage of tannin which it contains. It is light in weight and easily worked and does not warp readily. . . .

This lightness, freedom from warping, durability and reasonable strength, and the high percentage of valuable chemical substances which it contains, together with its great abundance have given chestnut a greater variety of uses than almost any other American hardwood. It touches almost every phase of our existence. It serves as a shade and ornamental tree on our parks and estates. Its wood is used in the building and decoration of our houses and the manufacture of our furniture. We sit down in chairs made of chestnut and transact our business at desks, ostensibly of oak, but generally of chestnut veneered with oak, we receive messages from the distance over wires strung on chestnut poles. We sit on a railroad train and read newspapers into whose composition chestnut pulp has gone, while our train travels over rails supported on chestnut ties and over trestles built of chestnut piles, along a track whose right-of-way is fenced by wire supported on chestnut posts. On the same train travel goods shipped in boxes and barrels made of chestnut boards and staves. Even the leather for our shoes is tanned in an extract made from chestnut wood. In the Fall we munch hot roasted chestnuts and many housewives feel that they are a necessary part of dressings of various kinds. At last when the tree can serve us no longer in any other way it forms the basic wood onto which oak and other woods are veneered to make our coffins.

Its Early History

The early settlers encountered chestnut pretty well up and down the eastern coast of the United States, and when food was scarce, if we are to believe our school histories, they were glad to make use of its succulent nuts as a serious part of their diet, even as did the Indians. . . . when the local pine was exhausted . . . oak and chestnut then began to be used and many Revolutionary and early nineteenth century houses were built of hewn oak and chestnut frames, oak floors, and chestnut sidings and shingles. . . . Country houses and barns are even yet frequently framed of local hardwood timbers, and one does not have to go back many years to find barns built of heavy hand-hewn chestnut beams put together with wooden pins. . . . In the Appalachian Mountains, even as far north as Pennsylvania, to this day log cabins are built of chestnut logs, sometimes in the round, sometimes hewn square.

The earliest use of chestnut still remains one of its important ones, for chestnut has been a fencing wood since Colonial times. Few woods split lengthwise easier and straighter than chestnut, or are lighter or more durable. Fence rails made of it will last a lifetime. The early settlers built their fences of chestnut rails, piling them in the familiar snake or zigzag fashion. . . . Later in the North a form of fence came into use in which the rails were mortised into the posts set in the ground. . . . Posts of larger size are frequently used for the foundations of shore cottages and other buildings which are built without cellars. . . .

The advent of the telegraph and telephone created a demand for large poles. At first, apparently, many woods were used indiscriminately, but for a long time the value of chestnut for this use as well as for trolley and electric light poles has been fully realized. Taking the country as a whole, cedar is the chief pole wood, but east of the Mississippi, where chestnut is available in large quantities, it outranks all other woods used for the purpose, and even taking the United States as a whole, 20 percent of the poles used are chestnut. . . .

The early settlers soon learned that chestnut did not make very desirable firewood, and their descendants have not forgotten the fact. Dry chestnut burns easily and quickly, but it snaps and crackles, throwing out sparks profusely. This makes it undesirable for the fireplace. Yet it is one of the best of hardwoods for kindling, since it splits easily and ignites quickly. . . . Sometimes chestnut is used in rural districts, where the gas range is not, as "summer wood." The fact that it ignites and burns quickly renders it desirable when a light, quick fire is wanted.

Chestnut Wood as a Source of Tannic Acid

. . . Chestnut wood is rich in [tannic acid]. Its tannin content averages more than 8 per cent, occasionally running as high as 12 per cent. . . . Over two-thirds of all the tannic acid produced in the United States is now extracted from chestnut wood and bark.

It is used in the manufacture of leather and the dyeing of silk. . . .

The industry of extracting tannic acid from chestnut wood is largely confined to the South. . . . The industry centers in southwestern Virginia, western North Carolina and eastern Tennessee, where some twenty plants, with a combined product of perhaps 1,000 barrels of extract per day, are at work. The process is very simple. The cordwood is ground up into small chips, placed in tanks and leached out by hot water. The product is then evaporated to dryness or the required degree of concentration. Although cordwood is generally used, sawmill waste is sometimes employed. . . . About 100,000 long cords of chestnut wood per annum are used in this industry in North Carolina alone, while Tennessee uses about half that amount, and the total production is reported to be about 250,000 standard cords per annum.

A few paper pulp plants in the South use chestnut in the manufacture of their product. The plant which uses probably the largest amount of this wood for the purpose has or had a contract to supply the Government with the paper for its postal cards. . . .

Log loader, Little River Lumber Company, in the Great Smoky Mountains, circa 1915. (Courtesy of Great Smoky Mountains National Park Library.)

Chestnut Lumber

Chestnut lumber is used for house construction, both interior and exterior. . . . Yet in spite of its many uses for building and construction it is much more in demand for house furnishing than house building. It is, in fact, one of our leading furniture woods, quite probably surpassing any one of the oaks in volume used, yet, with the exception of panels in wooden bedsteads, kitchen furniture and the less expensive chairs, bureaus, and tables, we see little furniture finished in chestnut. Its great use comes as core stock for veneers. . . . Tables, desks, bureaus, cabinets, and the like are often made of chestnut and covered with thin veneers of oak, maple, cherry, walnut or expensive tropical woods such as mahogany or rosewood. The essential wood of pianos is frequently chestnut.

There are two reasons for the popularity of chestnut in the furniture industry. First, it is abundant, light, holds its shape well, does not warp, is not affected by moisture, and can be obtained in wide widths. . . . Second, its open, porous structure, combined with freedom from knots, pitch or blemishes, and the frequent presence of numerous small holes. . . . caused by a boring insect, known as the chestnut timber worm, enable the glue which binds the core to the veneer to take a good grip. . . .

Coffins are hardly to be classified as furniture, yet they are made of much the same woods, and the process of manufacture is quite similar to that of many more cheerful articles. The coffin manufacturers probably use more chestnut than any other wood. It is used solid in coffins . . . of the less expensive grades, and as a backing for veneered coffins of higher price. . . .

. . . We have failed to mention chestnut as a shingle wood. Most of our shingles are of soft wood. . . . Chestnut is seventh on the list, but it is the leading hardwood. In 1909, 91,760,000 chestnut shingles were manufactured. . . . The above figure presumably does not include the large number of hand-made chestnut shingles made in the Southern Appalachians. . . Chestnut shingles are very durable and weather to an attractive shade. . . . It is . . . hard to get much chestnut shingle stock free from the worm holes previously mentioned, and these cause them to leak. It seems as though it ought to be possible to work up a market for chestnut shingles to be used as side shingles on cottages and suburban residences. Their attractive gray color when weathered is as pleasing as white cedar, and the supply is unlimited. . . .

"Gaining in Popularity"

In 1906 [the year of the first scientific description of the blight] the total amount of chestnut cut for lumber was 407,379,000 feet, board measure, of which amount Pennsylvania, West Virginia, Connecticut, and Tennessee produced over one-half. Chestnut has been gaining in popularity during the last few years, the cut of 1906 having been almost double that of 1899.

The wood is used principally for railroad ties, telegraph and telephone poles, posts, interior decorations, cabinet making, coffins, and for general construction purposes. Besides, the bark is used in large quantities for tanning, while both wood and bark are used for tanning extract. . . . In 1906 the total amount of chestnut extract consumed was 257,000 barrels and of chestnut bark 22,668 cords—a barrel containing 500 pounds and a cord 2,000 pounds.

In 1906 over 7,000,000 chestnut ties were purchased by the railroads.

New York Times, May 31, 1908

Processing post-blight chestnut at a portable stave mill in central Pennsylvania. (Pennsylvania Chestnut Blight Commission.)

Chestnut in the Future

Aside from its value for all sorts of uses, chestnut was long regarded as a valuable woodlot tree. . . . But its popularity was short lived, for today, notwithstanding all its good points, it is no longer upon the forester's list of desirable trees, and far from encouraging it, he is advocating its removal from the woodlot as speedily as possible. Enemies now attack this tree on every side, and it is very poor forestry to favor a tree against which nature has so definitely set her hand. . . .

One of these enemies has risen with almost drastic suddenness. Less than fifteen years ago the chestnut blight was unknown to the scientist or the woodsman. . . . At present it is found from Maine to North Carolina, and it is thought that it will all but exterminate the chestnut in the Northern States . . . and may invade the South with like disastrous results. . . . So the forester is recommending the removal of all chestnut of commercial value in the region of blight infestation in order that it may be marketed before it is destroyed. . . . Thirty years or less at the present rate of cutting will exhaust the supply of virgin chestnut timber in the Southern Appalachians. . . . If the blight and the other agents of destruction continue their devastation, it looks as though within our lifetime the chestnut will have to be added to that melancholy list of American plants and animals, like the buffalo . . . of which we say "formerly common, now rare." ∾

Thirty years or less at the present rate of cutting will exhaust the supply of virgin chestnut timber in the Southern Appalachians.

Leather, Tannin, and the Chestnut Tree

By William Lord

This article appeared in a different form in the fall 2004 Journal of The American Chestnut Foundation.

Leather is made from a variety of animal hides by a process known as tanning. Fresh hides consist primarily of protein and water. Tanning involves the replacement of a large portion of the water content of the hide with tannin, which bonds to the protein, giving the hide strength and stability. Tannin is a natural component of many plants that serves as a protection against predators and parasites. In America, from colonial times well into the nineteenth century, leather was produced by small industrial units known as tanneries, modeled from those common in Europe since the fifteenth century.

Tanning was a laborious trade, ever odious with foul-smelling animal remains, and stubbornly resisted change. The gristmill, the blacksmith, and the tannery were an essential part of every early developing community. While the miller and the smithy were receptive to advanced techniques, the tanner was never sufficiently goaded by circumstance to change. He acquired his most essential ingredient, tannin, from the bark of hemlock, oak, and chestnut, all of which were in plentiful supply.

The initial process of removing the hair from the hides required soaking in a lime solution and required up to a year. A tradesman known as a beamer then scraped the hide clear of flesh and remaining hair in preparation for the tanning pits. His strength rivaled that of a blacksmith. The work was exhausting, and beaming a dozen hides was a good day's work.

The "tan bark" was ground to the texture of a coarse sawdust. This chore relied on a horse that patiently walked around a low, circular enclosure, providing power to roll a large, cylindrical stone that crushed the tan bark—thus the "one horse" tannery.

The de-haired hides were alternated with layers of ground bark in a pit and then immersed in water. Tannin leached from the bark and slowly replaced the water in the hides. According to the wisdom of the tanner, the process was repeated by the strenuous effort of hooking the hides with long poles and placing them into adjacent pits for further treatment with more layers of tan bark. This process required several months, after which the hides were dried and then worked with oils, soaps, dyes, and other ingredients to perfect a finished product. The entire process might take two years.

Hemlock was preferred in the North; oak in the South. However, tanners often used a blend of hemlock, chestnut, and oak. They rated their tan bark like gourmets grade coffee beans. Leather tanned entirely with chestnut would be too hard and would crack easily. Tanned entirely with hemlock, it would be too soft. Oak bark could produce satisfactory leather in itself, but a good tanner knew the proper blends to fit the need.

Chestnut, although its bark was used, was not essential to the tanning process. But events in France brought a dramatic change with the development of a new method to extract tannin from the wood of European chestnut in concentrated form. Commencing in the early 1870s, an extract process could produce tannin that yielded a superior quality of leather. In America, rights to this process were purchased by the Champion Fibre Company. In 1908 it installed a huge combined tannin extract and paper mill in Canton, in western North Carolina. The site was chosen because of the abundance of native chestnut, which proved equal to the European chestnut as a source of tannin and also a superior pulp for paper.

At this time the chestnut blight was a known presence, having been discovered in New York City a few years earlier, but Champion officials perceived it as a distant threat that would never endanger the vast chestnut reserves in the southern Appalachians. Chestnut trees were felled and sawed into logs, which were hauled by ox teams or washed down mountain slopes in water-fed flumes to landing sites. Here the logs were hewn and split into uniform five-foot lengths and transported over narrow-gauge rails to the main line and on to the plant's storage yards.

The storage yard presented a vast, seventy-five-acre area with a high, row-upon-row aggregate of fifteen thousand cords—a two-month reserve supply. Wood was consumed at a rate of twelve cords per hour. At the plant the split logs were fed by a conveyer into five huge revolving chippers, reducing them "to small chips almost as quickly as one sharpens a pencil." The chips were screened to a uniform size, conveyed to overhead bins, and then poured into a set of thirty-six huge, steam-tight autoclaves. Boiling water within the autoclaves removed the tannin from the wood chips.

Chestnut acid wood collected, Coweeta Experimental Forest, North Carolina, 1942. (Photo by C. R. Hursh, courtesy of U.S. Forest Service Southern Research Station Special Collection, D. H. Ramsey Library Special Collections, University of North Carolina at Asheville.)

The extract was piped to evaporators, airtight metal tanks, for concentrating the extract, and the tannin-leached wood chips were conveyed to the pulp mill, there to make the "soft, clean, white wood pulp for paper manufacture."

The French method of extracting tannin from chestnut wood prompted change. A superior tannin product was dependably available as a liquid or as a powder and greatly shortened the time required to produce leather. This efficiency over the tan bark method resulted in the establishment of much larger tanneries that gradually replaced the small-scale, individualistic tanner.

When it began its Canton operation in 1908, Champion Fibre gave scant attention to the encroaching danger of the blight. Several years later, before the blight reached North Carolina in the early 1920s, R. W. Griffith, a company official, wrote an article on the company's operation. He considered forest fires as the greater danger. "The blight, which destroyed so many of the chestnut trees in the eastern parts of the country, fortunately never reached this area, and there is no immediate prospect of its doing so. The area, however, is not immune from the ravages of forest fires, but in the timberlands operated by the Champion Fibre Company . . . the underbrush is always cleared as the first precaution to be taken against fires, and this permits the development of a second growth [coppice], which becomes available for cutting in about twenty-five years."

Griffith may have been whistling in the dark even as he wrote. The blight flood inundated the chestnut of western North Carolina by 1924, when the U.S. Forest Service estimated the total stand of chestnut in the southern Appalachians at 33,700,000 cords. This resource was vital to the extract plants and the leather industry.

A study made by the U.S. Department of Agriculture and published in 1929 determined that blight-killed chestnut would still provide high-grade tannin: "There is no appreciable loss in tannin content in trees that have been dead for as long as 20 or 30 years."

In western North Carolina, and throughout the Appalachians, death claimed the chestnut giants, rendering the landscape bleak with their twisted, leafless forms. But the dead or dying trees prolonged the life of Champion's extract plant for many years, until the last ghosts were harvested in 1951.

Champion Paper and Fibre Company mill in Canton, North Carolina, circa 1924. (Courtesy of Great Smoky Mountains National Park Library.)

Coppicing

By William Lord

A version of this article was published in the fall 2004 Journal of The American Chestnut Foundation.

Coppicing, a practice of great antiquity, refers to the production and growth of shoots rising from a stump. In Neolithic times, tribes settling in Europe hacked down the forest with stone axes to clear land. They noticed that many of the broad-leaved trees and shrubs produced rapidly growing shoots, which they opportunely put to many uses. No tree has "outcoppiced" the chestnut. The Romans recognized this utility during their expansion in the Middle East, and through their effort the European chestnut, a native of Turkey, spread throughout the empire. The Romans introduced the chestnut to Britain, primarily to be a coppice tree.

During the following centuries, coppice culture of chestnut prevailed through much of Europe. A thorough system developed to produce the maximum and prolonged yield. A great number of the European settlers in America certainly were aware of how to coppice American chestnut in an optimal manner. Nonetheless, many did not. There were so many trees that indifferent management often prevailed.

In 1904, when the blight was first noted, approximately half the chestnut trees from Pennsylvania northward into New England were coppice.

In 1904, when the blight was first noted, approximately half the chestnut trees from Pennsylvania northward into New England were coppice. The embryonic U.S. Forest Service was energetically informing Americans how to best utilize their forest resources. Through the kindness of California TACF member Bernard Monahan, I received the 1904 Forest Bulletin No. 53 detailing how to manage chestnut coppice in Tidewater Maryland: Trees for coppice should be cut in winter. At this time the sap is concentrated in the roots, energizing the greatest growth. In addition the soil is frozen and thus prevents harmful compaction during the removal of the felled trees. Stumps should be cut at a slant and as close to the ground as possible. This will help prevent water from separating the stump bark from the trunk and facilitating the entry of harmful fungi/bacteria that could then spread to the sprouts. As many as forty sprouts may arise from the root crown. These should be thinned to the best six to provide them with all the growth energy. Some of the nut crop should be spared from human harvest and foraging hogs to permit regeneration. Cattle should not feed among coppice until the seedlings have exceeded a height of six feet. ~

"The Effects of Repeated and Bad Coppicing": Southern Maryland, circa 1904

Even before the arrival of the blight and when chestnuts were still very common, some thoughtful people worried about the future of the species. Reprinted here are cautionary excerpts from a U.S. Department of Agriculture bulletin originally published under the imprimatur of Gifford Pinchot, the founder and first director of the U.S. Forest Service.

(To: Hon. James Wilson, Secretary of Agriculture)
US Department of Agriculture, Bureau of Forestry
Washington, DC
JUNE 28, 1904

Sir: I have the honor to transmit herewith a report entitled "Chestnut in Southern Maryland," by Raphael Zon, a forest assistant in the Bureau of Forestry, and to recommend its publication as Bulletin No. 53 of the Bureau of Forestry. . . .

Very respectfully,
Gifford Pinchot, Forester

Most of the data were obtained in the southeastern part of Prince George County and the northwestern part of Calvert County. They include analyses of 1,245 large chestnut trees and of 426 seedlings for the growth in height and diameter; of 338 trees for the taper [taper was important for telephone and telegraph pole brokers]; and of 1,690 for the relation between stump-high and breast-high diameters, together with measurements of 1,269 one-year-old chestnut sprouts for the purpose of determining the best time and way of cutting chestnut for coppice [or sprouting]. . . .

The original stands of timber are mostly gone. The section studied was settled over two hundred years ago, and has remained principally an agricultural county ever since. Though the demand for chestnut timber in the early days was not great, it was used extensively even then for rails, fence posts, and vine props. . . . In more recent times chestnut has been cut on a larger scale and at a more rapid rate, on account of the increasing demand for chestnut ties and poles. . . .

The silvicultural system to which chestnut is best suited is "pure coppice." It must not be forgotten, however, that a chestnut stump can not go on coppicing forever. With each new generation of sprouts the stump becomes more and more weakened. . . . The effects of repeated and bad coppicing manifest themselves in the increasing number of dying chestnuts all over Maryland. . . .

The capacity of chestnut to produce sprouts from the stump in spite of the reckless and careless cutting now practiced may delay the entire disappearance of this most desirable of the trees possessed by the farmers of Maryland, but it will not save it from deterioration and eventually complete removal, unless efforts are made to provide also for its natural reproduction from the nut. . . . Although an abundance of seed is borne, the reproduction of chestnut from this source is exceedingly scant in Maryland. This is largely due to the fact that the nuts are a source of revenue. With chestnuts worth on an average $2.50 per bushel delivered in Baltimore, . . . the gathering of them is usually carried too far for the good of the woodlot . . . and the comparatively few which escape man are greedily devoured by the hogs which range freely in the woods, not to mention the squirrels and crows. If, after all, a chestnut seedling succeeds in coming up, the chances are that it will be destroyed by cattle. . . . [for] the use of the woodlot as a pasture is one of the chief enemies to the reproduction of the farmers' woods. To secure natural reproduction from the nut the woodlot must not be robbed wholly of its crops of chestnuts by turning them into money, the hogs must be kept entirely out of the woods during the season in which chestnuts fall and germinate, . . . and the young chestnut seedlings must be protected from the cattle until they reach the height at which no harm can be done to them. ❧

There is no tree which so quickly and surely reproduces itself from the stump, by sprouting, as the sweet chestnut. When a tree is cut in the winter or early spring, a thicket of sprouts come out around the stump, and in a few years time replace the weight and bulk of the original tree.

Colman's Rural World,
March 1883

Stump sprouts from a logged chestnut tree in West Salem, Wisconsin. (Photo by Frederick Paillet.)

Gifford Pinchot, Forester, Politician

The first American to become a professional forester, Gifford Pinchot was born in Simsbury, Connecticut, just after the Civil War ended in 1865. He grew up in New York City but spent his early summers with relatives in Connecticut and developed a love of the outdoors. Because of his father's business interests abroad, the family traveled extensively while Pinchot was a child.

After graduating from Yale University in 1889, Pinchot went to France to study forestry, because no forestry school yet existed in the United States. Shortly after Pinchot returned, Frederick Law Olmsted, the famous landscape architect and an old friend of Pinchot's father, recommended him to wealthy industrialist George Vanderbilt. Vanderbilt hired the young forester to tend to the badly abused land at his Biltmore estate and the better timber on his mountain acreage, near Asheville, North Carolina. It was the first official attempt in America to manage a forest with perpetuity in mind instead of liquidation. Pinchot set out to prove that good forestry could produce timber profits now as well as maintain the forest for future harvests.

Pinchot became a personal friend of Theodore Roosevelt, who in 1905 named him chief of the newly formed U.S. Forest Service. Together, Pinchot and Roosevelt made conservation a public issue and put it on the national agenda. After he married and settled in his family mansion, Grey Towers, in Milford, Pennsylvania, Pinchot remained active in conservation and progressive politics throughout his long and adventurous life, including serving two terms as governor of Pennsylvania. He died in 1946.

Simple Coppice

The following excerpt is from Gifford Pinchot's Primer of Forestry, Part II: Practical Forestry, *published by the U.S. Bureau of Forestry in 1905.*

It often happens, as in Pennsylvania or New Jersey, that a fire sweeps over the second-growth hardwood lands and fills all the young trees down to the ground; but the roots remain alive, and from them spring young sprouts about the bases of the burned trunks. After several years a second fire may follow and fill back the sprouts again, and other fires may continue at intervals to burn over the land, each followed by a new crop of sprouts. When a farmer does with the ax what is often done by fire he is using the system of Simple Coppice. Let us suppose a farmer has a woodlot covered principally with chestnut sprouts which he wants to manage for the steady production of railroad ties. He knows that chestnut sprouts are usually large enough for ties at the age of 35 years. In order to insure a steady yield of trees fit for ties, he divides the whole woodlot into thirty-five parts of equal productive capacity, and cuts one part clean every year. All the new sprouts that spring up on the part cut in any year are of the same age. At the end of thirty-five years, when the whole woodlot has been cut over, the thirty-five parts form a series of even-aged groups of sprouts from 1 to 35 years old. Every year the sprouts on one part reach the age of 35 years and are ready for cutting.

Many thousands of acres of American woodland, especially in New England, New York, Pennsylvania, and New Jersey, and in other places where chestnut is the principal tree, are treated under a rough system of Simple Coppice.

Pinchot's Legacy: William Ashe on Chestnuts

William W. Ashe was born in 1872 with a botanist's eye, and by the age of fifteen, when he entered the University of North Carolina (his native state), he had amassed enough specimens to fill a two-story building. In 1905 Ashe joined the U.S. Forest Service under Gifford Pinchot and worked there until his death in 1932. One of his greatest contributions to forest conservation was his extensive efforts to acquire degraded, logged-over lands for restoration as national forests in the eastern United States. Ashe was a prolific writer on a wide variety of subjects, including plant taxonomy and many aspects of farm and forest management. The excerpt below is from his pamphlet "Chestnut in Tennessee," (Tennessee Geological Survey Series), published in 1911, in which he gave a detailed overview of what chestnut trees need to thrive, as well as instructions on how best to manage a woodlot for chestnut tree production. He was well aware of "the chestnut bark disease, a very destructive parasitic malady from Virginia to Southern New England, no evidence of which was seen in Tennessee."

Chestnut is one of the most widely distributed trees of Tennessee, and the most important tree in the mountains of the eastern portion of the state, occupying large areas of land which have a low agricultural value. In many places in [the] mountains it forms as much as twenty-five per cent of the forest over tracts several thousand acres in extent. It is common on the slopes of the Cumberland tableland, especially on the sandstone soils which have a sufficient depth and are not too rocky.

Chestnut requires for its best growth, deep, moist loams or sandy loams . . . of considerable depth to permit the penetration of its ample, deeply ramifying roots . . . and [it] practically never [grows] on limestone soils. It makes excellent growth on highly acid soils. Although less exacting than yellow poplar, walnut or ash, in respect to depth of soil and amount and uniformity of moisture supply, it is more exacting than white oak, by which it is replaced on the drier soils. While chestnut makes moderate demands upon soil moisture, it does not require either a sweet or a fertile soil.

Chestnut requires for its best growth, deep, moist loams or sandy loams . . . of considerable depth to permit the penetration of its ample, deeply ramifying roots.

Chestnut is adapted to a wide range of climatic conditions. It flourishes from an altitude of less than 500 feet elevation in southwestern Tennessee, where the average annual temperature is 59 degrees Fahrenheit, to elevations of more than 5,500 feet along the Smoky and Unaka Mountain ranges, where the average annual temperature is below 50 degrees. Its best growth, however, is on moderately cool sites, such as shady slopes, coves, and elevated benches of the eastern mountains between 1,000 and 3,000 feet in altitude.

For seedling reproduction, chestnut requires only a limited amount of light: The seedlings will persist for many years under the shade of old trees, and when twenty to

Cutting fencing material, Chester County, Pennsylvania. (Pennsylvania Chestnut Blight Commission.)

thirty years old may not exceed 15 feet in height and 3 inches in diameter. As a rule, when the large trees which are overtopping these suppressed seedlings are cut, the seedlings respond quickly to the increased light and make accelerated growth.

Small trees are used for poles, posts, and ties; large, sound trees for lumber and shingles. Tops and low-grade wood are used for tannic extract, fuel wood, and paper pulp stock.

Chestnut bears seed or mast abundantly at intervals of a few years. In intervening years the seed crop is lighter, but seldom entirely wanting. The flowers appear in midsummer, too late to be killed by frost, but rainy weather, during the pollination period, may prevent the setting of the fruit and curtail the crop of nuts.

The sprouting capacity of chestnut is far superior to that of any other important hardwood growing in Tennessee. Until past the pole stage, chestnut suffers severely from fire because of its thin bark. Young chestnut is so subject to fire damage that it is of first importance to protect young stands. Old timber with thicker bark is less injured, though it cannot be burned without some injury. It is also necessary to protect young stands from cattle, since considerable damage results from browsing the foliage and young shoots. Chestnut is seldom thrown by the wind, and the stem rarely breaks unless hollowed at the base by fire. The leaders are sometimes broken by sleet and icestorms, and large branches torn away by windstorms.

The great number of uses to which the wood is put enable extremely close utilization not only of all portions of sound trees, including limbs and bark, but also a large amount of more or less defective wood. Small trees are used for poles, posts, and ties; large, sound trees for lumber and shingles. Tops and low-grade wood are used for tannic extract, fuel wood, and paper pulp stock. ~

A Constant and Growing Demand

From being stripped of its bark for Indian wigwams, laboriously chopped or sawn down by colonial farmers, to being harvested and processed on an industrial scale, American chestnut has fallen victim to its own abundance and utility. For its use in log cabins and barns, for framing, siding, shingles, fences, furniture, crates, and coffins, for telegraph and telephone poles, acid wood and pulpwood, this quick-growing, versatile tree was in constant and growing demand. By the early twentieth century, as the relentless advance of railroads was opening even the remote corners of Appalachia to large-scale logging operations, the newly arrived chestnut blight was in a position to deal a stunningly swift coup de grâce to this uniquely utilitarian species.

These images of chestnut logging reflect the increasing efficiency that accompanied the at-first gradual and then rapid disappearance of this tree from the American landscape. Clockwise from top left: *Portable sawmill in Pennsylvania; logger with chestnuts in Great Smoky Mountains; waiting for the logging train; logging chute, Little River Logging Company, Great Smoky Mountains. (Photos from Great Smoky Mountains National Park Library and Pennsylvania Chestnut Blight Commission.)*

Railroad ties of American chestnut ironically helped lay the paths that speeded the tree's disappearance from the landscape, both before and after the blight. The last quarter of the nineteenth century and the first decades of the twentieth saw railroads, both wide and narrow gauge, thread their way into the valleys and onto the mountainsides of the Appalachian heartland, bringing with them large-scale logging operations and even a new breed of locomotives.

Thunder in the Woods

By Les Line

It is a paradox that a strange-looking steam locomotive invented by a timberman from the flat pinelands of northern Michigan would come to play a leading role in stripping the virgin forests of the Appalachian Mountains.

Few of the men who felled nearly every white pine between Lake Michigan and Lake Huron in the second half of the nineteenth century are remembered today. But Ephraim Shay (1839–1916) merits an encyclopedia entry for conceiving the remarkable machine that bears his name. Shay owned a sawmill and general store in one of those ephemeral towns that popped up like mushrooms with the logging boom, then disappeared once the trees were gone. And he was frustrated with the performance of traditional "rod" locomotives, which were poorly suited for hauling long, heavy loads of logs from forest to mill over rough terrain.

In your typical wood- or coal-burning locomotive, high-pressure steam from the boiler is directed to brass cylinders at the front of the engine, one on each side. Each cylinder holds a large, horizontal piston. Flat arms (the main rods) connect the pistons to the locomotive's big driver wheels, which in turn are coupled to the other wheels by side rods. Injections of steam push the piston back and forth, each stroke rotating the drivers by a quarter-turn. And down the track you go.

Rod locomotives perform best on steel rails carefully laid on cross-ties embedded in stone ballast, with wide curves and gentle grades. Those conditions were impractical to meet in the North Woods, where rails, bridges, and trestles were made of a readily available material—wood—and rail lines were moved once a stand of pines was clear-cut.

Shay's locomotive, in contrast, is a geared engine. Its boiler is offset to the left side of the frame, and two or three cylinders are mounted vertically on the right side, near the cab. The piston rods drive a lengthwise crankshaft that in turn drives the four-wheel trucks through bevel gears on the shaft and the axles. There are no cylinders, pistons, etc., on the engine's left side. And smaller wheels compared to those of rod locomotives give the Shay a low-to-the-ground appearance. Loggers called them "sidewinders."

The Shay was specifically designed to meet the needs of the lumber mills. By using reducing gears instead of rods, Ephraim Shay's lighter-weight locomotive sacrificed speed for power, traction, and stability. Moreover, the crankshaft with its slip joints and universals was flexible enough to allow the trucks—the sets of wheels and axles on which a locomotive sits—full freedom of movement. As authors John Labbe and Vernon Goe wrote in their classic book *Railroads in the Woods*, "The Shay was an easy-riding engine and it was rugged and durable. It might strew the right-of-way with discarded parts, and its gears might be nearly devoid of teeth, but little short of complete derailment could thwart its progress."

There were no mountains in Michigan's Lower Peninsula (or the piney eastern Upper Peninsula, for that matter) and hardly any hills that were more than a bump on the landscape. So it's unlikely that Shay imagined his newfangled locomotive would prove a phenomenal success in mountain logging. Yet it could climb the steepest grades, swing around hairpin curves, negotiate frail tracks, and haul incredibly heavy loads. In time it would conquer the Appalachians, the vast coniferous forests cloaking the Pacific Northwest from tideland to the snow-covered crest of the Cascade Range, and California's awesome redwood and sequoia groves.

"The rapid rhythm of its three-cylinder exhaust became part and parcel of the logging scene," Labbe and Goe continued. "No one who has ever known it could forget it. A Shay thrashing its slow course up a heavy grade was lost in an aura of sound and smoke and steam." Thunder in the woods indeed.

History doesn't record the date when Ephraim Shay began work on his prototype. However, he sold the manufacturing rights to Lima Machine Works of Ohio in 1879, and the first production geared locomotive was shipped to a buyer in Michigan the next year. The cost was $1,700. By 1884 Lima had a thirty-four-page catalog of Shay models. And by 1945, when the last Shay was assembled, 2,761 engines had been turned out, a fair number of them going to other countries. They ranged in size from Lilliputian two-truck engines weighing less than ten tons, intended for use on modest narrow-gauge lines, to 150-ton,

Shay No. 3, Lima, circa 1903, at work in West Virginia. (West Virginia and Regional History Collection, West Virginia University Libraries.)

three-truck titans. Indeed, the Shay's design was so flexible that they were built for hundreds of specific jobs, including street running of freight trains in New York City. (Those engines had hoods so the moving pistons wouldn't frighten horses.) It's been said that no two were exactly alike.

More than two hundred Shays went to logging operations in West Virginia alone. Roy B. Clarkson, author of *Tumult on the Mountains*, a brief but richly illustrated history of lumbering in that state from 1770 to 1920, relates that the parade of sidewinders included the heaviest of its kind, a 154-ton model built in 1921 for West Virginia Pulp and Paper Company. The machine was later converted to a four-truck behemoth by nearly doubling the size (and, of course, the weight) of its water tank.

By the 1890s the Shays had company in the West Virginia woods—another geared locomotive called the Climax, which had a slanted cylinder on each side of the boiler and a central driveshaft. Climax engines, however, never really challenged the Shay for superiority in heavy-duty mountain logging. They were relatively small engines and became workhorses on tramroads and short logging spurs. A typical West Virginia tramroad, as described in Clarkson's book, was eleven miles long with rails made of three-by-seven-inch hemlock plies topped with a two-by-seven ply of maple or other hardwood and nailed together with seven-inch spikes. An iron strip might be laid on top. Ties were heavy slabs of wood, and the track was graded only in the roughest places. In such primitive circumstances, the iron wheels of a Climax needed flanges on both sides to keep them on the track.

Written descriptions of West Virginia's primeval forest before the 1870s, when mountain logging began in earnest, are sparse. But Clarkson's vivid re-creation will do. "When white men first trod the fertile bottomlands along the rivers," he wrote, "they saw immense oaks, walnuts, yellow poplars or tuliptrees, sycamores and other hardwoods. As they ascended the mountains they traversed growths of huge sugar maples, beech and yellow birch. On the higher plateaus and mountaintops they encountered forests of red spruce so thick that the forest floor had not felt the warming rays of the sun for centuries."

Climax locomotive and crew, Randolph County, West Virginia, circa 1900–1910. Note the slanted cylinder. (West Virginia and Regional History Collection, West Virginia University Libraries.)

The size of these trees is hard to imagine. American chestnuts with trunk diameters of ten feet or more thrived with chestnut oaks on the drier western side of the Appalachians. White oaks were the largest timber tree in the original forest, and one specimen felled by loggers was nine feet, ten inches in diameter at its base and 145 feet tall. A yellow poplar whose first limbs were eighty feet from the ground yielded twelve thousand board feet of lumber. One tree could fill an entire log train.

Before the railroad era, as Clarkson recounts, much of the timber cut in West Virginia was floated to mills in large rafts. But in the post–Civil War years, when a fast-growing population needed more wood, and groves near navigable streams were largely cut out, lumbermen turned their attention to steeper forests. And before the Shay, horses, mules and oxen pulled log trucks with flanged wheels along the aforementioned tramroads.

Still, there were ten million acres of original forest left when the rugged geared locomotives arrived on the scene. At the time, West Virginia had around five hundred sawmill towns that produced 180 million board feet of lumber a year. But by 1909 dozens of short and shorter logging railroads, totaling two or three thousand miles of track, threaded the mountains. (A "large" operator like the Greenbrier, Cheat and Elk Railroad had sixty-six miles of main track, not counting short-lived logging spurs. In contrast, the Strouds Creek and Muddlety Railroad was all of six miles long—and it wasn't the shortest line in the woods.) That was the year when lumber production by 1,572 mills peaked at 1.5 billion board feet. And only a million and a half acres of virgin forest remained.

In the post–Civil War years, when a fast-growing population needed more wood, and groves near navigable streams were largely cut out, lumbermen turned their attention to steeper forests.

Those long-ago lumber production numbers are not broken down by tree species. But given the fact that the American chestnut was a dominant tree in the Appalachian forests and its rot-resistant wood was prized for countless uses, from split-rail fences to finely polished coffins, the tree probably accounted for the largest share of the hardwood harvest in West Virginia and elsewhere. Indeed, many of those huge chestnut logs pulled and pushed from the mountainsides by laboring Shays were turned into millions of ties for America's expanding railroad network as well as poles for the telegraph lines that paralleled the tracks.

Ten years later the last remnants of the original West Virginia forest were essentially gone. The towering chestnuts, oaks, poplars, and other hardwoods and dark stands of hemlock and spruce were but a memory. One can argue that destruction of the Appalachian forests wouldn't have happened, at least to that extent, without Ephraim Shay's raucous invention. But worse was to come from coal strip-miners and, now, the removal of entire mountaintops to reach veins of black gold to feed power plants whose greenhouse-gas emissions threaten life on Earth.

Trees, at least, come back over time. ∾

There are 115 surviving Shay locomotives. Many of them hunker in silent display at railroading museums around the country, but others still thrash away on tourist lines. The best place to see Shays in operation is at Cass Scenic Railroad State Park in West Virginia. Cass was a booming town in its heyday, from 1908 to 1922, with three thousand mill employees turning 1.5 million board feet of timber into kiln-dried lumber or pulpwood every week. Today, Shay-pulled trains clamber over eleven miles of steep track to Bald Knob, the second-highest point in the state at 4,842 feet, or to the site of Spruce atop Cheat Mountain, once the highest town in the East, with a forty-room hotel and a pulpwood peeling plant. The Cass collection of six Shays includes the last one ever built.

Memories of a Noble Timber: Stumps, Sogs, Skeletons, and Wormy Wood

These oral histories, originally published as "Memories of the American Chestnut" in Foxfire 6 *(edited by Eliot Wigginton, Anchor Press/Doubleday, 1980) tell, in a way no scientific paper can, the meaning of chestnut trees to people in the southern Appalachians and the impact of the blight. The location is Rabun County, in the far northeastern corner of Georgia, and the date is 1980.*

Jake Waldroop:

I can show you some chestnut stumps now that are six or seven feet through, and they'd grow to be over a hundred feet tall, those chestnut trees would. Grea-a-a-at big, and they'd sprangle out, have a big clustery top to 'em. They most generally grew the straightest timber of any. As the old saying goes, "straight as a gun barrel." They didn't have too many low branches; they'd go way up without branches. On an average you could cut anywhere from three to four sixteen-foot logs out of a chestnut tree before you got into the knots. There was more chestnuts than any other one species of timber. Now you'd find some oaks and poplars once in a while that'd grow bigger than chestnuts, but if you take it on an average, the chestnut grew the biggest of any of 'em. And it grew fast.

[The wood is] slow to rot. Fact of the business is, if it gets down in there where no air gets to it, I don't know whether it'd ever rot or not. . . . There's old sogs that you can dig out and they'll be just as sound as can be—logs that have been laying there for hundreds of years. Old sogs. That's an old tree that's fell and gotten buried up in the dirt an' sometimes covered with moss. Now there was timber that was stronger than chestnut, but the one thing about chestnut, it was so much easier worked than the rest of it was. . . .

[People] used it for acidwood, pulpwood, telephone poles, cross-ties, fence rails, ditch timber, and they made furniture out of it. It made good framing and siding—you could use it about anywhere any other timber could be used. . . . Everybody built their own fences with chestnut rails. It was the best splittin' timber there was—wasn't anything equal to chestnut when it came to splitting. A good workingman, if he understood it all right, [if he] didn't have iron or steel hammers or wedges, would just make a white oak maul, then take dogwood and make a whole lot of wedges. Put them up and let them season. And when he was ready to build a fence, [he'd] take his ax and go out and chop down one of the [chestnut] trees. Then chop his logs off ten feet long and take that [wedge and maul] and split one hundred fence rails a day.

It made good firewood. Now you had to let it season—green chestnut wouldn't burn at all. It just refused. But when it dried out it was about as good a firewood as there was; you couldn't hardly beat it for nothin'. 'Way back we'd get chestnut for our stovewood. We'd get the dead [logs], bring them in, and bust them up—law, it was the finest wood you ever seen for stovewood. . . .

[Instead of chestnut], people'd go ahead and make crossties out of oak. Fact they could use about anything that growed for makin' crossties. But for telephone poles, they wasn't nothin' else here that they could use. Chestnut telephone poles is all they used that grow in this country. They went further down into the swampy country and got cypress. For framing you could take hemlock—it made almost as good a framing as chestnut did. You could make framing out of oak or poplar, but chestnut was the best framin' that they was. And people way back yonder, when they built log houses, they was all built out of chestnut. Now they could use poplar after the chestnut died out, but they preferred the chestnut 'cause it was easier worked. Most all the old log houses you see are chestnut. For fencing, now they had to change over to locust, sassafras, and mulberry for posts, but nothin' else took the place of chestnut for rails, because everything else was too hard to split. Them chestnut rails, oh you could make them—I've seen people take their ax and split a great big long log with just an ax.

It made good firewood. Now you had to let it season—green chestnut wouldn't burn at all. It just refused.

Seems like the poplar come back more than anything else. Chestnuts and poplar grew more in these bigger dark coves. 'Course the chestnut grew everywhere on the south sides and all, but its main favorite was to get in these dark north coves. That's where the biggest, healthiest chestnut trees were. More moisture anytime than there is on the south side. About the time that the chestnuts disappeared, the oaks grew more, and there were lots of acorns, and the hogs made it good on them, but they usually wouldn't get as fat as they did on chestnuts. . . .

People have been hunting sound logs awful close, but there are still some. I know of some that are just as sound as they ever were. Cut into 'em and they'd be plumb white inside. You take this downed wormy chestnut (that's what they get out of these old sogs), get that and make paneling out of it, and I guess it's selling the highest now of any lumber on the market.

Noel Moore:

One of the main uses of the chestnut tree when I was a boy was for telephone poles. They call 'em utility poles now, but back then they wasn't nothin' but telephone poles—wasn't any utility lines through this part of the country. They wouldn't use anything but chestnut back then because it would last so much longer than anything else and they could put it in the ground without having to treat it. It was light and easy to handle, and it was all handled by hand, you know. Pine is what they principally use now, but they won't use it unless it's pressure-treated or it won't last any time. But the chestnut would, it would last on and on.

Making barn timbers from blighted chestnut. (Pennsylvania Chestnut Blight Commission.)

They used it a lot for pulpwood when they first started to make paper—that's about the only thing they made paper out of was chestnut and poplar. They also used it for tannic acid—there's a lot of acid in the wood. Back then they would cut big enormous trees just to get the bark off 'em, and they would leave the rest of the tree just layin' there on the ground to rot. It'd be worth thousands of dollars now if we had wood like that, because it's so much better wood than anything that grows in the forest now. It made better framing lumber for building houses, [it was good] for siding because it wouldn't warp or split or rot, and it would take a finish good. Then they got to using it for furniture because it takes such a good finish; it polishes good, and the grain shows up good. It's a beautiful wood. . . .

After [the chestnuts] all died, the principal thing they used [them] for was pulpwood. The ground was coated with dead trees [and there were] dead skeletons stickin' up all over the mountains, big white skeletons. And the timber cutters would cut it in four-foot lengths and split it up and take it to paper mills, where they made it into paper. When it began to get scarce, the demand grew that much more for the worm-eaten chestnut, and all of it that had died was full of worm holes. They got to using that for finish work, for panel work—interior finishing. And the price has skyrocketed. The scarcer it got, the higher it got. You can find just a few places that you can find a tree that is sound enough that it can be sawed into lumber yet. If you can find one, you could sell it for more than a dollar a foot; that's more than a thousand dollars a thousand board feet.

Jack Grist:

Dad had a little grocery store in Dillard which was about fifteen by twenty feet. Most of his stock was kept under the counter because he didn't have room on the shelves to put it. And most of the store work was done by my mother when Dad was in the woods with the men cutting the poles. On his sales, a lot of the time it was a swap. A barter deal. He'd say, "Well, you brought so much chestnut, and it's worth (say) twelve dollars."

The man'd say, "Well, I need a sack of cottonseed meal, I need a dollar's worth of coffee, I need a bag of sugar." It was a swap deal. Lot of time people'd bring wood in, and on top of it they'd have a chicken coop full of hens. "How much you payin' for hens today?" "Well, so much." There was a man came every Thursday, picked those up and carried 'em to Greenville, South Carolina.

In 1924, Dad met a Georgia Power Company engineer, and he needed fifteen hundred poles twenty-five feet in length. He wanted chestnut, and he wanted 'em shipped from Dillard to wherever he wanted 'em. He asked Dad if he could get 'em for him in maybe two months. Dad said, "I'll get 'em before that if the weather's good and I can get things rolling like I want to."

The Georgia Power engineer came back to him (Dad was going along well on his delivery date), and said, "If you can give us the poles in four weeks, we'll give you a dollar for every pole." And they had ordered fifteen hundred, so that was a fifteen-hundred-dollar bonus, and he got 'em. He put everybody he could find with a crosscut saw to work. He lucked out a lot of times like that. . . .

I'd say that the biggest bulk of Dad's business as far as chestnut went, when it was still green, was for telephone poles, caskets, and acid wood. He was always a timber man from the time he was twenty years old. He was hauling lumber and logs way back that far. This country was literally covered with chestnut. As the saying goes, "You'd cut one down and two'd jump up in front of you." They were no trouble—they would just cut the tree and cut all the small limbs off it and load it on the wagon. In those days they didn't have trucks to haul with, so they had a couple of teams of mules or horses. They'd take the coupling out of the wagon, move it back maybe fifteen feet, and they'd load all the poles they could get on the wagon, then they'd tie a chain around them. That way they could come out the roads and into Dillard and into the pole yard. Then they'd measure twenty-five feet, and take a crosscut saw and cut the ends off. (That's what we used to cook with in the wood stove—it split real easy.)

Woman and a chestnut snag, circa 1910. (Shenandoah National Park Archives.)

When they were building the new road through Dillard, Dad became a good friend of the man that was building it. He, in turn, told the city officials [in Commerce, where he lived] when they needed some posts to contact Dad. Well, that spread, so the cities of Commerce, Jefferson, Brazelton, Winder, and some other towns ordered from him, and he shipped poles to each one of those towns, and they replaced the lines they had with new poles. Today you'd call him a broker. Everything he ever did was on a straight contract basis.

My dad always said that he lived out of the store, enough to live on. The money he made he made in the woods. He was just about born in the woods. He's walked just about every foot of all these hills, and he knew where every branch was.

Dr. John Brown:

In 1937 there were still some chestnuts here, but not too many—not as many as there were back in the latter twenties. Then I went off [to college] and I lost track of [the chestnut] until I decided to build a home in Charleston, South Carolina, when I was at the Medical University of South Carolina there. This was 1950. At that time I remembered that some of the most beautiful wood that I had ever seen, and some that was not indigenous to the Charleston area, was the American chestnut. So I came up [here] one weekend and tried my best to talk with the sawmill people around and tried to find some chestnut wood to put in the home I was building in Charleston. Lo and behold, I could find none; something had happened to the chestnut during these years of my absence from here. So I went to Scaly Mountain, where I knew that there were the most chestnuts of anywhere in this area that I had seen as a boy. I did find one sawmill man up there who had six thousand board feet of wormy chestnut which he had just stacked over in one corner of his lumberyard; no one wanted it. I mean he couldn't sell it.

Large old chestnut tree in the Pisgah range, North Carolina, 1910. (Photo by A. H. Graves, courtesy of U.S. Forest Service Southern Research Station Special Collection, D. H. Ramsey Library Special Collections, University of North Carolina at Asheville.)

So I said, "How much do you want for this?" Snow on the ground (this was wintertime), [and the wood] was covered with snow. We went over and looked at it.

He said, "Gosh, it's been here so long I'd almost give it to you to haul it off, but we do have some labor in this, so why don't you give me four hundred dollars for the whole stack."

Well, this was about four thousand board feet, as it turned out. I rented a tractor-trailer the next weekend. Snow was still on the ground, and we came all the way back up here from Charleston. Left Friday night, loaded up our chestnut, and got stuck in the snow with the tractor-trailer up there. I had to get pulled out, and I finally got back to Charleston on Sunday night with this load of chestnut, the most precious wood that I could have found. So we kiln-dried it and processed it. It was enough to do all of the woodwork, including the trimming and including paneling two rooms with wormy chestnut. And it was the only house in the lower part of South Carolina that had wormy chestnut in it. The newspaper, the *Charleston News Courier*, did an article on it and it was publicized quite well. We had a lot of visitors to see our house.

We moved from there in 1958 to Emory University and we had to sell our house. We certainly did hate to lose it. ~

Wormy Chestnut: Don't Blame the Blight

Today wormy chestnut panels the walls of attorneys' offices, boardrooms, and the custom interiors of comfortable homes partial to the "Country Look." I think it is commonly held that the major source of wormy chestnut was the millions of dead trees harvested after they were killed by the blight. Excellent research by TACF's Dr. Paul Sisco tells otherwise. Wormy chestnut is caused by the tunneling of the grub of the chestnut timberworm (*Melittomma sericeum*), a member of the family of ship-timber beetles, as it eats its way throughout the interior of the tree's trunk and major branches.

Sisco's research proves that wormy chestnut was well known to the timber industry long before the blight. It is also probable that the beetle attacks living as well as dead trees. Sisco quotes from "Chestnut in Tennessee," a 1911 pamphlet by William Ashe: "The chestnut timber worm causes the common defect known as 'wormy chestnut,' a defect which greatly reduces the value of much otherwise high grade timber." The fact that so much wormy chestnut is salvaged from the interiors of old barns and sheds indicates that it was not held in its present high regard. When and why did the change occur?

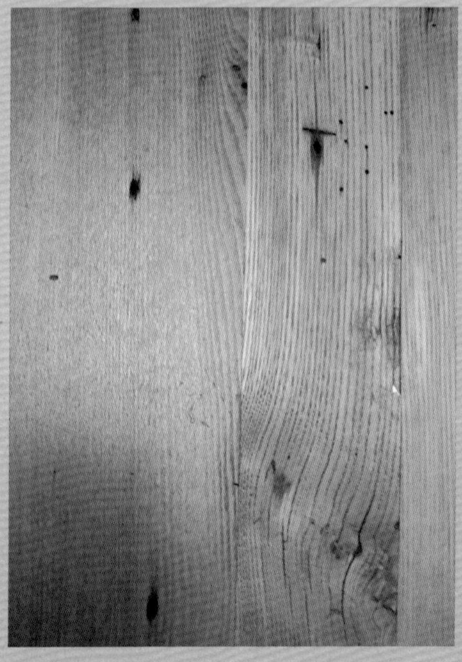

Wormy chestnut was common even before the onset of the blight. (Photo by Lou Bedor III.)

TACF member Jean Lam of Chestnut Ridge Park, Hubbard, Ohio, provides a reasonable answer: the present popularity and high status of wormy chestnut commenced with the affluence and increased leisure time following World War II. Wormy chestnut became and remains an integral part of the "Country Look." A market for wormy chestnut was present late in the 1940s. A retired telephone lineman informed Lam that at that time his company removed its fifty-year-old chestnut poles. They were milled into wormy chestnut boards and presumably found a ready market.

William Lord

The following are from memories of the American chestnut collected by The American Chestnut Foundation.

I am a woodworker by trade and have used chestnut as one of my principal woods for a long time. I first found some old boards, probably wainscoting, in a flea market around 1975. A few years later I found an actual chestnut sawmill in Sylva, North Carolina. I purchased 8,000 board feet of dentata, most sixteen feet in length and up to twenty-four inches in width, though most ran between six inches and twelve inches. It was rough-sawn but kiln dried. As we know, the wood has tannin in it, so the logs with little rot were hauled out of the hills and hollows of western North Carolina and Tennessee by horse. This was in 1978. The following year . . . I was working in Cashiers and heard of yet another chestnut sawmill. It appeared to be smaller, but unfortunately a large guy with a shotgun told me to get off the property, so I could never check it out. One thing did stand out, though. There was a log in the yard by itself that measured eight feet to nine feet in diameter, with a rot hole in the middle that was no more than six inches in diameter. The piece appeared to be twelve feet to fourteen feet in length and must have been something once upon a time.

David DiZinno, Wellington, Ohio, 2004

My dad was in the lumber business during my early youth, operating small sawmills, known as "ground mills" in our local area. The mills would be moved from cove to cove and the logs cut in the woods and skidded to the mill with horses. Always the predominant species he manufactured was chestnut, so it became involved in my first job. [When I was] about age 13, Dad had a mill in the valley that is now the watershed for the town of Mars Hill, North Carolina, near Asheville, North Carolina. This valley had the most prolific growth of chestnut I have ever seen. In the fall people would come into the valley pulling a sled with a single horse and take out sled loads of sacks filled with chestnuts for personal use and to sell on the commercial market. . . . I went with Dad to the sawmill that summer and took my first job (at ten cents per day plus room and board) doodling sawdust from Dad's mill which was cutting large chestnut logs. "Doodling" was a term used for shoveling the sawdust from beneath the saw into a wheelbarrow, rolling it away from the mill, and dumping it into a pile on the ground. . . .

The mills would be moved from cove to cove and the logs cut in the woods and skidded to the mill with horses.

By the time I volunteered in the Army Air Corps in the early 1940s, the chestnut blight had really taken its toll in our area. Hillsides that had hosted chestnut in the green of spring and the gold of fall were now covered with huge gray skeletons, bleakly outlined against the slopes. Quite often, as we sat on our porch in the cool of the evening, we could hear a heartrending "thud" and know that another giant had severed its final root connection to mother earth and assumed a prone position. This process continued until there were no skeletons left standing.

I followed [in] the footsteps of my father after I returned from World War II and entered the hardwood lumber manufacturing business, primarily serving the furniture

Portable sawmill using blighted trees, Pennsylvania. (Pennsylvania Chestnut Blight Commission.)

industry. It is a competitive business . . . I felt the need to not just be a "run of the mill" mill and embarked upon a plan to set us apart from the ordinary. The dead chestnut skeletons on the southern and western slopes could not defy the tendency of wood to deteriorate if it goes frequently from wet to dry, so they were rapidly rotting away. . . . The chestnuts lying on the northern and eastern slopes had become covered with moss, had a constant moisture content, and many of them still contained sound wood. With this knowledge, we thus embarked on our plan to introduce wormy chestnut as a specialty wood to once again produce fine cabinetry, picture frames, millwork, and wall paneling. We immediately doubled the raw price of the wood and sent crews through the mountain searching for chestnut "sogs," as we called them. It was much like prospecting for minerals, but produced many years of activity. . . . During those years, we were among the top three wormy chestnut producers in the world.

William A. Banks, from *Journal of The American Chestnut Foundation,* spring 2005; Banks was born in 1924 in Burnsville, North Carolina

Dad, born in 1872, said a friend, who I believe was J. P. Moore of Edray, West Virginia, was a carpenter, preacher, and ran a general store in the 1890s–1900s. Dad said he could marry you, later preach your funeral and bury you in a chestnut coffin, which was the best wood because the cloth lining stuck better when the glue caught in the wormholes and held tight.

Dave Sharp, Cincinnati, Ohio, 2002

European chestnut trees (C. sativa) *of souto de Quintela, near Lalin, in Galicia, northwest Spain. (Courtesy of Professor Ernesto Vieitez Cortizo.)*

THE RELATIVES

[A chestnut tree] on Mount Etna, which can be seen from the town of Aci, has often been mentioned by travelers. It is 160 feet in circumference, and has a hollow trunk in which shepherds find a retreat for themselves and their flocks.

— *Phrenological Journal and Science of Health,* April 1871

In Praise of the Chestnuts: Tasty, Nutritious, *and* Virtuous

By J. Hill Craddock

Chestnuts are good to eat. Chestnut trees have been cultivated for thousands of years for their sweet, edible nuts and were a staple food of traditional cultures in East Asia, Europe, and eastern North America. Migrating peoples have carried chestnuts far beyond the trees' native ranges, as far as South America, Australia, New Zealand, and the West Coast of North America. *Castanea mollissima* and *C. crenata* are grown in China and in Japan, respectively, and both species are grown in Korea. *Castanea sativa* is grown throughout the temperate zones of Europe, from the Caucasus and Persia in the east to Portugal and Great Britain in the west. The native North American species are *Castanea dentata* and *C. pumila*, but neither of these is cultivated for its nuts because of the chestnut blight disease and the rather smaller sizes of their fruits.

Korean native chestnut tree, probably C. crenata. *(Photo by Mahn-Jo Kim, courtesy of J. Hill Craddock.)*

Blight-resistant, large-fruited varieties of *C. mollissima* are grown in the eastern United States, and *C. sativa*, *C. crenata*, and hybrid chestnut trees are grown in the western U.S., where chestnut blight is less of a problem.

Chestnuts can be eaten raw, freshly harvested from beneath the trees or cured for several days to allow some of the starches to convert to sugars. Chestnuts can be cooked, roasted, candied, boiled, pureed, added to soups, sauces, and dressings, used as appetizers, first courses, main courses, side dishes, and desserts. Street vendors sell roasted chestnuts in some parts of the world, but in other places they might also sell boiled or candied chestnuts.

A storehouse full of dried chestnuts represented food security—and wealth.

Chestnuts are a perishable crop and must be treated as a recalcitrant seed to be kept viable until spring and protected from excessive drying and freezing. In the Alps, chestnuts were sometimes stored still enclosed within their prickly burs, mounded with chestnut leaves into large piles for overwintering. Certain varieties kept better than others did, and in the heart of the chestnut-growing world, long-keeping varieties were highly valued.

Traditionally, the bulk of the chestnut harvest would have been dried over a smoky fire and then cleaned of the shells for storage through the winter and into the following seasons. A storehouse full of dried chestnuts represented food security—and wealth. They were insurance against drought, flood, siege, and any of the many other calamities that could befall an agriculture based on annual grain crops. Taxes were levied in dried chestnuts in parts of medieval Italy. As evidence of their strategic importance, the trees themselves were included in official censuses right up through the Napoleonic era.

Dried chestnuts can be softened in water or milk and used in many of the same recipes that call for fresh chestnuts. But dried chestnuts also can be milled into a sweet flour and used in countless ways. Chestnut flour, in fact, was once one of the staples of Mediterranean cooking and especially so in the mountainous regions of Italy and Corsica, where chestnut culture became a veritable chestnut civilization. Almost every material need was provided for by the chestnut tree, not just food but also timbers, poles, wicker, tannin, and fuel from the chestnut coppice, and bedding for animals and even medicinal astringents from the leaves. With the grapevine and the olive tree, the European chestnut is one of the great pillars upon which Mediterranean civilization was built. Chinese and Japanese chestnut trees played similar and no less important roles in the civilizations of China, Korea, and Japan.

Like many common names for plants, the word "chestnut" means different things to different people. In England a "chestnut tree" is likely to be *Aesculus hippocastanum*, the tree we Americans call European horse chestnut. The genus *Aesculus* includes the North American "buckeyes," among them the Ohio buckeye. Interestingly, Longfellow's spreading chestnut was a European horse chestnut growing near his home in Cambridge, Massachusetts. When the tree was killed to make way for progress, its wood was used to build a chair that was presented to the aging poet by the local schoolchildren. The Children's Chair is currently on display at the Longfellow National Historic Site, at 105 Brattle Street in Cambridge. What we Americans call a chestnut tree, in England would be a "sweet chestnut," probably *Castanea sativa*, although other species have been introduced and are grown in Britain, including *C. dentata*, *C. crenata*, and hybrids. The French differentiate between *châtaignes*, essentially wild-type chestnuts, and *marrons*, which are the cultivated forms introduced from Italy since the late Middle Ages. The French marron cultivars are all propagated by grafting, are generally larger and better textured than the wild-type chestnuts, but most important, they should be free of multiple embryos (a serious defect for commercial processing). Euro-Japanese hybrid cultivars make up the vast majority of recently planted commercial chestnut orchards in Europe. *Castanea crenata* was introduced into Europe from Japan in the 1800s and cultivated for its exceptionally large nuts. Later, *C. crenata* was used in breeding efforts to combat the dreaded "ink disease" caused by species of *Phytophthora* and chestnut blight caused by *Cryphonectria parasitica*. In Italy, the term *marrone* refers to a particular set of cultivars with very limited geographic origins. Curiously, the Italian *marroni* are all male sterile cultivars. There are two other, very different plants called "water chestnuts"—*Trapa natans*, a noxious, floating, aquatic annual weed that is now infesting lakes and streams in some parts of the northeastern U.S., and *Eleocharis dulcis*, the perennial, grasslike sedge cultivated throughout Southeast Asia for its crispy, edible corm.

Like many common names for plants, the word "chestnut" means different things to different people.

Chestnuts are nutritious. Chestnuts are different from other tree nuts in that they have a relatively high carbohydrate content. About half of the fresh weight of chestnuts is starches and sugars. During the first week or so after harvest, some of the starch may

The Chestnut: Tree Crop Archetype

This mature chestnut grove in Boves, near Cuneo, northwestern Italy, resembles an old-growth hardwood forest in both structure and function. It yields significant ecological benefits, with consequences far beyond merely producing a nut crop, and provides the steward with a diversified income from sales of choice edible porcini mushrooms (*Boletus spp.*), chanterelles (*Cantharellus cibarius*), strawberries, and chestnut saw logs, in addition to the famous 'Garrone Rosso' chestnuts, prized by the Swiss chestnut roasters who buy most of the crop. The leaves and burs are raked into windrows along the contours of the hillside during the October chestnut harvest and are then buried by turning a furrow of earth down over the windrow using a large hoe. Next year's windrow will lie on top of this year's furrow, and the furrows, called *barrere* in Boves, will move slowly uphill as the cycle repeats year after year. In this way the entire orchard floor will be eventually turned under, directly incorporating all of the organic matter dropped by the chestnut overstory. Carlo Bellone, the owner, told me proudly that neither he nor any of his ancestors had ever burnt a leaf or brush pile, and that that was why their groves were healthier and were more productive than chestnut orchards in the areas where burning was practiced. The large gaps in the canopy result from harvest of enormous old trees sold to the tannery and from some timber sold to the sawmill. Interestingly, the cultivar 'Garrone Rosso' is well known also for the quality of its fine lumber that does not check or crack when milled. In the brush piles in the light gaps, Bellone had already grafted the seedling chestnut trees to scions of 'Garrone Rosso'.

J. Hill Craddock

Photo by J. Hill Craddock.

be converted to sugar, rendering the nuts sweeter to taste and improving their storage qualities. Fresh chestnuts contain only about 2 to 3 percent fat (or less), but the different types and amounts of lipids present are largely responsible for the flavor variations among the species and varieties of chestnut. Most tasters agree that the nuts of *C. dentata* and *C. pumila* are the most flavorful, while those of *C. crenata* are the least. Chestnut protein amounts to about 3 or 4 percent of the mass of the fresh seed, is of good quality, and is easily assimilated. There is no gluten in the protein of chestnuts, so they are readily digested even by folks who might be allergic to wheat. Chestnuts have appreciable amounts of vitamin C, thiamine (B_1), riboflavin (B_2), and folic acid (B_9).

Eating chestnuts can make the world a better place. The first chestnuts I ever saw were given to me by a friend and neighbor, John Todd, who was then the director of the New Alchemy Institute, in Woods Hole, Massachusetts. New Alchemy was a synthesis of aquaculture, horticulture, architecture, and biology. John told me they were the seeds of the rare American chestnut and that I ought to plant them. I had not yet heard the story of the American chestnut. The chestnut seeds were beautiful, shiny brown nuts. I planted them in my dad's greenhouse after keeping them for several months in moist peat moss in the refrigerator. Soon the seedling chestnut trees were growing in the nursery, and I began to realize what remarkable plants they were. My early interest in chestnuts was piqued by reading *Tree Crops: A Permanent Agriculture* by J. Russell Smith. First published in 1929 and revised in 1950, *Tree Crops* chronicles Smith's ambitious attempt to document evidence of the links between soil and perennial vegetation (prairies and forests), between healthy soils and world hunger, between the plow and soil destruction, and between topsoil and civilization.

Agriculture leads to environmental degradation when it depends on the plow to plant annual crops, because the plow destroys soil-building processes and causes erosion and loss of biodiversity. Exceptions include paddy soils and the alluvial soils of river bottomlands that are replenished by periodic flooding. Cropping systems based on perennial plants may mitigate the negative ecological impacts of agriculture, because in perennial agro-ecosystems soil-building processes flourish. Woody plants, especially very long-lived trees, can be cultivated using methods that mimic natural ecosystems in their stability, productivity, and complexity, requiring minimal inputs. Chestnut trees come very close to representing the archetypal tree crop. They are very long-lived; examples of *Castanea sativa* in Italy are known to be more than one thousand years old. And they provide annual harvest of delicious, nutritious, easily harvested, easily stored food. Because a mature chestnut orchard resembles a temperate hardwood forest in both structure and function, it provides significant ecological benefits, with consequences far beyond merely producing a fruit. The tree offers habitat to a great number of animal species and acts as the keystone in its community. It anchors the soil to steep slopes that would otherwise be almost completely unsuitable for any other form of agriculture and moderates the local climate by shading the understory and transpiring water into the atmosphere.

Chestnut protein amounts to about 3 or 4 percent of the mass of the fresh seed, is of good quality, and is easily assimilated. There is no gluten in the protein of chestnuts.

It serves as host for symbiotic relationships with fungi, including the choice edible chanterelle and porcini mushrooms whose niches are those of the soil's great decomposers and recyclers, mobilizing deep soil nutrients and minerals into the humus layers. The landscape value of the chestnut grove is almost unequaled by that of any other forest type, possibly because the grove is evocative of a simpler, quieter past, when our relationship with nature was based on the regular cycles of sun and moon and season.

Chestnuts are Slow Food. Countries in East Asia and southern Europe are still the leading consumers of chestnuts. Most of the world's chestnuts are consumed locally. The character of a place is intimately associated with, even defined by its dominant vegetation, and the great chestnut forests of Europe are a marvelous example of the symbiosis of human and tree. Likewise, the current distribution and importance of American and Asian chestnut trees reflect the centuries of coevolutionary interaction between human culture and the plants since the Pleistocene. Native populations of chestnut were brought into cultivation in all of these areas. Selection of superior individuals and subsequent propagation of them led to the eventual domestication of chestnut as a nut crop. Innumerable varieties of chestnut have been named, and many are still grown as graft-propagated cultivars. A few cultivars enjoy wide distribution, for instance the handful of exotic types grown commercially in the U.S., but the vast majority of chestnut types are grown only within very limited geographic ranges, often in the exact spot where they originated. Many cultivars are specialized for particular uses, such as the flour types with smaller, sweeter, easily peeled nuts, or the larger, dense-fruited kinds candied for *marrons glacés*.

Chestnuts reached their global nadir during the 1970s. A conspiracy of circumstances—catastrophic diseases, two world wars, cultural revolutions, the postwar boom, changing diets, and the almost insane economics of the global marketplace—contributed to the almost total loss of the American chestnut, significant erosion of European and Asian chestnut genetic resources, and the near extinction of the chestnut civiliza-

The Big Four

Nuts of the four larger *Castanea* species vary in size. They are, left to right: American, Chinese, Japanese, and European. By legend, the Romans encountered the chestnut at a town in Thessaly, Greece, called Castanea—thus its generic name.

Photo by Paul Sisco.

tion worldwide. Yet chestnuts are once again being planted all over the world, in the places that chestnuts have been grown traditionally, and in the places where chestnut growing has been introduced only recently. Advances in plant breeding and molecular biology promise us blight- and ink-resistant chestnut trees. New and newly rediscovered knowledge about the ecological benefits of tree crops shows that such crops make more sense now than ever. Exciting new awareness by food communities around the globe, working together to protect the heritage of food, tradition, and culture, will allow farmers and consumers alike to experience the pleasures of locally grown chestnuts. In 2002 The American Chestnut Foundation received the Slow Food Award for the Defense of Biodiversity because of its work and the vision to restore the American chestnut to the Appalachian forests. Chestnuts can be, and should be, a part of a healthy forest, a part of a healthy diet, and a healthy agriculture. ∾

Chestnuts (C. sativa) *of souto de Santa Rabelos at the town hall of Taboada, near Lugo in Galicia, Spain. (Courtesy of Professor Ernesto Vieitez Cortizo.)*

A World of Chestnuts

Chinese chestnut trees (C. mollissima*) behind a farmhouse in Pensacola, North Carolina. Farmers often planted a pair of Chinese trees behind their house after the blight took away the American chestnuts. (Photo by Paul Sisco.)*

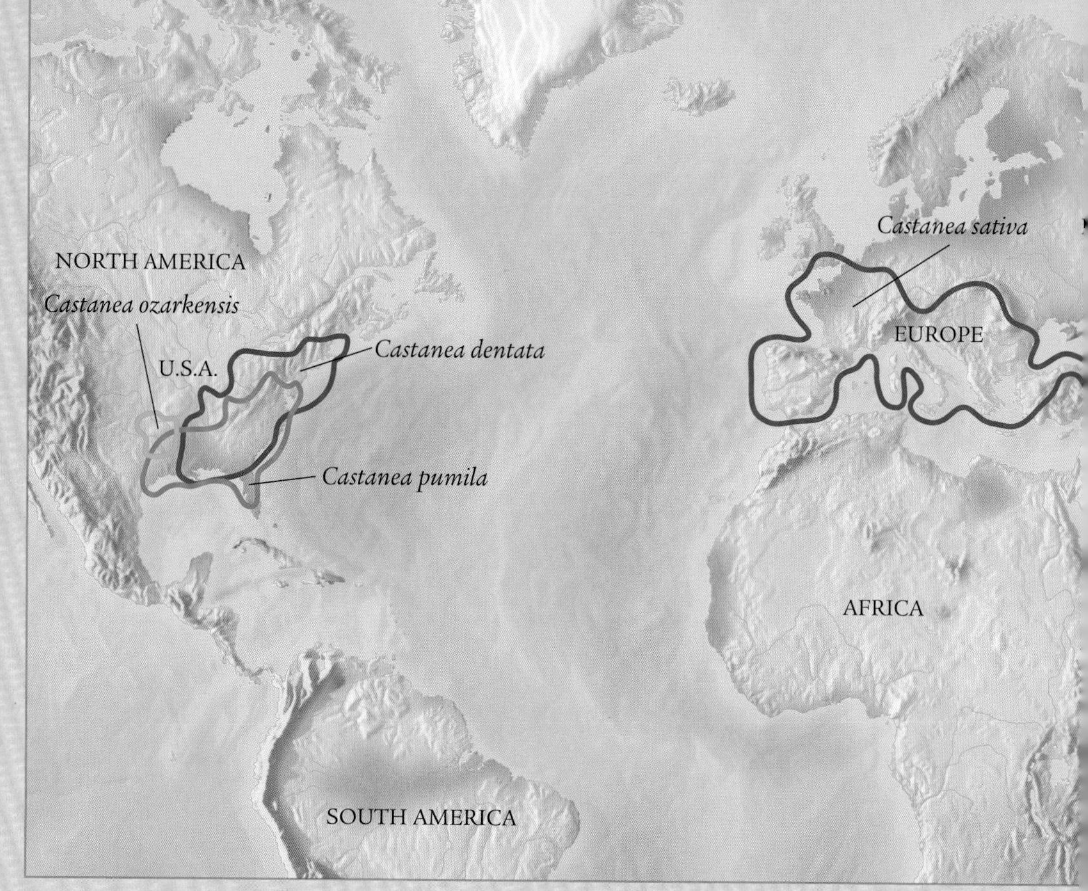

Castanea *species large and small are limited to the Northern Hemisphere in their natural range. The smaller* C. seguinii *(dwarf Chinese chestnut) and* C. henryi *(Chinese chinquapin) grow within the range of the Chinese chestnut,* C. mollissima, *while* C. pumila *(Allegheny chinquapin) and* C. ozarkensis *(Ozark chinquapin) overlap and grow slightly to the west of the natural range of the American chestnut.*

Chinese chestnut trees in Friendship Forest, near Chattanooga, Tennessee. These trees were planted in the 1930s by the Tennessee Valley Authority. (Photo by J. Hill Craddock.)

Budding catkins on Chinese chestnut (C. mollissima *Trucchi*). *(Photo by J. Hill Craddock.)*

Leaves of the Japanese chestnut (C. crenata).

Blossoming Japanese chestnut trees at the KFRI National Chestnut Gene Bank in Hwasung, Korea. (Photo by J. Hill Craddock.)

Japanese chestnut tree at Fort Defiance, North Carolina. (Photo by Paul Sisco.)

The "chestnut of a hundred horses" in Sant'Alfio, Sicily, on the eastern slopes of Mount Etna, is thought to be the oldest chestnut tree in the world, at more than three thousand years old. (Coutesy of Professor Ernesto Vieitez Cortizo.)

The chestnut is one of the most beautiful of trees, and deserves consideration on account of its ornamental character as well as for its material utility. [The chestnut] is said to have been found by the Romans, first at Castanea, a town of Thessaly, near the mouth of the Peneus, whence the fruit was named by them Castanea nuces, or nuts of Castanea. Some of the oldest and largest trees in the world now standing are chestnuts. One on Mount Etna, which can be seen from the town of Aci, has often been mentioned by travelers. It is 160 feet in circumference, and has a hollow trunk in which shepherds find a retreat for themselves and their flocks. It is called the hundred-horse chestnut, from a tradition that Joanna of Aragon once visited it, and that her whole party found protection beneath it from a sudden storm.

Phrenological Journal and Science of Health, April 1871

Leaves of the European chestnut.

A Forest of Chestnut: Russia's Western Caucasus

The western Caucasus Mountains near the Russian-Georgian border and the Black Sea are covered with an almost entirely deciduous forest that provides a sharp contrast with our image of the Rocky Mountains and Pacific Northwest, where montane forests are largely coniferous. In the panorama below, the lower slopes are dominated by European chestnut, oriental beech, and European hornbeam, with lesser amounts of oak, maple, linden, birch, poplar, and elm. Chestnut reaches its upper limit at about six thousand feet, where it is replaced by a mixed forest of giant firs, stunted beech, montane maple, and birch. Although there are about equal numbers of chestnut and beech trees per acre when averaged over the forest, the larger size of chestnut means that it constitutes the largest proportion in terms of timber volume.

Text and photos by Frederick Paillet

European chestnut and oriental beech dominate this mountainside forest near the Black Sea.

This single photograph captures the feel of the lush deciduous forests of the western Caucasus Mountains. The two dominant trees are oriental beech and European chestnut, the former with its silvery and smooth trunk and the latter characterized by vertical ridges and fissures. In the background are European hornbeam, growing as a smaller and generally more crooked tree.

Above: *Caucasian chestnut shows many features that are similar to what we know of American chestnut in pre-blight forests. American chestnut was known for its ability to regenerate from stump sprouts, often resulting in large trees with two or more stems rather than a single-stemmed tree originating as a true seedling. Many European chestnut trees in the Caucasus have multiple stems, suggesting origin as sprouts from a previously established tree.*

Below: *Most old photographs of large pre-blight chestnut trees in the humid southern Appalachians show relatively clean bark, free from extensive lichen and moss cover and not supporting much in the way of vines. In contrast, the even more humid climate of western Caucasian forests cause some chestnut trees to have bark literally covered with moss, lichen, and ivy vines.*

The Other American Chestnut and Two West Coast Cousins

By Frederick Paillet

This article appeared in a slightly different form in the fall-winter 1990 issue of the Journal of The American Chestnut Foundation. *Illustrations by the author.*

The American chestnut is the most familiar *Castanea* species in North America. This is the tree we've all heard about—the old forest giant with the valuable wood and useful nut crop. But the great chestnut has a lowly nephew in eastern forests, plus a couple of distant cousins on the West Coast. I first met the Allegheny chinquapin (*Castanea pumila* var. *pumila*) in the dry oak forests of northern Virginia during my chestnut research. At one time there were a number of named chinquapin species. But taxonomists now recognize only a single species with two varieties (*pumila*, the Allegheny chinquapin, and *ozarkensis*, the Ozark chinquapin). I had originally worried that the chestnut and chinquapin would be difficult to distinguish, but experience showed there wouldn't be a real problem.

Chinquapin leaves are slightly smaller, with much smaller teeth than chestnut leaves, and don't have the long, pointed chestnut tip (figure 1). The leaves also have their widest part two-thirds to three-quarters of the way to the tip, while chestnut leaves are broadest in the middle. At the same time, chinquapin leaves are decidedly fuzzy, and chinquapin twigs have a distinctive orange-brown color. Taxonomists have much more technical terms for these characteristics, but the bottom line is that the two species are easy to distinguish in the field, in spite of the great variation in chinquapin leaf shape and stem growth form.

figure 1. *Leaves and budding catkins (late May) and burs and nut (mid-September) from an Allegheny chinquapin in Virginia.*

I found chinquapin a pretty small shrub in the open forest in Virginia. My surveys in this area indicated that there were on the average about forty chestnut sprouts and fifty chinquapin shrub clones scattered over each acre of woodland. Almost all the chinquapin shrubs were much smaller and bushier than chestnut sprouts growing in the same woodlot—some less than six inches tall and bearing no more than three or four leaves. But the plant looks much more like a real member of the chestnut family when exposed to nearly full sun at the edge of a field. On some open-grown chinquapins I found stems with up to six burs, each holding a single acornlike nut—without the flat sides one associates with chestnuts at the supermarket, and nearly black in color.

figure 2. *Example of unusually large Ozark chinquapin in Arkansas (mid-November). This tree was about fourteen inches in diameter and more than forty feet tall. Such trees are now rare, but even larger specimens were common before the arrival of chestnut blight.*

My impression of chinquapin changed significantly when I had the opportunity to see the Ozark subspecies in its natural habitat (figure 2). Blight had already been in Arkansas for some time, but remains of old blight-killed chinquapin trunks as large as two feet in diameter littered the forest floor in places. Sprouting chinquapin clones showed growth form much like that of American chestnut wherever recent disturbance had eliminated the competition. The two obvious differences with chestnut were that basal sprouts originated from an extended area around the base of the tree rather than from preformed buds, and that released stems seemed to be expanding laterally after a few years of growth, rather than continuing the upward climb characteristic of chestnut. One gets the impression that Ozark chinquapin is attempting to fill the ecological niche occupied by chestnut in this Appalachian-like landscape where the latter is not present (figure 3).

Chinquapin is known to hybridize with chestnut, so one wonders why natural hybrids are so rare. The answer seems to be that chinquapin flowers almost a month earlier than chestnut. I found chinquapin blooming in Virginia in late May, while chestnut was flowering in late June in the same woodlots.

The chinquapin is a very close relative of the American chestnut, but there are several other chestnut relatives of more distant relationship in the mountains of California. The golden chinquapin (*Castanopsis chrysophylla*) is known to become a small tree in Oregon, but I found it growing as a low shrub on sparsely forested, rocky hillsides above Bear Lake in the San Bernardino Mountains about 9,000 feet in elevation. The dense evergreen thickets of low golden chinquapin shrubbery make one think of rhododendron, as do the dark green leathery leaves. Most stems were less than three feet tall, with a few approaching twice that stature

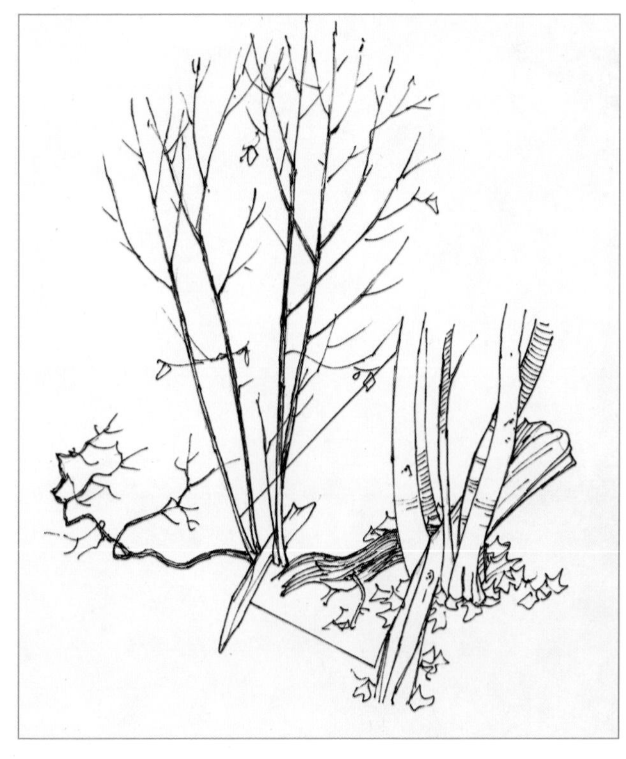

figure 3. *Example of Ozark chinquapin sprout clump in Arkansas, showing growth rates and stem form comparable to American chestnut. A falling snag apparently damaged an old and heavily suppressed chinquapin, resulting in the release of new sprouts. The sprouts were about twelve feet tall, had basal diameters of 2.5 inches, and branch nodes indicated the stems were four or five years old.*

in protected places. The clusters of very chestnutlike burs were just maturing in mid-July, while new flowers were still present on the tips of this year's growth. This "tree" seems to be the exact opposite of the great chestnut, growing as it does in the form of a knee-high shrub underneath the immense Jeffrey and sugar pines of the Southern California mountains.

I met the other California cousin of American chestnut in the famous Muir Woods, growing in the understory beneath magnificent redwoods. The tanoak (*Lithocarpus densiflora*) grows to a much more respectable size than the golden chinquapin but still doesn't make much of an impression underneath those redwoods. The evergreen leaves would seem to bear some resemblance to chestnut, except that they are so tough and leathery, and the edges tend to curl under, hiding the teeth. The fruit are really just acorns, except that the acorn cap has something like spines rather than simple scales.

Nonetheless, I was somewhat startled to see young tanoak saplings growing up into openings in the evergreen canopy, with much the same shape and appearance as chestnut saplings in New England. The trees had the same conical crown shape and branching pattern, and the semiglossy texture of the bark reminded me of chestnut, too. Another rather unfortunate parallel with chestnut is that tanoak is being decimated

Bur and nut of an Allegheny chinquapin. (Photo by J. Hill Craddock.)

Burs and foliage of an Ozark chinquapin. (Photo by Skip Mourglia, U.S. Department of Agriculture.)

by another introduced pathogen, the sudden oak death disease. A visit to the redwood forests at Muir Woods or Big Basin today reveals the reddened leaves of dying tanoaks almost everywhere.

One tends to think of the great forest trees such as chestnut, beech, and oak as well-defined species that have been around much as they are for all time. The distant and not-so-distant cousins of American chestnut suggest that there have been many different forms of these species over the 60 million or so years since oaks and chestnut first appeared on the earth. How many other interesting chestnut and chestnut-like trees have existed in habitats that we will never know, or became extinct in forests that no one ever saw? ∾

The distant and not-so-distant cousins of American chestnut suggest that there have been many different forms of these species over the 60 million or so years since oaks and chestnut first appeared on the earth.

Chestnut Introductions into North America

By Dr. Sandra L. Anagnostakis

When people find chestnut trees of any size growing in the New England woods they frequently call the Connecticut Agricultural Experiment Station in New Haven, hoping they have found an American chestnut tree resistant to chestnut blight disease. Usually the tree is Asian, or an Asian hybrid. In previous centuries chestnut trees were very important to the people on this continent. They took advantage of "new and different" material much more than is generally realized and were planting Asian species long before chestnut blight was discovered in New York City in 1904.

The first recorded importations were those of Thomas Jefferson, who brought cuttings to his Virginia home, Monticello, and grafted them on native American chestnut trees. When Éleuthère Irénée du Pont de Nemours (founder of the DuPont company) moved from France to Bergen Point, New Jersey, in 1799, and then on to Brandywine, Delaware, he brought many European chestnuts (*Castanea sativa*) with him. He imported more later, hybridized them, and planted them all over the area. By 1889 some of the popular varieties of *C. sativa* and *C. sativa* x *dentata* hybrids were 'Anderson', 'Bartram', 'Comfort', 'Cooper', 'Corson', 'Dager', 'Darlington', 'duPont', 'Miller', 'Moncur', 'Numbo', 'Paragon', 'Ridgely', 'Scott', 'Spanish', and 'Styer'.

The first recorded importations were those of Thomas Jefferson, who brought cuttings to his Virginia home, Monticello, and grafted them on native American chestnut trees.

In 1876 S. B. Parsons of Flushing, New York, imported lily bulbs through plant collector Thomas Hogg for his garden in Connecticut, and one of the baskets contained, instead of lily bulbs, seed of Japanese chestnuts, *Castanea crenata*. He planted the seed and gave seedlings to all his friends. Two of these are still growing very well in Connecticut—one in Old Lyme on the grounds of the Bee and Thistle Inn, and one in Cheshire behind the Congregational Church. Major importation of Asian chestnut trees began in 1882 when William Parry, of Parry, New Jersey, brought in 1,000 grafted *C. crenata* trees. Parry selected 'Parry' as his best but sold several other cultivars as well.

In 1886 Luther Burbank imported 10,000 nuts from Japan for selecting and hybridizing. In 1893 his "New Creations" catalog advertised his 'New Japan Mammoth' chestnut, and he sold three seedlings to Judge Andrew J. Coe of Connecticut. These were subsequently sold (in 1897) to J. H. Hale of South Glastonbury, Connecticut, who named them 'Coe', 'Hale', and 'McFarland' and sold grafted trees of the cultivars from his nursery and through catalogs as early as 1898.

Twenty-one cultivars of Japanese chestnuts were listed in T. H. Powell's 1898 Bulletin (Delaware Agricultural Experiment Station). These were discussed in gardening magazines such as the *Rural New Yorker* and advertised in plant and seed catalogs throughout the country. By the turn of the century, Asian and European chestnut trees were available by mail from many nurseries, such as Burbank (California), Parry Bros. (New Jersey), Hale (Connecticut), Kerr (Maryland), Biltmore (North Carolina), Boehmer (Japan), and the Yokohama Co. of New York and Tokyo. Chestnuts were grown as a crop in many places, and several U.S. companies in Pennsylvania and New Jersey were in business by 1900.

Chinese chestnuts are not mentioned in the early plant catalogs that I have seen, but plant explorers sent seed to the United States in the early 1900s. In 1903 Dr. Charles Sprague Sargent sent *C. mollissima* seed to the Arnold Arboretum near Boston, but no trees from this seed lot have survived. In 1908 E. H. Wilson sent the Arnold Arboretum seeds of *Castanea henryi* from western Hupeh (Hubei) Province, China, and one was planted in their collection. This tree survived better than most imports of this species but finally died in 1934.

Around the turn of the century several plant explorers were traveling around the world collecting plants that could not be found in North America. These people were often careful observers of plant ecology, and their notes make fascinating reading. After the Boxer Rebellion in 1901, travel in China again became possible, and several plant-collecting expeditions were undertaken. The most famous plant explorers are probably Ernest H. "Chinese" Wilson, who collected for an English nursery and later for the Arnold Arboretum; Joseph Rock, with backing from the National Geographic Society; and Frank N. Meyer, who was hired by David Fairchild to explore for the U.S. Plant

Threshing hybrid 'Paragon' chestnuts. (Patrick County, Va., Historical Society.)

Introduction Division of the U.S. Department of Agriculture. These men had very different personal styles, and their travels resulted in vast numbers of importations.

The USDA Bureau of Plant Industry started importing chestnut seed in the early 1900s and planting them in Savannah, Georgia, Chico, California, and at their headquarters in Bell, Maryland, near Glenn Dale. Walter Van Fleet worked with them for many years, followed by David Fairchild, R. Kent Beattie, George Flippo Gravett, and Fred Berry. They received plant material from Joseph Rock, Frank Meyer, Peter Liu, and Beattie himself. Contacts with missionaries in Asia yielded seed collections as well, and plants for distribution were assigned Plant Introduction numbers. In 1925 the Bureau of Forest Pathology started making collections of chestnut seed, primarily from within the United States, from native trees and those planted from introductions.

The devastating spread of chestnut blight disease in the first decades of the twentieth century gave new impetus to the development of hybrids of chestnut that were resistant to the fungus. Many people took up Frank Meyer's suggestion that hybridization of resistant Asian chestnuts with susceptible American chestnut might yield trees that could be grown in the United States, and hybrids made earlier to improve the orchard qualities of chestnut trees were examined for their resistance to chestnut blight disease.

Arthur H. Graves of the Brooklyn Botanical Garden started planting chestnut trees and making hybrids in the early 1930s. Trees were planted on his property in Hamden, Connecticut, and on land owned by the Connecticut Agricultural Experiment Station. His work was aided by Hans Nienstaedt and Richard Jaynes, who both did their doctoral research on chestnut at Yale University and the Connecticut Agricultural Experiment Station. Now that we can keep American chestnut trees alive with biological control by hypovirulence, breeding can more easily continue.

Species and hybrids of chestnut were distributed by the Experiment Station to homeowners all over the northeastern United States. Often records of origin are lost, tags are unreadable, or row lines are confused by the planting efforts of squirrels and blue jays. I try to identify mystery chestnut trees using leaf and twig characteristics. The pure species are relatively easy to identify, but the complicated hybrids must sometimes be a case of "best guess."

Species and hybrids of chestnut were distributed by the Experiment Station to homeowners all over the northeastern United States.

My file on chestnut history gets larger every year, as I find yet another catalog or letter from the early days of this century. Many fine Asian trees have withstood 50 to 120 years of New England winters, bugs, and blight. We can use these in present and future breeding programs, as long as we remember to write it down for the people trying to puzzle this out 100 years from now.

Food Notes: A Tasty, Nutritious Family

From various sources

The U.S. is the only country in the world that can grow chestnuts that does not have a commercial chestnut industry. The U.S. imports $20 million of chestnuts yearly because there are fewer than 500 acres of chestnut orchards in the U.S. It would take 10,000 acres of producing chestnut orchards to supply what we import! American-grown nuts can reach the market sooner, fresher, and bring a higher price than imports, which are often low in quality. U.S. consumption is less than 1 ounce per person per year, but 1 pound per capita in Europe and 2 pounds in Asia. It would take 120,000 acres of chestnut orchards to supply U.S. consumption at European levels, and create a $300 million new agricultural industry for America!

From the Chestnut Hill Tree Farm in Alachua, Florida. Chestnut Hill sells 'Dunstan' chestnut tree seedlings, a hybrid of Chinese and American trees.

Nutrients in Chestnuts

Chestnuts are high in fiber, have a good amount of protein, and the fats are more than 90 percent unsaturated fatty acids.

Nutrients in chestnuts given as the percentage of dry weight:

Species	Fiber	Protein	Fat	Carbohydrate
Chinese	14*	8	2	65
European	14	6	4	66
Japanese	14	8	0.4	90
American	19	10	10	40

*Note that since the fibers are carbohydrates, the numbers across will not necessarily add up to 100%.

From "Nutrients in Chestnuts," by Sandra L. Anagnostakis and Peter Devin. Northern Nut Growers Annual Report, 1999.

Comparison of Fats and Sugars in Chestnuts

Total lipid content was highest in the American chestnut followed by chinkapin, then European chestnuts, and lowest in the Chinese chestnut samples. . . . Magnitude of differences may be related to sensory preference for the American chestnut since it is well documented that lipids contribute to mouth-feel and flavor of many food products. Percent unsaturated fatty acid was high (average, 86%) with the content highest in the Chinese and American chestnuts. . . . The predominant [saturated fatty] acid was palmitic. Oleic was the major [unsaturated] fatty acid in the American and Chinese chestnuts and the chinkapins. European chestnuts contained mostly linoleic acid. These data attest to the quality of these nuts as a food product . . . since unsaturated fatty acids are more desirable nutritionally than higher levels of more highly saturated fatty acids. . . . Most of the sugar present was sucrose. . . . Differences in the quantities of sucrose were not significant by species. . . . Fructose and glucose were present in all species in very low quantities. ~

From "Comparison of Total Lipids, Fatty Acids, Sugars and Nonvolatile Organic Acids in Nuts from Four *Castanea* Species," by Samuel E. Senter, Jerry A. Payne, Gregory Miller, and Sandra L. Anagnostakis. *Journal of the Science of Food and Agriculture*, 1994.

Grande Dame of Comfort Food and a Chestnut Festival

Edna Lewis, who died in 2006 at age eighty-nine, was perhaps the nation's outstanding popularizer of southern country cooking. Lewis, the granddaughter of slaves, grew up on a farm in Freetown, Virginia, where she absorbed the rhythms of rural life. Though she later moved to New York and even worked for a time at the *Daily Worker*, she never lost contact with her southern roots, and her *Taste of Country Cooking*, which was published when she was sixty, has become a cookbook classic, admired as much for its writing as its down-home recipes. Her subsequent career as chef and food writer earned her plaudits worldwide, and she was designated *Grande Dame* by Les Dames d'Escoffier, a society of female culinary professionals.

When she was in her seventies, Lewis spotted a chestnut tree in the back of the Willow Grove Inn, near Charlottesville, Virginia, and encouraged the innkeeper, Angela Mulloy, to celebrate this rarity with a chestnut harvest festival—and thus a tradition was born. Mulloy, who was of Italian heritage, was no stranger to chestnuts and, recalling the tradition in Italy's Piedmonte, adapted it to Virginia's own Piedmont. Keeping with tradition, the festival begins with everyone roasting chestnuts, peeling off their blackened shells, dunking them in the season's fruity new wine, or *novella*, and savoring the tasty combination. A dinner follows that features chestnuts in every dish, along with Virginia wines.

European Chestnut Honey

By William Lord

A version of this article was published in the spring 2005 Bark, *the newsletter of The American Chestnut Foundation.*

Chestnut honey in America does not have the aura that prevails in Europe. Early records of honey from the flowers of the American chestnut are not for the most part complimentary. In 1887 two Pennsylvania beekeepers acknowledged that chestnut produced occasional crops that were of "bitter taste, dark in color and rank in smell."

This contrasts with the fond memory of north Georgia resident Noel Moore. In 1980, in *Foxfire 6*, he recalled a boyhood abundant with chestnut where the trees in bloom were "just like big, potted flowers standing up all over the mountains."

"And the blossoms gave one of the best honey crops we ever had. . . . Whenever chestnuts bloomed, in the morning, early, the trees looked like just the whole tops were alive with honeybees working on getting the nectar. They'd really go for it."

In Europe honey is absorbed within the mystique of the gourmet; descriptive phrases vie with the homage given to wine. Honey is venerated with a Lorelei allure enticing us to taste and enjoy. "Drizzle some on your favorite cake or ice cream . . . an earthy aroma . . . a refreshing floral taste that clings on the tongue long after the honey is gone . . . the robust flavor pairs well with strong cheese."

Throughout Mediterranean Europe nomadic beekeepers carry their hives to carefully selected sites among the blooming trees. Summers are sunny and dry, allowing the bees to ply their industrious ways with little hindrance from rain. One group concentrates on collecting nectar, another on collecting pollen. Chestnut pollen is an abundant source of high-value protein and may be more important to the bee than chestnut nectar. Beekeepers are aware of this and try to locate their hives remote from unwanted competition from plants with richer nectar.

Beekeeping is an ancient art in Europe. In Tuscany, amid the Apennines, records have been kept since 1508. An enduring rapport between man and bee remains in progress. European chestnut honey is available through the Internet. American chestnut honey, the kind known to Noel Moore, may be on the horizon. ∾

A False but Famous Relative: Longfellow's "Spreading Chestnut Tree"

The following article published in the Grand Forks Herald *in the year of his death, 1882, leaves no doubt that the tree made immortal in Henry Wadsworth Longfellow's beloved poem "The Village Blacksmith" was not an American chestnut but a horse chestnut* (Aesculus hippocastanum), *also known as a buckeye.*

Lydia M. Williard in *Phrenological Journal.* – In a little room out of Lady Washington's room—the Longfellow parlor—is a picture of the Village Smithy, and the spreading chestnut tree before it. All that is left now of the Smithy is this picture. Very much to Longfellow's regret and against his earnest expostulations, to widen Brattle street, the beautiful old chestnut tree was taken down. Early in the morning the choppers were at it. Like burning sparks from the anvil the chips flew in every direction, and soon a crash was heard and the cry went up, "The old chestnut is down!" The word ran from lip to lip. A crowd quickly collected, and all, rushing out from house to house just as they were, without coat or hat, each bore off some fragment as a souvenir, until an officer interfered and the plunder ceased. So the tree fell, but it was at last proposed to the city fathers that the children of the public school, by small subscriptions, should build out of its wood a great arm-chair for the poet's study. And when the chair was placed beside the mantel, the poet gave orders that every child might come to see it, and the tramp of little feet through the halls for months was the despair of housemaids. The wood is ebonized, the chair is perfectly black, the cushion and arms are of green leather. The castors are glass balls set in sockets. In the chair's back is a piece of beautiful carving, of horse-chestnut leaves and flowers. In other parts of the chair in graceful groups are finely-wrought horse-chestnut leaves and burrs. The verse beginning "And children coming home from school," etc. is raised in German text around the seat. On a brass plate under the cushion is a presentation inscription:

To
The Author of
The Village Blacksmith,
This chair, made from the wood of the spreading
Chestnut tree,
is presented as
An expression of grateful regard and veneration
By
The Children of Cambridge,
Who, with their friends, join in the best wishes
And congratulations
on
this anniversary,
February 27, 1879.

~

Sketch of the village smithy, Cambridge, by Henry Wadsworth Longfellow. The tree is a horse chestnut. (Courtesy of the National Park Service, Longfellow National Historic Site.)

Brothers Ben, left, and Rob Samels with their chestnut harvest under chestnut trees at the Samels Farm, Skegemog Point, Williamsburg, Michigan, in the fall of 1988. (Photo taken and hand-colored by Randall McCune.)

HEARTH AND HOME

Chestnuts are a cheap food, and they lend themselves well to many ways of serving.

— *Delineator* magazine, October 1910

Historical Chestnut Recipes

While in rural Appalachia the American chestnut touched nearly every aspect of life, elsewhere in the prosperous young republic, chestnut's influence was perhaps less obvious. Chestnut lumber was still utilitarian and widely used, though the nut itself was more an occasional treat than an economic staple. People did not depend on it for their livelihood.

In some cities, larger, imported chestnuts were available. Most of the dozen or so chestnut recipes in the 1896 Boston Cooking-School Cook Book *by Fannie Merritt Farmer call for French or Italian chestnuts, but these below do not specify. An American classic, the Fannie Farmer cookbook, as it came to be known, is still available in updated editions.*

To Shell Chestnuts.

Cut a half-inch gash on flat sides and put in an omelet pan, allowing one-half teaspoon butter to each cup chestnuts. Shake over range until butter is melted. Put in oven and let stand five minutes. Remove from oven, and with a small knife take off shells. By this method shelling and blanching is [*sic*] accomplished at the same time, as skins adhere to shells.

Devilled Chestnuts.

Shell one cup chestnuts, cut in thin slices, and fry until well browned, using enough butter to prevent chestnuts from burning. Season with Tabasco Sauce or few grains paprika.

Chestnut Soufflé.

¼ cup sugar.
2 tablespoons flour.
1 cup chestnut purée
½ cup milk.
Whites 3 eggs.

Mix sugar and flour, add chestnuts and milk gradually; cook five minutes, stirring constantly; beat whites of eggs until stiff, and cut and fold into mixture. Turn into buttered and sugared individual moulds, having them three-fourths full; set moulds in pan of hot water and bake in slow oven until firm, which may be determined by pressing with finger. Serve with Cream Sauce.

New Ways of Cooking Chestnuts

From the Delineator *magazine, October 1910*

In this country, except for turkey stuffing, little use is made of the chestnut, whereas abroad chestnut dishes of all kinds are very common. For one thing, chestnuts are a cheap food, and they lend themselves well to many ways of serving. So the French, the Spanish, and the Italian peoples, especially, send them to table served as vegetables plainly boiled, but masked with a good oil sauce. They have the nuts ground into chestnut flour of which they make good bread and various sorts of cakes and biscuits. They also boil them in sirup and serve them up as compotes; in short, in Europe chestnuts are considered very valuable food adjuncts and a great aid to cooking operations.

The chestnut differs from most nuts in its scant possession of oil, the fat giver, the warmth creator, the energy maker. But it is rich in starch. This is why a cooked chestnut is so mealy, so like flour, and this is the reason, of course, why the wise Spaniards and Italians can convert the abundant nuts into good chestnut bread. Though it has starch in such abundance, it is deficient in the gummy matter or dextrine that makes wheat flour viscid and tenacious and spongy when mixed with water into dough; so, in making chestnut bread, half the quantity of wheat flour is added to give the needed dextrine. . . .

In boiling chestnuts for the table, the deficiency of oil needs to be restored, therefore the peeled nuts are boiled in milk to which either butter or cream has been added. In boiling them for turkey stuffing, stock must be used, not water.

A good way to remove the brown outer shell and the inner skin, when the nuts are especially desired whole, is as follows: With a sharp knife make a slit in each chestnut; put them into boiling water for four minutes, take out and dry them. Then melt a little butter in a saucepan, and toss them about in this until every nut is coated with the butter and very hot. It will then be found that with the aid of a sharp-pointed knife both skins can be easily removed together leaving the nut whole, and ready for subsequent manipulations. The following recipes will be found delicious:

Chestnut Soup:

Take the outer rind from three-quarters of a pound of chestnuts, and put them in a large pan of warm water. As soon as this becomes too hot for the fingers to remain in it, take out the chestnuts, peel them quickly, immerse them in cold water, wipe and weigh them. Cover them with good stock, and stew gently for rather more than three-quarters of an hour, or until they break when touched with a fork. Drain them, rub them through a fine sieve, reversed, add one quart of good stock, a seasoning of mace, red pepper and salt, and stir often till the soup boils. Then add a quarter of a pint of cream. The stock in which the chestnuts are boiled may be added in part, or the whole may be used.

Curried Chestnuts:

Shell and blanch one pound of chestnuts; then stew in stock until tender. Melt one heaping tablespoonful of butter in a saucepan, fry in it one small sliced onion, one small sliced sour apple, one tablespoonful of curry powder, and a teaspoonful of chutney. Blend one tablespoonful of flour with one cupful of stock or gravy and add them. Cook till the apple is soft, then strain, add one teaspoonful of lemon-juice, half a teaspoonful of sugar, and simmer the chestnuts in this until they have absorbed the flavor. Serve with plenty of plain boiled rice. Curried chestnuts served with rice offer an excellent substitute for meat and vegetables. ∾

Chestnuts can be easily peeled. One way is to cut them in half and then quickly blanch them in boiling water. The blanched nuts are then easily peeled and can be frozen for use during the winter months. (Photo by J. Hill Craddock.)

Journey of a Chestnut Log

By John Egerton

"Excessive preoccupation with the South . . . is a bore," wrote Georgia-born author John Egerton in his 1974 book The Americanization of Dixie, *"but the opposite danger is in an assimilation of regions that spreads and perpetuates the banal and the venal." As a freelance writer or editor of eleven books and hundreds of articles that explore issues of race and region, Egerton battles the banal by celebrating the best aspects of southern life. His work has won numerous honors, including the 1995 Southern Book Critics Circle Award for* Speak Now Against the Day: The Generation before the Civil Rights Movement in the South. *His 1987 book* Southern Food at Home, on the Road, in History, *won Best Book on Food from the Culinary Institute of America, and in 2003 he was presented with a Lifetime Achievement Award from the Southern Foodways Alliance.*

"Many Southerners can still set a fine table and surround it with conversation and laughter and love," he has written. "It's an old Southern skill, a habit, a custom, a tradition, and it deserves to last as long as the corn grows tall." So it's natural that his encounter with a chestnut log culminated in a carving of a quintessential southern meal.

An elongated chunk from an old chestnut log is mounted horizontally above the fireplace mantel in my living room. It is just shy of four feet long and rounded lengthwise, with its concave side secured to the wall. On its convex face, where the bark once grew, an intricately detailed tableau has been carved, showing four people and a dog in a close-up, wide-angle, three-dimensional scene at their dinner table in a rural mountain home.

All the elements of this picture bespeak a bygone time. The table, which dominates the foreground, is covered with a cloth and set with plates and glasses. Steam rises from a bowl of vegetables, and a pan of plump rolls rests near the bowl. Across the table sits an older man in overalls, his billed cap hanging on one rail of his chair. Two youths flank him at either end, and an aproned woman stands just to the man's right, about to serve him from a platter she is holding. The dog waits beside one of the children, eyeing the scene intently. On the wall behind them, a tall cupboard and a keyhole clock are clearly visible (the time is twenty before six). Curtains blow gently to the sides of an open window, revealing in the distance a mountain ridge above an unpaved road.

All of these details are painstakingly carved into the dull gray-brown surface of the log, exposing a rich, vibrant, smooth-grained wood, the color and texture of which remind me of shelled pecans, of caramel. Nothing except the artist's knife has been applied to this indeterminately aged shard of "wormy chestnut," so-called because worms bored tiny holes into the barkless surface after the trees had died of disease and fallen to the forest floor. The worm holes, the straight and wavy lines of the wood's grain, and the mastery of the woodcarver all combine to deepen and enrich the character of this family gathered at their table, suspended in a time—the 1930s, perhaps—when the last of the mighty American chestnuts were dying on the surrounding mountainsides and falling in place, like soldiers at attention.

Throughout most of the eighteenth and nineteenth centuries, the chestnut trees of the Eastern United States were as important in their own way as hogs were to the pioneering and farming families moving west. For sheer utility, chestnuts were easily the first-choice trees; fast-growing, rot and drought-resistant, they yielded a hardwood that was easy to split, durable, not as dense and heavy as oak, and big—up to ten feet thick and a hundred feet high. When felled and cut up, chestnut trees were turned into everything from rail fences to houses and barns, from cradles to coffins to cordwood. And every year, in season, the tall sentinels rained down a harvest of nuts that fed the foraging livestock and wild game (as well as the people, who snacked on and baked with hearth-roasted chestnuts).

Then, with the arrival of the twentieth century, an exotic bark fungus attacked the trees, starting in New England and spreading south and west through the mountains of Appalachia. Within a generation, most of the big chestnuts littered the forests like highland logjams; in their place, shrubby sprouts of new growth emerged but never matured. The fallen trunks remained for decades, pocked with worm holes but resistant to decay, and from these came a continuing supply of chestnut lumber prized by furniture makers, barn builders, and rail-splitters. That source of serviceable "new" wood has long since vanished. The only American chestnut available now, at any price, was either made into furniture years back or somehow sheltered well enough to survive in prostrate silence in craggy forest glens.

"Grandma's Table," a chestnut carving by John Steely, mounted over the mantel of author John Egerton. (Photo by Bill LaFevor.)

It was just such a remnant of timber as this that my friend Clayton Braddock brought to me as a gift on a visit in the winter of 1995. Braddock (he went by his last name) lived with his wife, Jowain, an effervescent chanteuse, on a bosky, bouldered mountainside west of Blacksburg, Virginia. He was an engaging man—poet, picker, serenader, storyteller—and such a lover of wood and rocks that he chose to live in a house made of those elements, plus glass. A former journalist, he had reinvented himself as a college professor, but he was truly in his element while roaming the deep woods like a solitary druid, scavenging treasures, finding meaning and inspiration—clues to life's mysteries – in all manner of things that he lugged home to examine. One of these was that pin-holed chestnut log.

"I brought you a little piece of wood," he announced, with an eagerness in his booming voice. "It's wormy chestnut." The core of the tree had disintegrated, but what remained was hard and solid. From the curve of its outside surface, which felt firm and smooth to the touch, I guessed that it constituted about a fifth to an eighth of the live tree's girth. In my mind's eye I pictured a leafy chestnut, maybe seventy-five feet tall and as many years old, ten to fifteen feet round at its base, growing straight and stately on the slope above Braddock's house, long before he or the house had come there. No telling how long ago it had toppled, or when the worms had drilled their way to its heart.

I ran both hands along the curve. "It's smooth," I said, "like a piece of driftwood, or a chunk off a ship's mast." We stood there for a minute, thinking. Finally I asked him, "What can I do with it?"

"Carve something on it," he replied, so quickly that I knew he had already thought it through.

"Like . . . what?"

"Oh, a scene of some kind—a landscape, an interior. A mural in wood, in bas relief, or whatever that sort of raised image is called. Knowing how much you and Ann like to cook, I was thinking you might want to do a food scene, something like that."

"The Last Supper?" I responded, smiling.

"Well, some supper—maybe a picnic, or a banquet. Let your artist think about it. You don't want to be too prescriptive. Let it be a creative thing."

I could see it—see something, anyway—and I knew where to go with it. "I've got another mountain friend in Virginia," I said, "practically a neighbor of yours, though I don't think you've met him. Lives down near Meadows of Dan. He's a woodworker, a carver, a furniture maker, does beautiful pieces, small and large. I bet he'd like to carve on this, just to see what he could do with it."

John Steely was in some ways a mirror opposite of Clayton Braddock: tall while Clayton was short, focused rather than frenetic, quiet to the point of being taciturn instead of projecting a boisterous bonhomie. They had some wonderful qualities in common, though; both were creative (albeit in different media), and incisive, and authentically self-realized—"all wool and a yard wide," as I once heard someone described. The genuine article. Comfortably at home in their own skin. I always wanted to bring those two great friends of mine together, but I waited too late; Clayton is gone now, relocated to another energy stream, no doubt still cheerfully searching for that enchanted forest where good druids dwell in peace.

Steely worked wood, and his wife, Mary Dashiell, was a potter, high on a ridge of the Blue Ridge Mountains. Their workspaces were as overflowing with sentient pleasures as a colony of elves: softly polished, buttery smooth tables and chairs that smelled of poplar, pine, walnut, maple; whimsically colorful pottery fishes and birds that whistled like flutes; and in the kitchen, something fresh and aromatic usually bubbling on a back burner.

John eyed the chestnut hulk silently, rubbing his chin. I didn't wait for him to ask me what I was thinking. "I was thinking," I said, "that you might carve a scene here on the curved face."

"A scene." He kept it in his steady gaze. "Anything in particular?"

"No, not really. Maybe something having to do with food."

"Food," he echoed. Then, after another long pause, he looked up and said, "Well, leave it here. I'll see if anything occurs to me."

That was all; nothing more. I saw Steely again, a few months later, but he didn't

Detail of "Grandma's Table," carving by John Steely. (Photo by Bill LaFevor.)

mention the chestnut piece. More time passed—a year, maybe two. Then, on another trip to Virginia, I was giving a talk to a small group when I spied my man in the back of the room. After we adjourned, he came up to greet me, and we chatted amiably for a few minutes.

Then Steely said, "I've got your chestnut out in my car." His words were casual, almost like an afterthought or a prelude to parting. I had been hoping for something more definitive. Had he just brought it back to me unchanged? I tried not to let him see disappointment in my expression.

"Okay, let's go get it."

"Well, I just started cutting on it, and that's what came out. It was fun to do. I liked the way the wood took my knife."

When he opened his trunk and lifted it out, I was speechless. All around the border of the convex side, the dull brown skin of the log remained as it had been, but within that oval band were faces, shapes, contours, angles—all of a different shade of brown than the weathered rim. The etched images were as clearly identifiable as figures in an impressionist painting—a Renoir, a Monet. Better yet, Steely's images were enhanced by the grain of the wood, the worm holes, a slash or two that might have been axe cuts, even a couple of punctures that appeared to have been made by nails or bullets. The carved eyes of his figures seemed to follow me around.

"It's amazing," I finally managed to say. "How did you do it?"

John shrugged. "Well, I just started cutting on it, and that's what came out. It was fun to do. I liked the way the wood took my knife. I didn't know how well the chestnut would work, but I understand now why it used to be a popular choice for furniture making."

I ran my fingertips over every face, over the food and the furniture. It was as if these images had been buried in the log, waiting for an artist, a master carver with the right sharp tool, to cut away their protective cover and set them free. "It's almost like they've been in there all along," I said.

"Yeah, well . . ." He left the rest unsaid.

After a minute I asked, "Do you know who they are?"

"I think so," John replied, "sort of. When my brother and I were young, we used to go to Arkansas in the summertime to visit our grandparents. Those memories have stayed with me. So I guess that's us. My grandmother was a wonderful cook. I can still taste her hot rolls, fresh vegetables, fried chicken, pork chops."

I was starting to taste them too. There where Steely and I were standing, in the gathering dusk, I remembered that it was suppertime. "Let's go get something to eat," I said. "I'm starving."

We had to work out the details of our transaction. No fee had been discussed. I told him there was no way I could pay him what his carving was worth, because it was priceless. He had already done some calculating, and handed me a piece of paper. "Here's how many hours I worked on it," John explained, "and I'm charging you fifteen dollars an hour."

By almost any measure, the total was ridiculously low. I told him that, but he wouldn't budge from his numbers. I was getting a unique work of art, a piece that could not be duplicated, for a fraction of what it would bring at auction. "It's a steal, Steely," I protested.

"Just write the check," he ordered, softly but firmly.

When the late-afternoon sun peeks aslant at the figures in "Grandma's Table," their raised faces throw tiny shadows off to one side. The grain of the chestnut adds lines of age, of character, as fittingly as those from the carver's hand. In the shifting, fleeting beams of natural light, the color of the wood seems to flow across the textured surface, like honey on sliced bread.

Every time I look up at this wonderful creation, I think of Clayton Braddock, who rescued the chestnut from a forest bed, and lived to see and admire the destiny he had made possible for it. And I think of John Steely, who found his grandmother's welcome table buried in that log, and brought it back to life, just as lovers of the mighty American chestnut are striving now to rescue the tree from its genetic grave.

"You don't look back along time but down through it, like water," the Canadian writer Margaret Atwood has said. "Sometimes things come to the surface, sometimes they don't. Nothing goes away."

Nothing. And that includes "Grandma's Table." ∾

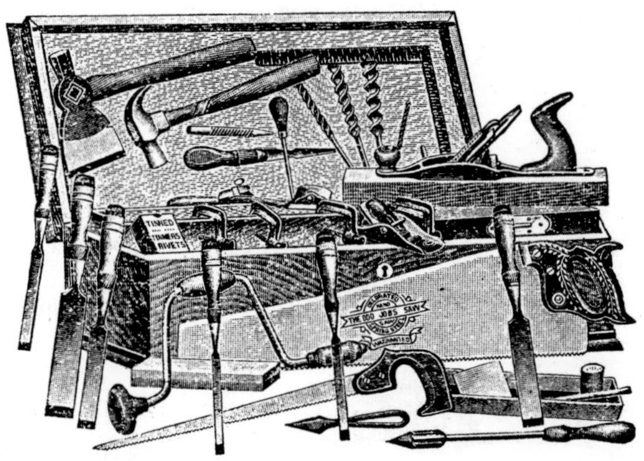

A Fenced-in Forest

In much of Appalachia, chestnut trees not only supported abundant wildlife, but also sustained free-range livestock. At the same time, the tree's wood was the favored material for the ever-present rail fences that kept the roaming livestock out of farmers' crops and gardens.

The Split-Rail Fence

By William Lord

The rail fence is an American original, perhaps devised by a provident but unknown settler in colonial Virginia. Its various names indicate its place of origin and appearance. It is known as the Virginia, the zigzag, the snake, or the worm fence. It required much more lumber than the post-and-rail fence of contemporary Europe, but it was perfectly suited to America, rich in forests and open space. A split-rail fence was much easier to construct. It required no digging and could be used on almost any type of terrain. It required no nails and only a few simple tools.

Even today a rail splitter uses the same tools the pioneer did: an ax, a saw, wedges, and a maul or sledgehammer. And even a saw isn't essential.

Lincoln the Rail Splitter, *circa 1909. (Prints and Photographs Division, Library of Congress.)*

Over time it was discovered that chestnut made the best rails. It was rot resistant, comparatively light, and easiest to split. Trees generally eight to twenty-four inches in diameter were cut down and then sawed into ten- to twelve-foot lengths. A wedge was placed in the center of the butt end, vertical to the ground, and then struck with the maul. The wedge opened up a crack of two or more feet along the log. A second wedge was placed in the crack and pounded with the maul, extending the split. This would generally loosen the first wedge, and it could be placed ahead of the second wedge to complete the split. Some rail splitters could split a chestnut log with the first wedge.

As the great tracts of forest were cut down, the chestnut's superior ability to sprout and grow several straight stems at the stump provided an even better source for rails than did trees from seed. Seedlings grew much slower, and the trunks of some were twisted and produced uneven rails.

Setting the first course of rails, with its zigzag pattern, was called "laying the worm." If deemed necessary, the crossed ends were placed on a flat rock for stability. More rails were then added, to whatever height was necessary. A pair of rails was usually placed in the manner of an "X" over the top of each intersection of the zigs and zags, to form a "lock" to resist the violence of weather and the push of livestock.

Abraham Lincoln was known as a rail splitter and also as a practical joker. He often entered rail-splitting contests. He outsplit one foremost contender by slipping a black gum log into his pile. Black gum is very knotty and difficult to split, and Abe won hands down.

The Chestnut Commons: Fence-out vs. Fence-in

By Ralph H. Lutts

The following is excerpted from the author's "Manna from God: The American chestnut trade in southwestern Virginia," in the journal Environmental History, *July 2004.*

For mountain folk, chestnuts were more than a source of food for themselves; the nuts were an abundant communal resource. Animals, such as hogs, turkeys, and cattle, were allowed to range freely in these Blue Ridge counties of Virginia without regard to property lines until well into the twentieth century. They grazed, foraged, and watered wherever they wandered. The free-range agricultural tradition was widely practiced in the South from colonial times and was strongly supported in the mountains, where farmers often owned large tracts of unimproved land. This practice was particularly beneficial to slaves, small landholders, renters, sharecroppers, and to the poor who did not own enough land to support their animals. This open-range tradition was upheld in 1900 by the Virginia Supreme Court of Appeals, which declared that "the rule of the common law which requires the owner of animals to keep them on his own land or within enclosures is not in force in [Virginia] . . . and the owner of animals, being under no obligation to restrain them, is not liable for damage done in consequence of their straying on the unenclosed lands of another, unless he drives them there."

Rail fences like this one were built to keep foraging animals outside the fence, rather than inside.

If an animal damaged a neighbor's crops, there were few grounds for legal action unless that animal had broken through a fence. People were required to fence their neighbors' animals out, rather than fence their own animals in. A county board of supervisors had the local option to pass an ordinance requiring owners to keep their animals on their own land. However, at the beginning of the twentieth century, only one Virginia county, Accomac, required residents to fence in their animals. The Blue Ridge counties of southwestern Virginia did not begin to require this until long after the blight wiped out the American chestnut. Thus, much of the unfenced rural landscape of this region was a grazing and foraging commons. The ubiquitous rail fences that surrounded household gardens and farm crops bore witness to this. Although individuals owned the land, their unimproved acreage was a communal resource open to everyone's animals.

Chestnut rail fence in north central Virginia. (Photo courtesy of the Connecticut Agricultural Experiment Station.)

Cattle, hogs, and domesticated turkeys foraged through unfenced pasture and forest. In the autumn, hogs and turkeys fattened on the bounty of acorns and chestnuts. Hogs were important because their meat could be salted and stored through the winter by people who lacked refrigeration. Although the animals foraged across property lines, there was great respect for ownership of the animals.

Ownership of hogs and cattle could be identified by unique patterns of notches and holes cut in the animals' ears. The marks were sometimes registered at the local courthouse. An unmarked young hog born in the woods, however, could be claimed by the first person to find it. Farmers who lived at a lower elevation or had few chestnuts nearby sometimes fattened their hogs by hauling or driving them to more desirable locations to forage on chestnuts. Abraham Helms recalled, for example, that his father would take his hogs to Patrick County's Jones Mountain to fatten them.

Der Keschdebaum

Pennsylvania German tradition and the American Chestnut

By Doris Armstrong Goldman

This article appeared in a slightly different form in the fall-winter 1994–95 Journal of The American Chestnut Foundation.

The Pennsylvania Germans (also know as Pennsylvania Dutch, or *Deitsch*), originally lived in rural areas where the American chestnut tree was common and thus played an important role in the culture and daily lives of these people. The Pennsylvania Germans came to America between 1710 and 1820 from places where European chestnuts were grown and are still appreciated in cooking, such as Alsace-Lorraine, Switzerland, and especially the Pfalz, or Palatine, region of western Germany. In a book on British medicinal uses of plants published in 1772, Dr. R. Brookes says that chestnuts are "windy and hard to digest, so they seldom agree with any except laborous working people," but he added that chestnuts were much eaten in continental Europe and were prepared by boiling or roasting. Since the Pennsylvania Germans were already familiar with chestnuts, they probably made use of the American nuts soon after they arrived.

Many of the Pennsylvania Dutch words for tree parts use the very "flat" sort of Pfalzer German spoken in regions where chestnut was important to daily life, rather than formal High German. "Chestnut tree" would be *Keschdebaum* (*Kastanienbaum* in High German). The chestnut bur or fruit husk was *Igla* or *Keschdigla*, the nuts were *Kesche* or *Keschde*.

"Chestnut tree" would be Keschdebaum (Kastanienbaum *in High German). The chestnut bur or fruit husk was* Igla *or* Keschdigla, *the nuts were* Kesche *or* Keschde.

The Pennsylvania Germans learned so many of their folk remedies from the native American Indians that to *brauche mitt*, which meant to use a folk medicine or charm (a *Brauchmittel*) was "to powwow" in English. Like the Indians, they treated whooping cough with a medicine prepared with the liquid left after boiling chestnut leaves in water. The Indians also used a tea of chestnut leaves as a sedative and tonic, and used the bark as a dye and as a treatment for worms. They also cooked with chestnut meal and chestnut oil. The Pennsylvania Dutch used durable, rot-resistant chestnut wood for furniture, musical instruments, coffins, shingles, houses, barns, and for long-lasting fences, barrels, and pump parts. Chestnut was considered to be poor firewood.

Chestnut tanbark, which was used for tanning leather, was prepared first by removing the bark in the spring, when the sap was ascending, with a tan spud, or *Rinnascheeler*. Then the material was ground up fine and soaked for several days to extract the tannin, which would be used to work the leather.

Chestnut timber was cut in August and December, probably during relatively slow periods on the farm, and preferably during the old moon, which they believed was the time when the wood would be free of worms.

Among carpenters and woodworkers, American chestnut was often the favorite wood both for personal preferences and utility's sake; the wood was used for a wide variety of purposes. One barn built in central Pennsylvania in the 1800s still stands and is made completely of chestnut.

Fence making, as described by Alan G. Keyser in *Pennsylvania Folklife* in 1971, also involved chestnut. Field fences, the favorite being the split-rail style, were constructed largely of chestnut wood. Posts, when used, were chestnut or locust, hewn with a broadax to be about six and half to seven feet long, and were sunk deep enough to leave a little more than four feet above ground. So that posts would "grow into the ground" and not be frost-heaved, they were set when the old moon was waning, or were set upside down. Posts were spaced eleven feet apart and were connected by twelve-foot-long chestnut rails.

In the spring, children used to slip the bark off chestnut shoots to make whistles called Keschdpeifa *(chestnut pipes).*

The family kitchen garden, often called a four-square garden because of its layout, was surrounded by a picket fence or *Glabbordfens*, partly for display and partly to keep animals out. Each eleven-foot section was called a *Gfach*. Only two rails were needed to support the pickets, which were made of chestnut, oak, or pine, and spaced about an inch apart. One family made pickets by splitting four-foot-chestnut logs into billets four to five inches wide and six to seven inches thick and then into six or seven pickets. A forty-five-degree saw cut at the top put a point on the picket. The white picket fence celebrated in American culture was certainly a part of Pennsylvania Dutch home life. Typically many of the wooden structures on the farm were whitewashed, which gave a neat appearance and helped preserve the wood.

Elsewhere in the garden, chestnut bordered the raised beds and made boardwalks and cold frames. Grape arbors and poles for hops and beans were made from chestnut or red cedar.

In the spring, children used to slip the bark off chestnut shoots to make whistles called *Keschdpeifa* (chestnut pipes), and in the fall they had to go out to the woods to help gather chestnuts for harvest. Some children disliked the task because the spiny burs pricked their hands and feet. A proverb used when someone pouted or made a sour face (for example, after stepping on a chestnut bur!) was "En Maul macha wie en Fuchs wanner Keschdigla fresst," or "The fox makes a terrible face when he eats a chestnut bur."

Several Pennsylvania German proverbs collected in the early 1900s about chestnuts predict the size of the nut crop judging by the weather in early summer. These may have a factual basis, because if it's too rainy or cold during pollination and fertilization or fruit set, the crop is poor. "Wann uf di Pingschte regert, gebts ken Keschte" means "Rain on Pinkster means no chestnuts." Pinkster (Whitsuntide or Pentecost) usually falls in mid-May. "Wann di Maeriche nass iber der Baerik get, gebts ken Keschte" means "When the Virgin gets wet as she goes over the mountain, there will be no chestnuts"—in other words, when it rains on the visitation of the Virgin (July 2, the day commemorating the visit of Mary to her cousin Elizabeth), the chestnut crop will fail. "Wann regert uf der Tschann Hus, gebts ken Nuss" means "When it rains on Jan Hus's Day (July 6), there will be no nuts." Jan Hus was a Czech religious reformer burned at the stake in the 1400s. "Wanns regert uf der Siberschlefer gebts ken Keschte" means "When it rains on the day of the Seven Sleepers (July 27) it gives no chestnuts." The Seven Sleepers were early Christians who, it was said, were walled up in a cave and instead of dying, fell asleep for several hundred years, until all the Roman Empire became Christian.

Some of these proverbs are nearly identical to proverbs from western Germany, but this one is truly American: "Wanns uf der firt Tschulei regert waern di Keschte waermich," which means "When it rains on the Fourth of July, the chestnuts will be wormy."

Finally, in the fall, "Fil Hikerniss, Haselniss, Walniss un Keschte bedeite en haerter Winter," or "Full hickory nuts, hazelnuts, walnuts, and chestnuts foretell a hard winter." ~

Pennsylvania Dutch country was rich in chestnut lore, much of it brought over from the old country.

Living in Chestnut

In its simplest form, chestnut timber, as dressed or undressed logs, was used early on to build cabins, barns, and sheds, and where it was plentiful it was the favored wood for such purposes. Many of our ancestors literally lived in chestnut boxes, often roofed with chestnut shingles.

Right: *Like many others of its kind in Appalachia, this chestnut cabin is still in use.* Below: *Six or seven chestnut logs were enough for a full story on this cabin. (Great Smoky Mountains National Park Library / Tennessee Valley Authority.)*

When asked by a boyhood friend to design buildings for the resort community of Linville in the North Carolina Blue Ridge northeast of Asheville, architect Henry Bacon developed a symmetrical, rustic equivalent of his favored neoclassical style (Bacon later designed the Lincoln Memorial in Washington, D.C.). From the 1890s to 1913, Bacon designed several buildings for Linville, including its well-known and often photographed All Saints Episcopal Church. He used native chestnut throughout, both inside and out, including walls clad with shingles of chestnut bark. The combination of this most democratic of materials with Bacon's elegant style and balance resulted in a uniquely American woodsy classicism.

The Bacon-inspired Eseeola Lodge in Linville. (Photo by Meghan Jordan.)

"The Studio," designed by Bacon, was the residence of Edgar Love III in Linville. (Photo courtesy of Hugh Morton estate.)

Above: *All Saints Episcopal Church, believed to be the last building Bacon designed in Linville.* Right: *The church interior. (Photos by Meghan Jordan.)*

A Down-Home Wood

By Chris Ditlow

Even in brick and frame houses in towns and cities, chestnut wood was everywhere, though its presence was not always apparent. The following article appeared in slightly different form in the fall 2004 Journal of The American Chestnut Foundation.

If I walked into my home town of Harrisburg, Pennsylvania, in 1890, where would I find American chestnut being used? Well, it wouldn't be in the governor's house as finished trim work. You might see it in the governor's attic, however, used as rough framing, or as shingles on the roof. Or you may find it in the carriage house out back. More likely, you'd find it in the wood pile, waiting to fuel the kitchen woodstove.

If chestnut wood was used for finished trim work, it was most likely in the small-town train station or the Victorian-era row house. I've seen varnished chestnut millwork in some of these old homes, on finished doors and paneling. Next door would be identical trim made of pine with a coat of paint on it. The person with the chestnut preferred an inexpensive wood. Chestnut was just pennies more than clear pine.

Chestnut was plentiful. However, the wormholes commonly found in chestnut degraded its value and made it less desirable than most other hardwoods. I've seen old tally sheets with various woods offered for sale. When chestnut is listed, you'll also see it marked "clear" in brackets, indicating no visible wormholes. Indeed, today, when hardwood is graded, insect damage in a board will not allow for sale by grade rules.

In those days, only chestnut showing minor bug damage was considered appropriate for millwork. It was never used in a home as finished flooring because of its softness. It was used as flooring in the barn, however, or as rough flooring in the attic or in a warehouse, and it was frequently used as sheathing boards on the roof.

Chestnut woodwork in C. K. Sober House, Northumberland County, Pennsylvania. (Pennsylvania Chestnut Blight Commission.)

Old outhouse on a dairy farm near Barnardsville, North Carolina, still has much of its original siding of American chestnut. (Photo courtesy of Doug Gillis.)

Because of its abundance in the pre-blight days, chestnut was taken for granted. I have read many vintage woodworking publications on millwork and cabinet making, and chestnut is rarely mentioned. It would have been a favorite of the less skilled country cabinet maker who specialized in utility cabinets such as jelly cupboards, because it was so easy to hand rip and plane. But if a client wanted a quality cabinet, it would be made of walnut or cherry.

Because of its abundance in the pre-blight days, chestnut was taken for granted.

In the early machine-furniture industry, clear grade chestnut boards were manufactured into inexpensive consumer goods such as iceboxes or bedroom furniture. But chestnut was most useful at that time for lumber core plywood, because it was easy to dry and very stable. The plywood had a solid chestnut core, five-eighths-inch thick, covered with a more desirable face veneer such as quartersawn white oak, a favorite style around 1900. This technique was used in most "oak" furniture from the 1890s until World War I, when the styles went to colonial revival. The chestnut "subparts" were still common until the 1950s, when dead chestnut began to play out of supply.

In my opinion, if the blight never occurred, the abundance of chestnut trees would cause it to still be a secondary wood, used more for pallets than for finished goods, similar to poplar's use today.

But that's all changed. I've bought and sold salvaged chestnut, and the ironic thing is that the first question the buyer asks me is how many bug holes does the wood have. Bug holes! A character never considered in a bygone age. Chestnut has very nice workability features that today's craftsmen like. Also, its high tannic acid content makes it easy to darken by fuming with ammonia, a feature traditionally used in mission oak styles.

Chestnut was a common, easily dried and processed wood that was not appreciated until its demise. We always reflect on the past, and the warmth of chestnut's brown color, bug holes and all, adds to its charm as it ages like a fine wine. Let's all pray that TACF can restore it to its proper place in our eastern forests. ~

Music of the Earth

By Demarron Leif Meadows

Music lives in the earth. Music is born into life, sprouts up from the ground, up through the trees. The music of the earth lives in the maples, poplars, and the mighty chestnuts. The craftsman builds the instrument from the chestnut and captures the music in the instrument, and on a morning when the fog wisps and swirls, the music is released. Released to the mountain air it floats across gardens and green fields and mates with birds and their songs until it lands on the trees and returns to the earth from which it came.

The resourcefulness of the people throughout the Appalachian chain is never more evident than in their musical instruments. Craftspeople take pride in their choice of locally available wood for their instruments. To honor a culturally important tree, many musicians chose to use the once abundant chestnut in their instruments. Often combinations of walnut, chestnut, cherry, cigar boxes, groundhog hides, and tin cans created unique instruments that characterize not only the creativity of Appalachians but also the diversity of the land and culture.

A chestnut dulcimer and chestnut guitar. (Photo by Robin Acciardo.)

Though few instruments survive from the days when the country was young and chestnut trees dominated the landscape, we do have reports of chestnut being used in homespun instruments. I recall my great uncle's homemade banjo, made with chestnut and a groundhog hide. Contemporary instrument makers frequently use chestnut for dulcimers, thus honoring a historically important wood and a regionally unique instrument.

Commercially, chestnut was used for pianos in the early twentieth century. Wood of the American chestnut holds true to its shape, was historically abundant, and most important is not affected by moisture. These qualities made chestnut desirable for the construction of pianos. Also the porous structure facilitated gluing and application of veneers while providing superior strength. In 1915, the *American Forestry* journal stated, "The essential wood of pianos is frequently chestnut, onto which other woods are veneered."

Personally having played a chestnut guitar crafted by a Kentucky instrument maker, I attest to the mellow sound that seems to belong around a campfire in East Kentucky mountains on a summer evening. At these times I feel the connection of people and the land on which they live. Maybe someday, when the chestnut is restored to the landscape, we can release the music into the air, and it will fall upon the chestnuts and once again return to the earth from which it came.

Higher Society

The uses of chestnut wood were not always strictly utilitarian, as these two examples illustrate. The lobby of the former DeWitt Clinton Hotel in Albany, New York, was handsomely paneled throughout in native chestnut, while a chestnut Windsor-style bench in the Winterthur Museum is a model of simple elegance.

Below left: *Clinton Hotel photo from* American Lumberman; below right: *Windsor bench photo courtesy of Winterthur Museum.*

From my youth, I can remember seeing the stark white skeletons of dead chestnut trees, and marveling at how tall and straight they stood.

—Erle E. Ehly, Philadelphia

A ghost chestnut, victim of the blight. (Photo courtesy of the Connecticut Agricultural Experiment Station.)

GHOST TREES

You could just see the trees dying. You could see them changing from time to time. One would die; the leaves would turn brown and fall off in the middle of the summer. Maybe the next would go ahead and finish out the summer. But people couldn't believe it. They thought they'd come back.

—Noel Moore, from *Foxfire 6*

"A Serious Disease"

Dr. William A. Murrill, assistant curator at the New York Botanical Garden, spent much of 1905 investigating the illness that was destroying chestnut trees in the botanical garden and elsewhere. In 1906 he published the first scientific description of the blight fungus and how it operates, excerpted below, from "Serious Chestnut Disease," in the Journal of the New York Botanical Garden, *Vol. 7, No. 78, June 1906.*

A serious disease of our native chestnut, which threatens the extinction of this valuable tree in and about New York City, was brought to my attention last summer by Mr. H. W. Merkel, of the New York Zoological Park, and has been under investigation here since that time.

The immense number of dead and dying chestnut trees in the Zoological Park first caused Mr. Merkel to suspect the presence of a destructive fungus. . . . The same disease has been found to exist among the chestnuts of New Jersey, Maryland and Virginia. . . .

Dr. William Murrill, assistant curator at the New York Botanical Garden, stands atop a victim of the blight. (Courtesy of Mushroom, the Journal of Wild Mushrooming.*)*

In its effect on the host, this fungus may be classed with the most destructive parasites; the parts attacked being so vital and the attack so vigorous that young trees often succumb in one or two years.

In its effect on the host, this fungus may be classed with the most destructive parasites; the parts attacked being so vital and the attack so vigorous that young trees often succumb in one or two years, and older ones soon lose branches of such size that the vigor of the entire tree is materially impaired and its beauty and usefulness practically destroyed. It is not the primary effect of the fungus on the living tissues of the tree, widespread as this effect often is, that causes the greatest damage; but the secondary effect of this injury on the remaining portions of the trunk or branch affected; for it is the habit of the entering mycelium to proceed in a circle about the affected portion until it is completely girdled. This girdling habit is due to the stoppage of the circulation up and down the stem at the infected point and the growth of the mycelium toward the current of water and food supply, which is more and more deflected by the invading fungus until finally cut off altogether. . . .

The present supposition is . . . that infection takes place only through wounds; or, possibly, through the lenticels. Wounds are, unfortunately, only too frequent, especially in the case of a tender, rapidly-growing tree like the chestnut, which has the additional misfortune of attracting lumbermen and nut-gatherers. If it escapes winter injuries to its trunk, the spring storms are sure to break the smaller branches and abrade the surfaces of the larger limbs; if it is not disfigured by the green fly and twig-borer during summer, it is sure to be mutilated by savage hordes of small boys in autumn. Even the ubiquitous squirrel may spread the disease with tooth and claw while cutting off ripe burs and racing up and down the trunks; while every bird and insect that rests upon an infected spot is liable to carry the spores upon its feet or body to other trees. Mice, voles and rabbits often make wounds about the base of a tree and carry the spores in their fur. All during the growing season spores are being developed in countless numbers, and these are liable to fall into even the slightest abrasions of the bark and germinate.

"The Practical Extermination of the Chestnut Tree"

"All Chestnut Trees Here Are Doomed": so reads a headline in the New York Times *in the summer of 1911. It had been five years since the first public recognition of the seriousness of the blight; the increasingly fatalistic outlook for the future of the tree can be charted from a selection of articles from the* Times, *in its reports from ground zero of the blight in North America.*

Chestnut Trees Face Destruction — Trees Worth Millions Dying in This State from a Canker for Which There Is No Remedy. Eats Beneath The Bark — Sprays and Other Attempts to Check Spread of the Parasite Unsuccessful — Trees in Botanical Park Doomed.

The wail of the chestnut tree lover is heard from all parts of New York, Long Island, and adjacent country. Thousands of trees, amounting to millions of dollars in value, are dying, the victims of the most deadly plant parasite known, the chestnut canker, (Diaporthe parasitica Murrill) for which there is no known remedy. Within the last two years from $5,000,000 to $10,000,000 worth of chestnut trees have been lost in New York and the immediate vicinity. . . . In the New York Botanical Garden, where the original investigation and study of the destructive fungi has been made, they have lost 300 trees, and are only waiting for Winter and workmen at liberty to cut down as many more.

It means the practical extermination of the chestnut tree in this part of the country, Dr. William A. Murrill, Assistant Director of the New York Botanical Garden, an expert in fungi, who has made a thorough study of the chestnut canker, told a Times reporter yesterday. He believes a law should be passed preventing the sending of the infected chestnut to other parts of the United States, and he has already warned other countries, Italy in particular, where the chestnut is an important article of commerce and food supply, against importing our chestnut in any form, for fear of infection. . . .

Hundreds of letters are received at the Botanical Garden, contain[ing] almost piteous appeals for help from people whose trees are dying. . . .

"This chestnut canker, which is a fungus growth, works under the bark of the trees," says Dr. Murrill. "The spores from the fungi are formed in the Fall and disseminated in the Spring, not by millions, but by billions. Everywhere there is a crack in the bark of the tree, made by the wind or by the claws of a squirrel, these spores are deposited, and the work of destruction begins. We at first thought that cutting away the affected part and covering with coal tar might be successful, but we found that it was not. A tree sometimes takes the disease in twenty places at once, and they may be in the highest branches of the tree, where a squirrel could hardly reach them. . . .

The wail of the chestnut tree lover is heard from all parts of New York, Long Island, and adjacent country.

["]We first learned of the canker when Mr. Merkel discovered it in the chestnut trees in the Zoological Gardens in 1905, and then upon examination it was found in the trees of the Botanical Garden. The fungus shows in minute dots the orange-red fruit on the outside of the bark, which sounds hollow when tapped. The affected parts gradually die as the fungus encircles the branches and trunk, and it will kill a tree with a trunk two feet in diameter in two years. . . .["]

New York Times, May 21, 1908

The Costly Blight of the Chestnut Canker
Rapid Advance of a Disease Which Will Ultimately Destroy, According to Dr. Murrill, All Our Chestnut Trees

That all the chestnut trees in the United States are doomed to destruction by a mysterious disease called chestnut blight, or canker, is the gloomy prediction of Dr. W. A. Murrill, Assistant Director of the New York Botanical Garden. Ever since the first appearance of the disease, three years ago, he has been making an exhaustive study of its effects. Now he asserts that there is nothing to be done against it; that it must run its course like all epidemics. So rapid are the ravages of the blight that he advises that all chestnut timber in the country be cut and used before the trees still unaffected by the canker succumb to its attacks.

According to Dr. Murrill the damage already done by the disease in New York and contiguous States is somewhere between $5,000,000 and $10,000,000. . . . One instance observed by Dr. Murrill personally will give some idea of the rapidity and seriousness of the disease. When he went to live two years ago, at the little suburb of Bronxwood Park,

A fencerow of stricken chestnut trees in Pennsylvania. (Pennsylvania Chestnut Blight Commission.)

just east of the Botanical Garden, there were at least fifty chestnut trees growing near his home. Now not one is left. . . .

"The disease may be recognized," Dr Murrill continued, "by the dying of the bark in patches. On the smaller twigs the pustules appear through the lenticles in the bark; on the larger branches and trunks it is first noticed in the cracks of the bark. The effect of the fungus is to girdle the tree in a short time, and cut off the supply of nourishment and water from the roots. . . . This fungus is the most rapid and destructive known, being able under good conditions to kill a large chestnut tree in from two to three years."

New York Times, May 31, 1908

Mysterious Blight Kills Chestnut Trees By Thousands
No Remedy for It Has Yet Been Found and the Area
Is Increasing Rapidly — Estates Of Col. Roosevelt,
John D. Rockefeller and Miss Helen Gould Suffer.

There is no known remedy for this chestnut blight. It attacks all chestnut trees alike, whether in a millionaire's park or a farmer's woodlot.

At the moment Col. Theodore Roosevelt is one of the worst sufferers. More than 1,000 trees in his Sagamore Hill estate are showing the mouldy orange spots and withered leaves of the disease. These trees in the vigor of their growth must be destroyed.

It is the same story at John D. Rockefeller's estate in the Pocantico Hills and at Miss Helen Gould's on the Hudson. . . . Nearly all the chestnut trees in Bronx Park are gone. Fully 20,000 trees in Forest Park, Queens, have been attacked; about 17,000 of them are dead or have been cut down, and another year will see the passing of the rest. . . .

"How shall we know this menace to our parks and forests?" asks [*sic*] the sufferers. There is no mistaking the blight when it appears. The owners of chestnut trees note it first as small orange-red spots appearing on the bark of the chestnut trees which sounds hollow when tapped. On the young limbs and sprouts the blight produces a round, sunken patch of discolored bark, often with cracks running up and down. . . . When these signs appear many advise cutting down the tree at once and saving the lumber. For the tree is doomed. . . .

To place the loss at $10 for each tree, as was done with the 10,000 reported in Pennsylvania, is making the estimate very low indeed. Large trees have been valued at not less than $100. . . . The largest trees have been known to add $1,000 to the value of a suburban lot. . . .

Dr. Haven Metcalf of the Laboratory of Forest Pathology in the Department of Agriculture at Washington advocated cutting away the diseased portions and spraying the rest of the diseased tree. An appropriation of $2,000 was obtained in New York and spent in cutting, plastering, quarantining, and spraying with Bordeaux mixture the chestnut trees in Bronx Park. But these remedies were without results.

New York Times, October 2, 1910

There is no known remedy for this chestnut blight. It attacks all chestnut trees alike, whether in a millionaire's park or a farmer's woodlot.

Cutting out infected trees, Bedford County, Pennsylvania. (Pennsylvania Chestnut Blight Commission.)

All Chestnut Trees Here Are Doomed — Blight Extending All Over This Country and Not One May Be Left Standing. Last Two in Bronx Dying — There Were 1,500 In Beautiful Grove There — Death of the Chestnuts Has Improved Hemlock Forest.

There are a few people who write to the Botanical Garden to say that the real cause is the general wickedness of the people of the United States.

The chestnut blight or canker is still a great piece of wickedness in the tree world. Dr. W. A. Murrill, Assistant Director of the New York Botanical Garden, has just returned from a trip to Virginia, where he saw the spread of the dreaded thing. People outside New York, he says, are only now beginning to realize what a serious thing it is.

There are a few people who write to the Botanical Garden to say that the real cause is the general wickedness of the people of the United States. It is a scourge for sinfulness and extravagant living, and private prayer or perhaps a grand religious revival might stay it. . . .

Pennsylvania, whose Forestry Department values the chestnuts of the State at $50,000,000, has been the first to take up the matter on a large scale. After a special message from Gov. Tener the Pennsylvania Legislature voted an appropriation of $275,000 to fight the plague. Various methods are under consideration, and vigorous quarantine methods will be carried out, though quarantine for a tree plague is a difficult matter when the wind, migrating birds, and even the squirrels with cheerful ignorance carry the spores for miles and miles. The squirrels are among the most dangerous propagators of the disease for short distances, for the spores must find a place where the bark is scratched and broken to enter and make a home, and the sharp claws of the squirrel make the necessary abrasions and admit the spores at the same time. . . .

New York Times, July 30, 1911

Pennsylvania Takes the Lead

Although scientists for the U.S. Department of Agriculture established a lab in 1907 to study the chestnut disease, the federal government had little authority to deal with this kind of emergency. The states were essentially on their own. Pennsylvania was the only state that attempted an organized, methodical response to the blight. In 1911 the state legislature passed a bill creating a "Commission for the Investigation and Control of the Chestnut Tree Blight Disease in Pennsylvania." Five citizens were appointed to the commission and given a budget of $275,000 to study and halt the blight's spread. So widely was the blight distributed in eastern Pennsylvania that it was already deemed beyond control there, but a field force of more than thirty men was deployed to the western half of the state. Their goal was to implement a method advocated by Dr. Murrill after he had identified the fungus and its mode of operation: to find and destroy isolated infestations ahead of the main front, and thus to try to stop the blight's movement. The men had the authority to cut down and burn blighted trees, including the bark on the stump. Some 30,000 trees in thirty-six counties were eradicated by 1913, when the commission submitted its final report.

That report stated: "The progress of the disease in the western half of the State has been set back five years. . . . The Commission closes its work with regret, knowing well that the blight will now spread over the state without hindrance. . . . One of the most valuable results of the Commission's work was the establishment of the fact that the wood of a blighted tree is entirely fit for use, and if utilized soon after the death of the tree from blight, can be disposed of in the regular way and at normal values."

Removing infected bark in Pennsylvania. Such steps proved futile. (Pennsylvania Chestnut Blight Commission.)

The commissioners concluded their work with a question still relevant today as imported, invasive, nonnative species continue to severely damage American ecosystems: "It seems necessary to call sharp attention to the real lesson to be learned: the necessity of more scientific research upon problems of this character. . . . We have seen that the blight might have been kept out of the country in the first place by inspection [of imported nursery stock], or once in, that it might have been destroyed, or at least checked before it had gotten widely distributed. But instead it was permitted to enter, and to spread for many years without scientific notice. . . . Are we doing any better now with reference to the future?" ~

The Pennsylvania Chestnut Tree Blight Commission, 1911–13

By William Lord

Pennsylvania made the maximum effort to control the chestnut blight. The blight had all but destroyed the American chestnut in most of New England, New York, New Jersey, Delaware, and eastern Pennsylvania. The commission was determined to stem the advance and save its most valuable forest resource and the virgin stands yet untouched by the blight in the southern Appalachians.

In 1904, when the blight was first detected among the 1,400 chestnut trees in New York's Bronx Zoological Park, it did not cause undue alarm. An occasional yellowed branch was noted among the overall greenery. But alarm bells rang the following year. Dead, leafless branches on trees of all sizes prompted a call for help. W. H. Merkel, the park forester, had never seen anything like it. William A. Murrill, a mycologist at the New York Botanical Society, identified the culprit as a fungus new to science, and he named it *Diaportha parasitica.* He published his findings in 1906 and noted that this "blight" was already present among the chestnuts of New Jersey, Maryland, and Virginia.

The blight was identified in Pennsylvania in 1908, north of Philadelphia on the estate of Harold Pierce, a wealthy and influential businessman. He and neighboring landowners were very concerned about the welfare of the many, magnificent trophy chestnut trees gracing their properties.

The Pennsylvania Forestry Department sent a team to investigate. The blight was spreading westward, not only through the estates, but all along the border adjacent to New York and New Jersey. Governor John K. Tener and the legislature responded by creating the Pennsylvania Chestnut Tree Blight Commission in 1911. The commission consisted of five members, serving without pay, and was vested with the power to enact and enforce regulations.

The commission followed a blight control program authored by Haven Metcalf and J. Franklin Collins of the United States Department of Agriculture. They found reliable evidence that the blight had infected American chestnut on western Long Island "at least as early as 1893." They further observed "that the disease advances but slowly in a solid line, but instead spreads from isolated centers of infection, often many miles in advance of the main line of disease," radiating in all directions from its principal locus in New York City and western Long Island. The isolated centers of infection also radiated in all directions, coalescing into one another and into the advancing main line. They served

Felling and peeling bark from a diseased tree in Pennsylvania. (Pennsylvania Chestnut Blight Commission.)

as springboards for further advance of the infection. Metcalf and Collins reasoned that if the isolated centers could be located and eliminated, the overall speed of the advancing blight would be greatly reduced and enable a more effective attack against the main line. They further proposed removing all chestnut within a ten- to twenty-mile "immune zone" facing the main line of infection.

They tested their method in the field from 1908 to 1911 by canvassing an area within a thirty-five-mile radius of Washington, D.C., and locating fourteen isolated infections. Each area was visited yearly, and the diseased trees were cut and burned.

Their plan was published in USDA Farmers' Bulletin 467. "Up to the present time [June 1911], the disease has not reappeared at any point where eliminated and the country . . . is apparently free from bark disease, although new infections must be looked for as long as the disease remains unchecked."

Murrill had described the blight as a previously unknown fungus. No one knew where it came from or why it was so lethal. Metcalf and Collins proposed that it came from Japan on imports of Japanese chestnut nursery stock.

The commission was not too concerned with where the blight came from. It was here and destroying their most valuable timber resource. In 1911, when field work began, 40 percent of Pennsylvania was hopelessly infected, from the northeast corner of the state southwest to its midpoint at the Maryland border. A team of more than thirty men was deployed to canvass counties west of the main line of infection. Isolated outbreaks were located in four widely separated western counties, and the owners were directed to cut and burn all diseased trees, including the bark on the stump. In each of the four counties the outbreak was traced to infected nursery stock.

In 1911, when field work began, 40 percent of Pennsylvania was hopelessly infected, from the northeast corner of the state southwest to its midpoint at the Maryland border.

The commission was convinced that success required the concerted involvement of all the states throughout eastern America with a vested interest in saving the chestnut. Governor Tener invited every state east of the Mississippi, excepting Wisconsin, Illinois, and Florida, to attend a convention held in Harrisburg on February 20 and 21, 1912. Pennsylvania was now actively showing the way and hoped for regionwide participation.

Lack of consensus on two paramount issues doomed the conference from the start. Scientists in attendance were sharply divided on the origin of the blight and what to do about it. Some held that the blight was probably of foreign origin. This was evident from the swiftness with which it spread among an apparently defenseless host with no prior exposure to its lethal attack. The chestnut composed about 25 percent of the forest within its range and provided a plentiful and nourishing food for the parasite to feast and prosper on. Therefore it was imperative that a concerted effort be made now by all the states. Research to learn more about the blight and devise improved methods of control could be conducted concurrently.

Other scientist delegates believed the blight was caused by a native, normally harmless fungus that had become an opportunist parasite on chestnut trees subjected to a combination of stresses during recent years: drought, severe winters, frequent forest fires, and poor coppice management.

Because of coppicing, the chestnut was now much more abundant in the mid-Atlantic states north into New England than when the first European settlers arrived. As the original forest was cut, chestnut increased over competing trees owing to its superior sprouting ability. Coppice, or coppicing, referred to the growing and harvesting of the sprouts, when they reached sufficient size, for poles, rails, ties, and posts. The rapid growth of the chestnut sprouts following each cutting taxed the food supply stored in the roots. By the early 1900s the chestnut sprouts had been harvested several times, and many trees were weak and unthrifty.

Scientists who believed the blight was caused by a native opportunist saw no need to engage in an expensive control program. They maintained that the chestnut would recover on its own with a return to normal weather and good forest management.

Following a welcoming speech by Governor Tener, J. Franklin Collins addressed the convention and advised the delegates to begin a blight-control program immediately and also conduct concurrent research. He was followed by F. C. Stewart of New York, where the blight had spread through the southeast portion of the state. Stewart had accompanied Metcalf and Collins on an inspection of the isolated outbreaks near Washington, D.C., in December 1911. They had found two new infection sites not included in the original fourteen reported in bulletin 467. The infected trees were, Stewart reported, "discharging millions of spores at the very moment Dr. Metcalf was writing his statement that the country within a radius of 35 miles of Washington was apparently free from the disease."

The proponents of the Pennsylvania plan, led by deputy state forester I. C. Williams, spoke with eloquence and fervor, time and again receiving the applause of the delegates. Do the best we can now. Give the cut-and-burn method a chance. During the final hours of the convention, Williams engaged in a lively debate with Dr. Murrill, the man who first identified the blight fungus. Murrill had tried the cut-and-burn method in New York City and western Long Island and considered it a hopeless task. He advised the states to monitor the disease and to apply funding for research to determine better means of control. The states could best serve their citizens by expediting the sale of chestnut lumber. Williams remained a warrior and promised that Pennsylvania would continue the fight. He had no support from Delaware, New Jersey, and southern New England, where the blight was overwhelming. Some of the New York delegates at least hoped for Pennsylvania's success. Maryland, West Virginia, and Virginia agreed to participate.

Murrill had tried the cut-and-burn method in New York City and western Long Island and considered it a hopeless task.

Keller E. Rockey, a commission forester, gave a progress report at the annual fall meeting of the Northern Nut Growers Association in 1912. Progress and hope. Seldom did the commission need to take legal measures. In most cases the owners were "anxious to get rid of infected trees and our field men are given hearty support by individuals, granges and other organizations." The commission held well-attended meetings where the blight was described and literature distributed. Exhibits were placed "in about 30 county fairs" and at schools and colleges. The Boy Scouts were enthusiastic volunteers.

The coming year would tell the tale. "It is the expectation that by the end of January 1913 all scattered spot infections will be removed from the territory west of the line previously mentioned [where infection is already complete], and that, to the best of our knowledge, these western counties will be free from blight. In 1913 the field force will be concentrated on the advance line and the work will be carried eastward."

This optimism was not to last. In 1913 the commission was heavily engaged in removal of diseased chestnut along the advance line, but the blight spread through and beyond, despite the best efforts of the commission. All field work ceased on July 25, 1913, twenty-four months after it began in August 1911. The commission had identified 37,510 infected trees and removed 30,705. According to a report by G. F. Gravatt of the USDA, a limited effort of blight control continued in Maryland, West Virginia, and Virginia until 1915, when all government work ceased.

Notwithstanding its failure to control the blight, the commission had many noteworthy achievements: its research scientist Paul J. Anderson described the life history of the fungus in detail and placed it in the genus *Endothia,* and its studies confirmed that the fungus's transmission in nature was primarily by wind. The commission also contributed to the passage of the first federal plant quarantine law in 1912.

The blight continued its devastation beyond Pennsylvania and through the southern Appalachians at an accelerated rate. The leading edge of heavy infection reached North Carolina in 1923 and within two more decades invaded virtually every bypassed cove and hollow from Maine to Georgia. ❧

Chestnut Trees Doomed. Blight Spreads Uncurbed over Appalachians, Says Forest Expert

Cincinnati, Oct. 12 (AP).—The chestnut blight threatens to destroy every chestnut tree in the Appalachian Mountain forest region, said E. H. Frothingham, director of the Appalachian Forest Experiment Station, Asheville, N.C., before the Appalachian Logging Congress here today.

"A terrible blight, the chestnut blight, is spreading irresistibly over the Appalachian Mountain forest region," said Mr. Frothingham. "It has already killed millions of chestnut trees and it will kill millions more, until virtually every chestnut tree has been wiped out. The best thing to be done is to chop down the good remaining chestnut trees, worth millions of dollars, use them up and permit nature to grow other kinds of trees in their places."

Mr. Frothingham said that every effort to check the ravages of the blight had been in vain.

New York Times, Oct. 13, 1926

A ghost forest in Shenandoah National Park, Virginia. (Shenandoah National Park Archives; copy by John Amberson.)

Memories of a Fallen Giant

The following oral histories are from Foxfire 6 *(edited by Eliot Wigginton, Anchor Press/ Doubleday, 1980). The location is Rabun County, Georgia, and the date is 1980.*

Marie Mellinger (a naturalist in Rabun County):

In 1938, eighty-five per cent of the chestnuts in the Smoky Mountain National Park had been affected or killed by the blight, so you see, it moved westward very quickly. . . . When you go through the mountains you see what we call sprout forests. The sprouts grow up [from old stumps] and they grow up maybe ten to fifteen feet, and then the blight gets them and they die back again. But there are some big old trees left—there's one on top of Brasstown Bald [in Georgia], and the whole tree is dead except for one branch that sticks out, and that one branch blooms and bears chestnuts. Because of the grain and the silvery color, the [dead] chestnut trees are called ghosts. Wherever the bark was opened up, secondary things would get in—various kinds of fungi, worms, and bark beetles—and all the bark would come off. Chestnut wood lasts longer before it decays than any other wood, and the worm holes that people like so much in chestnut were made after the blight killed the trees.

Because of the grain and the silvery color, the [dead] chestnut trees are called ghosts. Wherever the bark was opened up, secondary things would get in—various kinds of fungi, worms, and bark beetles—and all the bark would come off.

Several species of oak, and some hickory has come in to take the place the chestnut used to fill. Even though these trees also produce nuts, people say there are fewer squirrels and turkeys than there used to be. But of course, there are a lot of other factors in there, more logging, more developments, more roads, more everything.

Jake Waldroop:

The blight hit here around 1938 and on up to '42 or '43. . . . It came from out of the East and was traveling West. Where we lived up yonder, [there] was bi-i-i-g chestnut country right across from us, we would [watch it], and it went right on and traveled West. You could just almost see [the trees] a-dying, they died so fast. After that blight hit, the bark went to falling off of 'em. Two or three years after that the trunks began to [weaken] and a windstorm'd come up and it'd be awful to hear them trees a-fallin' in the chestnut belt.

[The blight would] just hit them trees. A band'd go right around the tree and it'd girdle that tree, just go around it, and the tree would die. When we were clearin' up new ground in these coves, why you could take your ax and go to a chestnut tree and just hack it, didn't have to cut it down, just hack around it, and it would die. Well, that's what the blight did. Just went around that tree and it'd die. It grows on, still tries to grow, and some of the sprouts will get as big as my leg, then that girdle [will] come around it and it'll die. I've known of a few in the last few years that'd get up big enough to bear chestnuts and then they'd die.

People couldn't understand it at first. Finally the Forest Service found out it came from Asia, shipped over in lumber or something, got into the United States, and got started. The worst lick to ever hit the South, and the United States, in the timber line, was when they lost the chestnut timber.

You just can't imagine how much it changed the looks of the mountains when the chestnut timber all died. When the chestnut was there, why, it was usually a solid growth of it. And when it died, it left great patches that just looked bare. People didn't pay too much attention [when the chestnut first started dying], but later they began to realize what was happening, and they tried to save every piece of it. People go back in these mountains yet and hunt for these old sogs I told you about. Now where that blight hit 'em, first the bark would fall off, and then the wood would go to crackin'. Sun cracks. And them cracks would be about every six inches plumb around that tree, and they'd go plumb to the heart, and all you could do with that then was make pulpwood out of it. It wasn't no good for saw logs. Couldn't get enough of it without a crack. But one never did get too dry or too dead but what they could get the acid out of it. . . .

You just can't imagine how much it changed the looks of the mountains when the chestnut timber all died.

Very seldom do you ever see [a ghost chestnut tree]. They're all down now. You might once in a while find one, but not often. Lots of stumps, and sprouts where young growth tries to come back. Some of 'em will get up maybe eight to ten inches through, then that girdle, that strip come around and it dies. That blight was the awfulest lick that the South ever got. It hurt everybody because so many people could get to work because of the trees. They could get telephone poles, or make crossties, pulpwood for tannic acid or paper. Economically, it was the worst blow this area ever had. It gave all the mountain people employment; they could work at that chestnut. A lot of people log now, but it's nothin' like it was back then when the chestnut was still here.

Noel Moore:

When the blight hit, you could just see the trees dying. You could see them changing from time to time. One would die; the leaves would turn brown and fall off in the middle of the summer. Maybe the next would go ahead and finish out the summer. But people couldn't believe it. They thought they'd come back. And it moved from year to year. After people saw what was really happening, it really dawned on them what a tragedy it was. The government did some research on it when it first started getting real bad. But the old-timers in the mountains here blamed it on the worm. You'd go back and cut down a dead chestnut and it would be full of worm holes. And they thought that was what was killing the chestnut. But the worm came after the chestnut died.

The blight is a fungus that gets in the sap, under the bark. It just goes around and cuts [the sap] off, and that kills the tree. The bark is thick and you can take that and peel

Dead chestnut, bulldozed for removal. (Shenandoah National Park Archives; copy by John Amberson.)

it off. And there's a layer almost an eighth of an inch thick that's real gummy, [full of] sweet sap. You take a knife and scrape it up and it's real good just to eat—[it has] a sweet, creamy taste. And that's what the fungus strikes. And the fungus can't live underground; that's the reason we still have a few young [sprouts] come up yet. [A sprout will] make a little sapling before the fungus happens to hit it, because the roots underground are still green. And they'll come out and grow. Usually [the trees] died pretty well in clusters. You could see [the blight] moving across the mountains from one side to the other, or from the bottom to the top.

There was a mountain just across the valley from where we were living at that time. It was a ridge like. It wasn't very tall and it was covered up completely with chestnut trees. All of 'em were young trees. They was some of 'em as much as twenty-four inches in diameter. And that's where we'd usually go to get our crop of chestnuts. But they all died in one summer. Every one of 'em. They just quit having nuts. There weren't any more. And there [used to be] thousands of bushels of 'em shipped out of these mountains to cities. They was sold in the fruit stands and sidewalk stores in all the big cities because everybody liked them, you know. They were cheap.

That was one of the greatest losses of natural resources that this country has ever suffered. It affected everybody that had anything to do with timber in any way because the best crop of mountain wood was completely destroyed. 'Course, it lasted several years after they all died, because people kept going in the woods and getting [dead] timber. But it wasn't like it would have been if they'd kept growing and people could have kept cutting them green. What a money crop that would be on the mountains if the blight hadn't come. ∾

The remains of a chestnut stand, Shenandoah National Park, Virginia. (Shenandoah National Park Archives; copy by John Amberson.)

The following is from memories of the American chestnut collected by The American Chestnut Foundation.

In 1925 my parents bought a 147-acre farm adjacent to a smaller farm owned by relatives in the northeast corner of Maryland. I was about eight years old at the time. A steam-powered sawmill had just harvested about twenty of the forty acres of wooded land on the farm. The remaining twenty acres of woodland had been harvested earlier and now grew young mixed hardwoods averaging twenty-five feet in height. This new vigorous growth was evidently resulting from the opening to sunlight that had occurred when the big chestnuts had died several years earlier. The chestnuts' skeletons were lying helter-skelter and at all sorts of angles throughout the woods. They had fallen against one another or against some unwanted oak or beech or other undesirable tree when the sawmill had harvested the wood eight or ten years earlier. The bark from the chestnuts was mostly gone by 1925. The exposed wood was very light in color, about the color of bleached cattle bones.

During the next several years, my friends would join me on adventures into this "haunted" environment. We'd see how high we could climb a leaner or how snug we would feel in the great holes left where a root system had been partly pulled out when the eighty-foot tree had toppled during a windy storm. In retrospect, it appeared they tumbled one or a few at a time, not as a big group might in a violent thunderstorm where they'd probably all fall in one direction. A favorite game was trying to run through the forest without ever touching the ground, like a raccoon, opossum, or squirrel might travel, transferring from tree to tree, the path dictated by the erratic patterns made by the fallen chestnuts. The remains of the mighty chestnuts that had lodged in living, supporting trees could be seen for many years. ~

Clarence Wherry Brown, 2002. Brown, who was born in 1917, still lives on his family farm in Cecil County, Maryland.

Walking among the Ghosts

By Gregory R. Weaver

This article appeared in slightly different form in the spring 2003 Journal of The American Chestnut Foundation.

Today, many species of trees reach record size in the southern Appalachian Mountains. Growing conditions are nearly ideal, with abundant rainfall, a moderate climate, and fertile soil. Until its demise in the last century, the American chestnut was an important part of the southern Appalachian ecosystem.

Because of the rot resistance of chestnut wood and the prior sheer abundance of the tree, there are many remaining stumps, standing trunks, and logs that help us understand how magnificent the chestnut forest was and how devastating is the loss of this tree. Knowledge of where chestnut formerly thrived is important to plan for restoration of the tree and to direct efforts where they are most likely to be successful.

William Ashe's 1911 "Chestnut in Tennessee" says that American chestnut was most plentiful in the Unaka and Smoky Mountains of eastern Tennessee but also common on the Cumberland Plateau and the Highland Rim. Preferred sites were elevated benches of north and west slopes and crests of northern spurs from 1,800 to 3,500 feet in elevation. American chestnut grew there in pure stands of 100 acres. Chestnut was less important in the central basin around Nashville and in the western part of the state.

Standing old chestnut trunk, bleached white by the sun, 2001. (Photo courtesy of Hugh Irwin.)

The American chestnut tree grew to immense size. An article in the *Scottsville (Ky.), Argus* in 1876 told of a nine-foot-diameter, 230-year-old chestnut tree that was split into 700 rails.

Tree cover has increased in Tennessee over the latter part of the twentieth century. Many of these second-growth forests are visually attractive and have a great diversity of flora and fauna. However, to find the best remnants of the chestnut forest, it is necessary to go to the remaining old-growth forests. The largest old-growth forest in Tennessee is in the Great Smoky Mountains National Park. The park's 540,000 acres straddle the Tennessee–North Carolina border. Estimates of the amount of old-growth forest range between 20 and 60 percent of the park's acreage, with most recent estimates closer to the lower figure.

The Great Smoky Mountains Natural History Association has published a map showing the areas of old-growth forest in the park. Look for the chestnut logs and stumps in these forests at mid elevations. Large chestnut logs and stumps are plentiful along the Ramsay Cascades, Porters Creek, Gabes Mountain, and Gregory Bald trails. Look for straight trunks with a reddish color. If protected from the weather (upright trunks, for example), the surface may be smooth. Logs that have been exposed to decay develop long longitudinal furrows. In the Smokies, these logs are usually covered with moss, but the reddish color can still be seen. In areas of less rainfall, such as middle Tennessee, gray lichens grow abundantly on the logs, sometimes hiding the reddish color. Chestnut heartwood often rots first, leaving many of the logs hollow.

Differentiate chestnut from red oak and hemlock. Red oak has a typical oak grain pattern. If bark can be seen on the log, that is an obvious clue; the bark is long gone from chestnut. The sapwood of hemlock is lighter, and small branches are more common, even on larger trees. Neither red oak nor hemlock logs develop the long, deep longitudinal furrows typical of chestnut.

The Park Service and Civilian Conservation Corps cut down many of the dead chestnut trees near the trails for safety reasons years ago. However, many large trunks are still standing several feet away from the trails. These are more easily found in the winter, when the understory plants have lost their leaves.

Stump sprouts are living American chestnut trees that sprout from old root systems. They rarely attain substantial size before the trunk is killed by chestnut blight. Stump sprouts are common in some areas of the park. Look for them along the first 1.5 miles of the Ramsay Cascades Trail, at mid-elevation on the Gregory Bald Trail, and along the crest of Sugarlands Mountain. Interestingly, many of the areas where old chestnut logs are the largest and most plentiful (implying good chestnut habitat) do not have many stump sprouts. Perhaps the growing conditions for other species of trees are good there too and the stump sprouts have lost out to competition.

The Grotto Falls Trail passes through an old-growth forest dominated by hemlock. There are a few impressive chestnut stumps along the way, but overall, chestnut logs are not as common as along the Ramsay Cascades Trail.

If bark can be seen on the log, that is an obvious clue; the bark is long gone from chestnut.

Dead American chestnut trunk on the Gregory Ridge Trail, Great Smoky Mountains National Park, Tennessee, 1997. (Photo by Gregory Weaver.)

Other old-growth forests in Tennessee can be found in the Cherokee National Forest, including Holtzen Mountain (Pig Oak Branch); Joyce Kilmer Memorial Forest (Slickrock and Citico wilderness areas, which extend into North Carolina); Falls Branch Scenic Area (Monroe County); Big Frog Mountain (Polk County); Roan High Bluff (on Roan Mountain); Fall Creek Falls State Park; and Piney Falls State Natural Area. There are also old-growth forests in Frozen Head State Natural Area and at University of the South (Dick Cave), the Hatchie River National Wildlife Refuge, and at Overton Park in Memphis.

Most of the old-growth forests in Tennessee are accessible to the public. An unfortunate exception is Savage Gulf State Natural Area, whose reportedly magnificent mixed mesophytic forest is closed to visitation. ❧

[I] have been busy for several days collecting specimens of this bad chestnut bark disease and taking photos of same.

—Frank Meyer, letter from China, June 1913

Frank Meyer, intrepid and tireless plant explorer for the U.S. Department of Agriculture, in Wutai Shan, Shanxi Province, China, February 26, 1908. Meyer tracked down the source of chestnut blight in China and Japan. (Photo from U.S. National Agricultural Library, Beltsville, Maryland.)

THE SCIENTISTS

This northern Chinese chestnut is not a lumber tree but attempts might be made to cross it with the American species trying to give the last one more hardiness and resistance against disease.

—Frank Meyer

The Man Who Tracked Down the Blight

By William Lord

Frank N. Meyer, the man who discovered the source of the chestnut blight in East Asia, was born Frans Nicolas Meijer in Amsterdam, Holland, in 1875. From his youngest days, he was fascinated with plants, and this aptitude was recognized by his less-than-affluent parents. At age fourteen he was sent to work in the Amsterdam Botanical Gardens, where he caught the eye of the man in charge, world-famous horticulturist Hugo de Vries. Meyer was not one who responded to arbitrary orders, but he would work from dawn to dusk if properly motivated. De Vries saw that Meyer needed to be handled with care but was well worth the effort. With help from his mentor, Meyer completed several university courses in botany. He became head gardener in charge of the experimental garden.

But Meyer had dreams of world travel, perhaps inspired by the exotic plants in the botanical gardens. He observed and studied these strangers from foreign lands and wanted to see them in their native terrain. At night, when he was walking home from work, his musings might lead his footsteps into a dusky distance, where he would simply sleep in a haystack.

America was Meyer's horizon of choice. He arrived in 1901 and found work in Washington, D.C., with the U.S. Department of Agriculture. But staying put and making his fortune held no appeal. His call was to travel and explore, to find plants that would benefit mankind and earn his due of praise and recognition. The following year he spanned America to California and continued on to Mexico. From the Pacific port of San Blas he journeyed cross-country to the Gulf of Mexico, traveling several hundred miles of the distance on foot. In the remoter areas he slept outdoors or in the native huts and dined as the natives dined. During his time in Mexico he mailed eight varieties of seeds, each carefully described, to the USDA Plant Introduction Garden in Chico, California.

His work impressed David Fairchild, head of the newly formed USDA Foreign Plant Introduction section. Mexico, in the remote regions visited by plant explorers, was plagued with banditry. Meyer was not only a dedicated plant explorer but also resolutely brave. Whatever the odds, he would complete his mission. Would he be interested in becoming a plant explorer for the USDA, Fairchild inquired, beginning with a trip to China? We can only imagine Meyer's joyful acceptance. The two men became lifelong friends.

Meyer arrived in Peking (Beijing) in the fall of 1905 to commence three years of plant collecting. A stranger in a strange land, he was very much on his own. He was funded by the U.S. government and had an official document authorizing him as an agricultural explorer to enter "Manchuria and other parts of China," but with vaguely written orders—"see what you can find and send." By one means or another he organized his own small caravans of two-wheeled carts drawn by donkeys or mules, with drivers, coolies, and interpreters. They braved sandstorms, snowstorms, and typhoons. They withstood attacks by robber gangs. He and his interpreters somehow made themselves understood in rural regions where dialects often changed from town to town. The value of currency also varied from town to town; some wanted silver coins, some wanted brass or copper, some accepted paper money issued in China, Hong Kong, or Mexico. Nonetheless, Meyer covered a huge area radiating from Peking to Hankow (now Wuhan) and Shanghai to the south and through northeastern China to Korea and Siberia. He would travel between major cities by train and then assemble a caravan for local exploration. He collected and shipped plant material to the Washington office, to the USDA Plant Introduction Garden in Chico, and to the Arnold Arboretum of Harvard University.

Meyer was not only a dedicated plant explorer but also resolutely brave. Whatever the odds, he would complete his mission.

Throughout much of mountainous northern China, deforestation had produced a wasteland. Meyer found native trees surviving on the undefiled grounds of old temples. From one such site north of Peking he collected chestnut seeds in the fall of 1907 and included them in a shipment of forty-five parcels to Washington.

He returned to America in 1908, a new celebrity whose words were received with respect and admiration at tuxedo events and at agricultural experiment stations across the country. China, more so than Mexico, was strange and unknown to most Americans, and Meyer had the allure of Marco Polo. Meyer enjoyed his celebrity but soon tired of the formal affairs, preferring the company of people at plant introduction gardens, agricultural colleges, and experiment stations, where he could learn their specific needs. But nothing pleased him more than to see some of his "discoveries" growing in health and promise.

In 1909 he was off again, this time by way of Europe, visiting botanical gardens in England and on the Continent. He entered Asia north of the Black Sea, plant exploring and collecting thousands of miles through remote terrain to the Siberian-Mongolian border. At this point, 1911, local warfare prevented travel into China, and Meyer returned to America by way of England. He landed in April 1912 on the *Mauretania*, one day after the maiden voyage of the *Titanic*.

In February 1912, two months before Meyer's return, the Pennsylvania Blight Commission had sponsored a meeting in Harrisburg attended by concerned scientists to discuss means of saving the American chestnut from a strange and devastating predator. The commission was seeking to engage all states with an interest in the chestnut in a concerted effort to control the blight. In this regard the meeting did not succeed, but it brought into focus two opposing views on the origin of the blight. Some believed the pathogen was a native, normally nonlethal fungus taking advantage of trees stressed by several years of drought and other environmental factors. Others maintained that the blight was of foreign origin.

Both Fairchild and Meyer were undoubtedly aware of the meeting, but they were busy preparing for Meyer's next trip to the Orient. Meyer left for Peking, again by way of Europe, arriving in England in November 1912. At the time of his departure, neither the blight nor the chestnut was part of his agenda.

Haven Metcalf, a plant pathologist at the USDA, believed that the blight had come to America by way of nursery stock imported from Japan. At this time the Chinese chestnut was virtually unknown in America, but the Japanese chestnut was a common orchard and park tree. Metcalf had observed that the Japanese trees were resistant to the blight. In the fall of 1912, about the time of Meyer's departure, supportive evidence came from a far-off chestnut orchard in British Columbia, where the blight was found in chestnut nursery stock imported from the Orient. Metcalf contacted Fairchild, who informed Meyer in China by letter, dated February 26, 1913, to search for evidence of blight infection on the Chinese chestnut. He also mailed specimens of diseased bark.

In May Meyer wrote that he had received the fungus specimens and planned a special trip to a mountainous area about a hundred miles eastward from Peking and just south of the Great Wall. He found what his friends hoped he would find. The letter of discovery was written in early June, 1913.

> Here I am sitting in a Chinese inn in an old dilapidated town to the northeast of Peking, between tsun hua tcho [Zunhua?] and Yehol [Jehol; now Chengde]

and have been busy for several days collecting specimens of this bad chestnut bark disease and taking photos of same. It seems that the Chinese fungus is apparently the same as the one that kills off the chestnut trees in north eastern America. I hope to send a cablegram through the American Legation in Peking about this discovery, to the Secretary of Agriculture. I am also enclosing a small piece of bark with this fungus on it. More material I hope to send off from Tienstin [Tianjin] and Peking. Here are my main observations. This blight does not, by far, do as much damage to Chinese chestnut trees as to the American ones. Not a single tree could be found which had been killed entirely by this disease, although there might have been such trees, which had been removed by the ever active and economic Chinese farmers.

Dead limbs, however, were often seen and many a saw wound showed where limbs had been removed. Young trees and trees on level, poor soil were much more attacked than old trees or trees growing on richer, sloping soil at the base of rocks and hills. The disease is apparently losing its virulence and the wounds on the bigger majority of the trees were in process of healing over. The Chinese ascribe this disease to the workings of caterpillars, grubs and ants, which are very freely found beneath the bark on these diseased spots and the main trunk and branches.

"It seems that the Chinese fungus is apparently the same as the one that kills off the chestnut trees in north eastern America."

To combat the disease they scrape the bark clean every winter or early spring. The strips of bark are all collected, tied up in bundles and sold as fuel.

This Chinese chestnut does not grow to such size as the American one. Trees over 40 feet are rare. They are of low branching habits with open heads, more or less the way of European chestnut, Castanea vesca [*C. sativa*]. The lumber is hard, but even a good sized tree produces relatively little good lumber. Old wounds are to be observed here and there on ancient trees showing that 40 or 50 years ago similar outbreaks of fungus disease have taken place.

The maximum age of these Chinese chestnuts seen in its native habitat seems to be between 250 and 300 years, but when that old they are already in decay. The tree is not a fast grower and does not begin to bear until 12–15 years old. The soil best suited to these is a warm, well decomposed granite, with perfect drainage, in which locality they love the lower slopes of hills and mountains where they will be sheltered.

The valleys and ravines in the lower altitudes of the Rocky Mountain regions would probably supply congenial localities for these chestnuts.

This northern Chinese chestnut is not a lumber tree but attempts might be made to cross it with the American species trying to give the last one more hardiness and resistance against disease.

The nuts of this Chinese chestnut are not as large as those from the European or Japanese forms, but they are very sweet and are in great demand in China.

> What is the remedy used in America against the blight? What I see of it I would suggest spraying of the trunks and branches in spring time before the leaves come out, with an emulsion of an oily substance, like diluted tar, diluted crude petroleum, diluted whale oil with lime, etc., anything that would cover up these fungi with something sticky and biting, that would prevent them from spreading their spores and would greatly lessen the chance of healthy trees catching this fungus by making their bark not a good receiving place for spores floating in the air. Of course this only applies to districts where the blight is just starting or where it has not made its appearance as yet.
>
> In places where it is very serious I suppose the only thing is to cut down all trees which are attacked and to make a chestnut free belt between the affected region and the non affected one. I am, of course, not an expert at this problem and I simply offer these suggestions as they come into my head while thinking about possible means for checking this terrible blight.
>
> The great chestnut district of North China lies in the mountain valleys between the town of San tuning [likely Santunying] and the great Chinese wall, 4 to 5 days journey by carts from Peking to the northeast and one and one half to two days journey by carts from the railroad station, Tang shan [Tangsha] on the railroad from Tienstin to Shan hai kwan [Shanhaiguan]. Most of the trees seem to be of original growth, but also plantations have been made at the foot of the mountains and hills.
>
> And now I have a few questions to do, which I hope you or somebody else may seem fit to answer. Who is the man who first thought this chestnut bark fungus might occur in China and what were his reasons for thinking so?
>
> Where was this fungus first found? On Long Island, isn't it? Could it have been brought over in shipments of Japanese plants? If so, this same disease might occur in Japan. Have you written to someone living near a chestnut district in Japan?
>
> You say in your letter of Feb 26 that if I discover the same species in China, it will affect the whole chestnut blight situation in American. Please state in what way.

David Fairchild might have replied with something like, "How much does this mean to us? Let me count the ways." The men at USDA believed they had the method and means to control the blight.

Through 1914 and most of 1915, Meyer traveled southwest and southeast through China, now very alert for the Chinese chestnut and the blight. He collected blight specimens from native trees, in March 1914 in Shangtung (Shandong) Province by the Yellow Sea, and in September 1914 from Shensi (Shaanxi) Province to the west. The following year, in June, he collected blight specimens in Chekiang (Zhejiang) Province. These were received by eager scientists at headquarters. Writing from Chekiang, Meyer remarked, "Well, I have a few interesting discoveries to report. First, there are many specimens of Castanea mollissima scattered at the bases and on the lower slopes of the hills around here, and these chestnuts are seriously attacked by the bark fungus and in my estimation are going to succumb to it these coming years."

At Fairchild's request, Meyer went to Japan and was again successful in collecting the blight fungus, from a Japanese chestnut in mountains about a hundred miles north of Tokyo, in September 1915. Meanwhile, C. L. Shear and other USDA scientists made careful comparison tests between the "American" and "Chinese" fungus. They found that the spores from each source grew identical colonies of mycelium when cultured in the same media. When mycelium from either source was inoculated into American chestnut trees, the same type canker developed. Bark peeled away from a canker revealed the telltale mycelial "fans" at the leading edge of the expanding lesion.

Meyer's time in Japan was brief but productive. He found the blight to be quite prevalent, but, surprisingly, it was not recognized as such. Two of his Japanese associates wished to see the evidence, and Meyer located some infected trees near Tokyo.

Meyer returned in October 1915, arriving in Seattle to an enthusiastic welcome from Fairchild. To Meyer's surprise and delight, Fairchild had journeyed across the continent from Washington and was there to greet him at the pier. Meyer stood at the rail shouting his exultant conviction that the blight had come to America by way of Japan. Then he was deluged with immigration officers and newsmen. The good friends finally got together and "spent half the night talking."

"Work is to me what medicine is for sick people."

Meyer and Fairchild visited the Chico Plant Introduction Garden in California, where many of his introductions were now flourishing, some doing better than in their native land. There were dwarf, sweet-tasting lemons, drought-resistant almonds, and some of the Chinese chestnut hybrids developed by USDA's Dr. Walter Van Fleet. Then Meyer left on a triumphant tour of nurseries and experiment stations across America. But his élan was jolted by the depressing news that a large shipment, "representing almost eighteen months hard work," had been destroyed by a hurricane during a layover in Galveston.

By mid 1916 Meyer was Orient-bound again, to explore previously unvisited central China. The chestnut was now a prominent part of a very demanding agenda. America was headed for war, giving Meyer's exploration and collecting an added urgency; he sought seed and scions of a blight-resistant native pear, for a drought-resistant peach, and for every species of native chestnut, and on and on and on. A younger Meyer had remarked, "Work is to me what medicine is for sick people." But Hupeh (Hubei) Province in central China would test his stamina and resolve to the extreme: "If I had seven bodies I could use all in my work," he remarked. Most of his travel was on foot, accompanied by his interpreter and any animals available to cart his collections. Malaria and dysentery were endemic, and the country was immersed in constant warfare. On February 1, 1918, he wrote to Fairchild from Yichang, in Hubei Province:

> The more I travel around in Hupeh, the more I am impressed with its immenseness, nothing but mountains and valleys and hills and dales. Put the state of Montana across Georgia and neighboring states and you have some idea of topography and climate of Hupeh. No one man can ever cover this whole province on foot and really one cannot travel otherwise; there are no real roads, nothing but trails and accommodation and food-supplies of the poorest imaginable. As I am writing we hear the rickety noise of rifle fire, for the Northern and Southern troops are at battle only a mile or so north of the city. That we do not live "at ease," you can easily imagine.

He found the Chinese chestnut, *C. mollissima*, and also the dwarf chestnut, *C. seguinii*, growing on the mountain slopes and hills of central and western Hubei. Over time he was able to ship scions and several hundred pounds of Chinese nuts and a lesser amount of dwarf. All plant material was carefully prepared and transported in sturdy crates, but the time and layovers required to make the long journey down the Yangtze River to Shanghai and then across the Pacific handicapped his effort. On average, about half the nuts germinated, and one valuable shipment was almost totally ruined, probably owing to overheating during a layover. Fortunately, a few of the nuts had sprouted and, "these we shall save."

"As I am writing we hear the rickety noise of rifle fire, for the Northern and Southern troops are at battle only a mile or so north of the city. That we do not live 'at ease,' you can easily imagine."

Meyer found an abundant presence of the blight. He wrote to Fairchild in February 1918: "I noticed plenty of Endothia parasitica in cultivated as well as in wild Castanea molissima right from Ichang [Yichang] to beyond Hsing shan hsian [Xingshan]. On some places it was very serious, especially one day's journey N.W. of Hsing shan hsien in wild trees. Please communicate this to Dr. Shear. I got some wild chestnut tho' for which please see No. 2458a and 2459a."

Walter Van Fleet, a retired physician, had become the head plant breeder for the USDA. At times he played violin sonatas for the benefit of his hybrid pears, raspberries, roses, and various chestnuts. It is probable that Meyer sent him some Chinese nuts at the time he discovered the blight in 1913. Fairchild, in October 1917, described a scene that would have gladdened Meyer on his return.

"You would be immensely interested to see his dwarf hybrids between the chinquapin and the Japanese chestnut, but you would be particularly interested in his rows of Castanea molissima, some of which, though only six or eight feet high, are already in fruit."

Van Fleet's chestnut orchard, in Bell, Maryland, was near a large grove of blighted chestnut, but the Chinese trees were "resisting the blight very well," according to Fairchild.

Meyer was loved and honored by his fellow workers. Van Fleet's chestnut orchard was one of many rewards he would have enjoyed. But he never made it home. En route on the night of June 1, 1918, he disappeared from aboard a riverboat headed for Shanghai. His body was found ashore a few days later, and he was buried in Shanghai. The cause of death was never determined, but his health had seriously deteriorated. He may have fallen or jumped into the dark waters of the Yangtze. ~

Dr. Walter Van Fleet, Renaissance Man

Dr. Walter Van Fleet (1857–1921) was a practicing physician who abandoned his profession at age thirty-five to become a horticulturist who would become world famous. Garden lovers know him as the medal-winning originator of many popular rose varieties. Apparently he had no formal training as a plant breeder, but he combined the discipline of his medical training with omnivorous reading and application. He also became known in the fields of ornithology, taxidermy, photography, and as an associate editor for the *Rural New Yorker,* an influential farm paper. To this add his talent with the violin, and we have a renaissance man.

During the last decade of the nineteenth century, Van Fleet became interested in the chestnut genus, primarily for nut production. "The advent . . . of certain large-fruited and early bearing chestnut varieties of the European and Asiatic types, some appearing to be natural hybrids between the exotic species and our native chestnut . . . suggested . . . the possibility of breeding all the accessible species . . . in a systematic manner," he later wrote in the *Journal of Heredity,* in 1914. At this time three tree species were available, the Japanese, European, and American chestnuts, and the shrub-sized native chinquapin.

Van Fleet waxed enthusiastic over the promise of a cross between the Paragon, "the best variety of the European type," pollinated with American, and with crosses between the chinquapin and the Japanese.

The blight reached his Paragon-American hybrids in 1910 and destroyed them within a few years. He noted the marked blight resistance of the Japanese varieties, providing an early clue to the blight's Asiatic origin.

Around 1911 Van Fleet accepted the offer of the U.S. Department of Agriculture to be in charge of its program to develop a blight-resistant chestnut, including a timber tree. He and his wife occupied a rose-covered cottage on the grounds at Bell, Maryland. By this time seed from the newly discovered Chinese chestnut was being imported, and Van Fleet incorporated its blight-resistant genes into his program. Both the Japanese and Chinese chestnuts were orchard trees, lacking the required height of the timber-producing American and European varieties. Van Fleet considered the American and European "entirely useless in breeding for disease resistance."

Van Fleet died in 1921 convinced that the blight resistance of the Japanese and Chinese species ensured a future for the chestnut as an orchard tree but less so as a timber tree. He had just begun working with a new species, the tall timber-type Chinese chinquapin, and had written, "It is fervently to be hoped that the species will resist the disease." This hope was not realized.

William Lord

A Pathogen without Rival

By Frederick V. Hebard, Mark L. Double, and William L. MacDonald

The distinguished British ecologist Charles Elton probably underestimated the scope of the dispersal of the earth's biota and the calamities that would ensue when he stated in 1958, "A hundred years of faster and bigger transport has kept up and intensified the bombardment of every country by foreign species, brought accidentally or on purpose, by vessel and by air and overland from places that used to be isolated."

Immigrations have resulted in the worldwide distribution of organisms since nomadic groups of humans wandered across the earth. But in the last 400 years and particularly since the eighteenth century, an ever-increasing array of species has been transported to new geographic locations. This has been most evident with immigrations to North America from Europe and Asia. In part, the increased trade that accompanied the Industrial Revolution was responsible for this migration. Likewise, people in search of religious freedom, relief from famine, or the promise of a better life traveled to new lands. With people came their plants and animals, and with the plants and animals came the pests and pathogens they harbored. The very existence of the microscopic world surrounding us was virtually unknown.

Knowledge of microorganisms began to emerge only during the latter half of the nineteenth century. The Irish potato famine beginning in 1845 provided the impetus for some of the first insights into the role microorganisms play in plant disease. Hundreds of thousands of people in Ireland died, and one and a half million immigrated to the United States, primarily because of the potato famine.

In the last 400 years and particularly since the eighteenth century, an ever-increasing array of species has been transported to new geographic locations.

One of the first individuals to investigate fungi as a cause of plant disease was Heinrich Anton de Bary, known as the father of modern plant pathology. In the 1850s and '60s de Bary and others proved experimentally that a fungus-like organism was responsible for the blight killing the potatoes. De Bary also proved that fungi and similar organisms caused other notable plant diseases, such as rusts and smuts of wheat and mildews of grapes. His work finally helped dispel the common belief that plant diseases were incited by mysterious vapors and that the fungi associated with diseased plants arose by spontaneous generation.

The first major work examining the pathology of tree diseases came during the latter half of the nineteenth century when Robert Hartig, a German forester, determined that fungi on tree stems represented the fruiting bodies (conks) of fungal filaments buried in the decaying wood. Thus, tree diseases were shown to be similar to other plant diseases.

In spite of all the significant microbiological findings, there is little evidence that anyone anticipated what would ensue when microorganisms were moved intercontinen-

Dead chestnut tree with sprouts arising from the root collar.

tally. At the time, plants and animals moved without regulation. For North American trees, the results were and continue to be devastating. The microorganisms responsible for white pine blister rust, Dutch elm disease, and larch canker were among the first to become established. But most notable was the importation of *Cryphonectria parasitica* on Japanese chestnut nursery stock, probably between 1880 and 1895. This fungus initiated one of the greatest natural disasters in the annals of forest biology, killing American chestnut trees on more than 200 million acres in eastern North America. Chestnut blight remains the most destructive disease known for any host, including trees, other plants, animals, and humans. It killed approximately four billion American chestnut trees, leaving few trees that survived infection. Fortunately, extinction of the species has been prevented by a continuous cycle of sprouting from the root collar, infection, death, and resprouting.

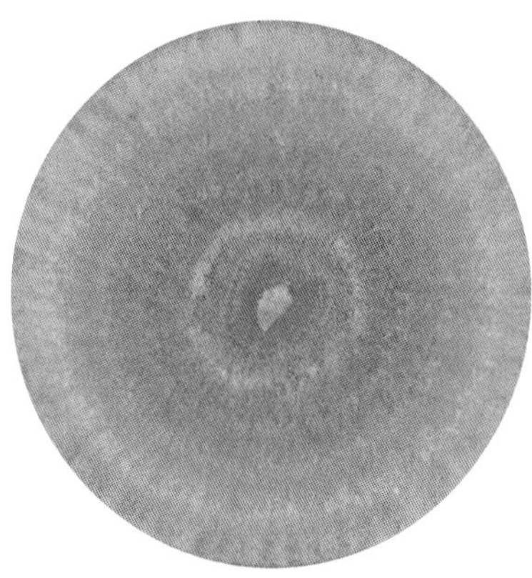
Petri dish containing a virulent colony of Cryphonectria parasitica.

The blight fungus *Cryphonectria parasitica* was first identified in 1905 by William Murrill, a noted mycologist, who worked at the New York Botanical Garden, next to the Bronx Zoological Park, where chestnut blight was first noticed in 1904. The organism was classified as a member of the largest group of fungi, the ascomycetes, and was similar to other ascomycetes that were known to incite such plant diseases as peach leaf curl, plum pockets, larch canker, stem rot of sweet potato, and black knot of plum.

Name of the Fungus

Scientists use a formal system for naming organisms. This system, using Latin, was devised in the mid-1700s by the Swedish physician and botanist Carolus Linneaus. Every known living creature has been given a two-part name. The first part of the name is the genus, followed by the species name. Examples of this system include human beings (*Homo sapiens*) and the infamous dinosaur *Tyrannosaurus rex* (commonly referred to as *T. rex*). The chestnut blight fungus has gone through several name changes. It was first named *Diaporthe parasitica* by Murrill in 1906. That name was changed to *Endothia parasitica* in 1912. In a more recent examination of some of the specific characteristics of the fungus, the name was changed in 1978 to *Cryphonectria parasitica* because of similarities to other members of the genus *Cryphonectria*.

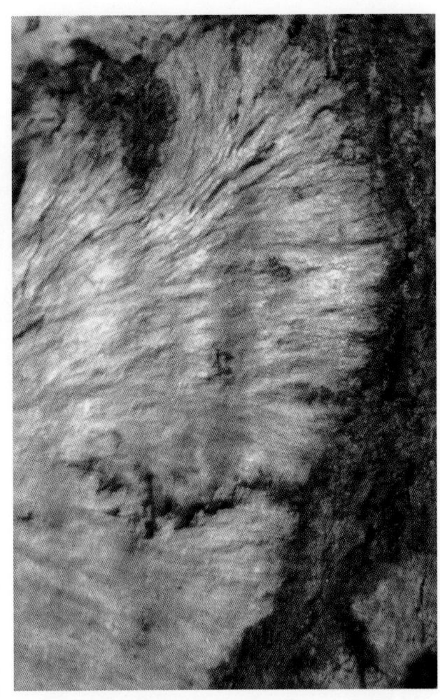

Mycelial fans formed by Cryphonectria parasitica *within infected bark of American chestnut.*

C. parasitica is a bark pathogen because infection results in areas of dead bark known as cankers. On trees with more than one canker, each canker is the result of a separate infection. Once an infection occurs, the fungus grows rapidly in the bark, producing an elaborate network of fungal filaments known as mycelial fans. If the fans encircle a stem and extend down to the wood, the vascular systems carrying the tree's life-sustaining sap are destroyed, killing the stem beyond the point of infection. This results in death of the leaves on the killed stem and the flagging symptoms that gave rise to the common name of the disease, chestnut "blight."

The fungus has numerous entryways into the tree, but most are associated with wounds. In 1906, soon after the discovery of chestnut blight, Murrill suggested a number of agents that might be responsible for the wounds that give entrance to the parasite: lumbermen, nut gatherers, the green fly, the twig borer, squirrels, birds, insects, mice, moles, and rabbits. He later suggested that dead twigs were a channel of entrance, since he often found them at the center of cankers. The evidence remains the same today; wounds are essential to the infection process. Regardless of its means of entry, the chestnut blight fungus found a very suitable host in North America.

Flagging symptoms of blight on young American chestnut sprouts.

On the highly susceptible American chestnut host, the blight fungus commonly extends throughout the bark down to the wood. In contrast, on resistant hosts, such as the Oriental species, the blight fungus often is prevented from extending to the wood, creating a superficial canker. When cankers extend to the wood, the fungus usually forms bright orange, pimplelike structures on the surface of the bark. These structures are the tops of fungal tissues, called stromata, that form beneath the bark and erupt through it. On superficial cankers that do not extend to the wood, stromata seldom erupt through the bark.

Virulent canker on a young American chestnut tree. Inset: *Close-up of orange pimplelike structures which are the stromata of* Cryphonectria parasitica.

Two types of fruiting bodies are produced within the orange stromata: the pycnidia, which produce hundreds of thousands of microscopic, single-celled, asexual spores called conidia; and the pear-shaped perithecia, which produce larger, two-celled sexual spores called ascospores.

The conidia often are exuded during warm, humid periods in a sticky mass of spores. They are moved mainly by rain and primarily are connected to the local spread of the organism, giving rise to new cankers on the same or nearby trees. Conidia also can hitchhike in water droplets or on the feet of birds, squirrels, insects, and other animals over longer distances. Conidia can persist in the soil and in the digestive systems of mites that eat stromata. The ascospores, in contrast, are forcibly expelled from the mature perithecia, to be picked up by air currents, and are considered to be important for long-distance spread of the blight.

Hypovirulent canker on chestnut. This superficial type of infection seldom extends to the wood, and few stromata are produced.

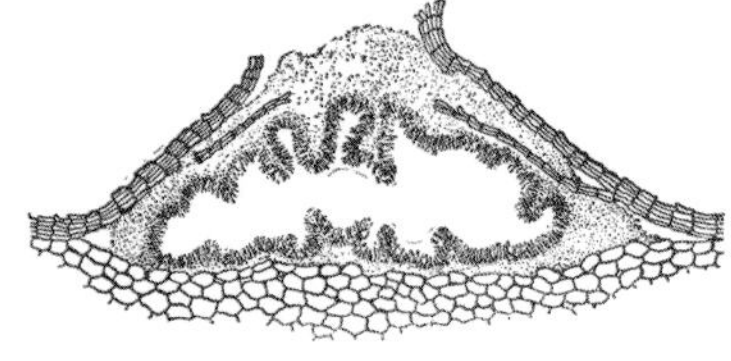

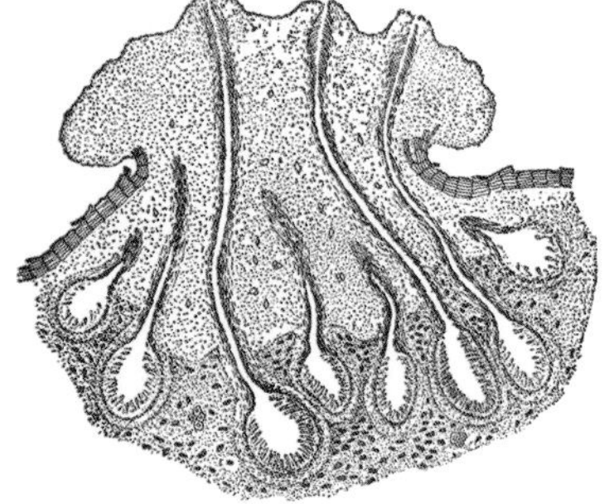

Above: *Drawings of a pycnidium (top) and perithecia (bottom), asexual and sexual reproductive structures, formed within the orange stromata imbedded in the bark (F. D. Heald, 1913).*

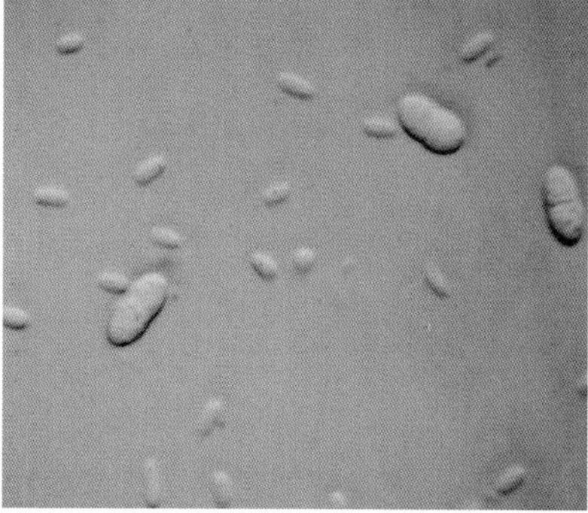

The smaller asexual conidia and the larger sexual ascospores viewed by light microscopy.

Hypovirulence: A disease of *Cryphonectria* emerges

In the 1930s *C. parasitica* was discovered in Europe and began devastating European chestnut trees, just as it had the American chestnut. The prospects for the European chestnut looked similarly bleak. However, in the early 1950s Antonio Biraghi, an Italian plant pathologist, noticed that some chestnut trees in Italy were recovering from blight. Biraghi advanced two hypotheses to explain the recovery: first, that the blight fungus had become less virulent, and, second, that the European chestnut tree had become more resistant.

A recovering chestnut stand similar to one observed by Biraghi. The dead branches are evidence of the initial blight epidemic; the new growth is associated with reduced virulence of the fungus, allowing for the regrowth.

Jean Grente, a French mycologist, subsequently established that reduced virulence in the fungus was a principal factor in the recovery. Grente took bark samples from numerous cankers, from which he isolated the chestnut blight fungus. Much to his surprise, many of the isolates that grew from the bark of the recovering trees were greatly reduced in pigmentation. Rather than the bright orange color typical of the killing strains, these isolates were much paler; in fact, many of them were nearly white. He experimented with the white isolates in the laboratory by pairing them side by side with orange isolates in petri plates. He noted that the orange isolates often grew normally for several days and then began growing like the white isolates. Grente attributed this color change to the transmission of an infectious agent from the white to the orange isolate. However, not all pairings resulted in this shift in pigmentation. When no change in appearance occurred, he showed the infectious agent was not successfully transmitted, a situation now attributed to genetic differences between the white and orange strains.

Grente discovered another unique and important feature of the white isolates. When he inoculated them into the bark of European chestnut, they produced significantly smaller cankers than did the orange isolates, prompting him to call them "hypovirulent," meaning less virulent. Since his pioneering research, other scientists have determined that the infectious agent represents a unique virus, now called a hypovirus. To date, several hypoviruses have been identified that infect the chestnut blight fungus, and three types have been shown to reduce the ability of the fungus to cause lethal cankers. These hypoviruses produce a variety of changes in the metabolism of

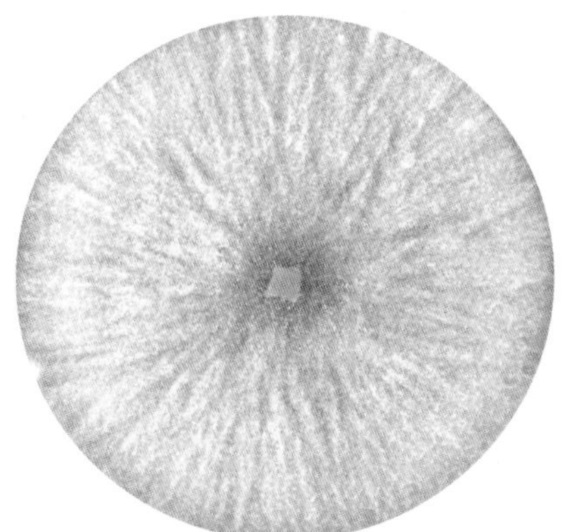

Petri dish containing a hypovirulent colony of Cryphonectria parasitica. *Note the reduction in orange pigmentation compared to the virulent colony.*

Petri plates each containing a pairing of virulent and hypovirulent colonies of Cryphonectria parasitica. *The plate on the left is an example of successful hypovirus transmission; the white arrow indicates the area that acquired hypovirus. No transmission occurred in the plate on the right.*

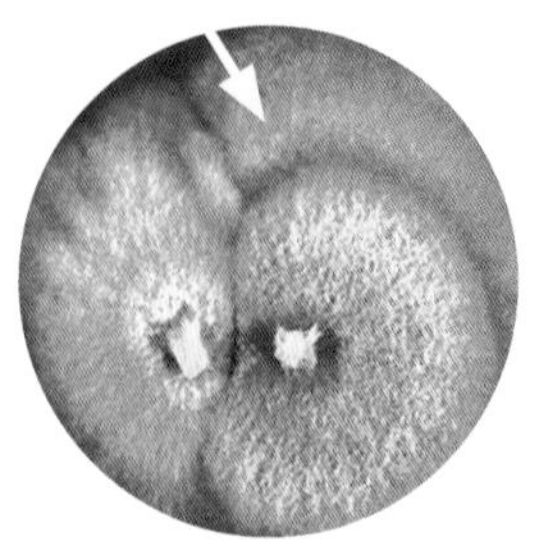

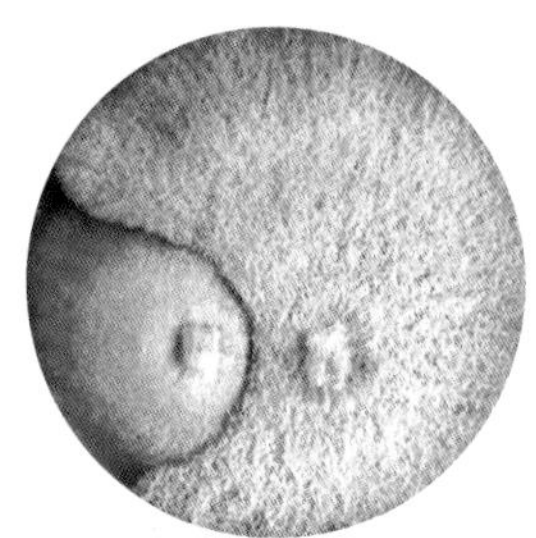

the fungus, but one of the most important alterations, relative to biological control, is the reduction in its ability to cause disease. Essentially, the fungus has acquired its own disease.

Hypovirulence as a biological control for *C. parasitica*

The beauty of Biraghi and Grente's discovery is that the phenomenon of hypovirulence they described is associated with significant, naturally occurring biological control of chestnut blight in numerous regions of Italy. Additionally, Grente was able to effect biological control of blight in France by treating cankers with hypovirulent strains, mimicking the biocontrol occurring naturally in Italy. On a larger scale, there is promise that hypovirulence also can be used for biological control of *C. parasitica* on American chestnut. Unfortunately, this promise has yet to be realized in forest settings in North America. There are three factors that may be impeding biological control of blight with hypoviruses.

First, the European chestnut, although susceptible to blight, is not as susceptible as American chestnut. The European species is able to withstand the initial onslaught of virulent strains longer, and is not as damaged by them. This increased resistance may mean virulent strains have more time to acquire hypovirus and be controlled.

A Benign Relative of *C. parasitica*

C. parasitica has relatives in the genus *Cryphonectria*. The closest is *C. radicalis,* a species known in North America and Europe; *C. parasitica* is a native of eastern Asia. Both species are almost identical in appearance when cultured in the laboratory, but they differ slightly in the size of their ascospores. What is most significant is their difference in ability to cause disease in chestnut. *C. parasitica* causes a serious disease on American and European chestnut and can infect Oriental species, while *C. radicalis* is a relatively benign pathogen. Both fungal species may have originated as one but diverged as they coevolved with their respective hosts. Why *C. parasitica* became a very capable pathogen while *C. radicalis* did not remains an intriguing question.

At present, C. parasitica *holds the upper hand in what must be considered a biological imbalance. Whether it will continue to do so over long biological periods is debatable.*

Second, European chestnut tends to occur in pure stands, so when blight initially kills a stand, most of the regrowth is by sprouting chestnut. This persistent population of sprouts supports many virulent infections that in turn acquire hypoviruses, resulting in the remission of blight. In contrast, the eastern hardwood forests of North America contain numerous tree species. These other species often shade and compete with new sprouts that arise from the stumps of blight-killed chestnut, either killing the sprouts and entire stumps outright or allowing only very slow growth. These small, suppressed understory sprouts do not support epidemics of the chestnut blight fungus and the concurrent development of hypovirus infections necessary for the remission of blight.

Finally, within the natural range of American chestnut, numerous strains of the blight fungus can often be found at any one location, unlike in Europe, where one strain usually predominates in an area. For hypovirus transmission to occur readily, strains need to be genetically similar. In an analogy using human blood types, someone with type "A" blood cannot donate to someone who is type "B." The same principle holds true for isolates of the chestnut blight fungus, as Grente previously demonstrated. In eastern North America, an area decimated by chestnut blight, many different strains of the fungus exist. Some localized areas can contain as many as thirty-five or more different strains. Thus, hypoviruses probably can spread from canker to canker much more easily in Europe than in the United States.

At present, *C. parasitica* holds the upper hand in what must be considered a biological imbalance. Whether it will continue to do so over long biological periods is debatable. Certainly there are examples of successful biological invaders whose effects eventually have been lessened by other pathogens, parasites, or predators. This appears to be the case for European chestnuts growing in Italy, as hypoviruses play an ever-increasing role in the natural biological control of the disease.

Likewise, for the chestnut host, there may be an ongoing natural selection process for blight resistance. If this is occurring, the limited sexual reproduction of American chestnut taking place is undoubtedly a bottleneck to the process. Although the goal of The American Chestnut Foundation and other organizations is to breed blight-resistant American chestnuts, it is unclear at this time whether these efforts will produce resistant trees that will grow well in forest settings. Resistance through breeding, coupled with hypovirulence, may provide the successful combination necessary to control blight on American chestnut. ∾

Old Soldiers Never Die

By William Lord

When our soldiers die in combat, we vow that their sacrifice will not be in vain. Historians describe campaigns in hallowed tones, lest we forget. Arthur Harmount Graves (1879–1962) was a soldier who campaigned with the armament of a plant breeder to defeat the blight and produce a blight-resistant, timber-type chestnut tree. He made progress, but final victory eluded him.

Graves sought to replace the American chestnut rather than to resurrect it. He observed the different species of chestnut and sought to combine specific traits to produce the desired trees. To produce a timber-type chestnut, he worked primarily with the Japanese, Chinese, and American species.

Graves arrived on the chestnut horizon in 1910, a total Yale man; graduate, PhD, and then a professor at the Yale School of Forestry. The blight had spread into Connecticut from points of origin in and around Long Island, New York, and grabbed the attention of the thirty-one-year-old professor. He became a campaigner for the chestnut for the rest of his life.

Graves was an early motorcycle enthusiast and found cycling an ideal way to cover the countryside. He could leave the road and traverse lanes and paths no Model T would dare. He reconnoitered areas around his Connecticut acreage and observed the blight invader decimating the chestnut.

In 1911 F. W. Rane, the state forester of Massachusetts, arranged to have Graves do a motorcycle chestnut reconnaissance. Graves scouted the entire state, June through August, and found the invader to be more prevalent than anyone had realized. In February 1912 Graves attended the Pennsylvania-sponsored Conference for Preventing the Spread of the Chestnut Bark Disease, in Harrisburg. The principal speaker from Connecticut was George P. Clinton. The Pennsylvania hosts had recently begun an ambitious program to combat the blight and were seeking to construct a concerted attack, involving all the chestnut states from Maine to Georgia. Clinton demurred. The blight was so omnipresent in his state that combat was not an option. He believed that the blight was a normally harmless fungus that was opportunistically pillaging a tree weakened by an unnatural sequence of severe winters and droughts and that the chestnut would recover with the return of milder weather.

The Pennsylvania Blight Commission produced a series of bulletins describing the blight and the work that was being done in an effort to contain the fungus. Whether or not he agreed with Clinton, Graves made no comment published in the transcript of the conference. He did comment on a Pennsylvania proposal to stop the spread of the invader by eliminating all chestnut trees within a ten- to twenty-mile-wide zone bordering the main line of advance. He also mentioned his motorcycle scouting with deserved pride. "If this sort of work is going to be taken up by the State, it seems to me it would be a good plan to delimit all areas which contain no chestnuts. I have the honor, Mr. Chairman, to be the gentleman who went through the State of Massachusetts on a motor cycle . . . and I found a great many areas there which had no chestnut at all, and some such areas I am sure occur in Pennsylvania, so if you are going to take up this method, it seems to me such areas ought to be marked out and then start west of those."

Graves had not motorcycled through Pennsylvania as he had through Massachusetts. Chestnut blight was present in every county. The buffer zone was partially cut but then abandoned because the blight had already jumped over it. The blight was so overwhelming in its advance that the Blight Commission stopped field operations in 1913.

From the onset of his call to duty, Graves was ever on the lookout for the appearance of trees showing resistance to the blight. In 1918 a bright hope faded. "About 75 trees were found situated on the island of Manhattan itself, also some near Jamaica, L. I. [Long Island], and some near Valley Stream, L. I., which showed unmistakable resistance to the blight . . . in many cases showing Endothia cankers with healed margins, and often with swollen areas where lesions had formed on branches, indicating a struggle on the part of the host tissue to overcome and occlude the parasitic growth. Furthermore, inoculations with the fungus in these trees showed that the parasite grew at a much lower rate than in ordinary non-resistant trees, a result which was based on data from hundreds of inoculations. . . . Vigorous seedlings from these trees are now growing at the USDA at Bell, Maryland. . . . So far, however, no especial resistance has been shown by these seedlings nor the grafts." Graves concluded that the resistance of the trees was due to their "favorable environment coupled with their inherent vigor, rather than any other specific inherent character of resistance." Nonetheless, he noted, "This . . . does not explain the fact that the fungus when inoculated into these trees grew more slowly that in ordinary trees." Graves never gave up the hope that resistance would occur by mutation.

Arthur Graves with one of his trees. (Courtesy of the Connecticut Agricultural Experiment Station.)

In 1929 Graves presented a paper at the twentieth annual meeting of the Northern Nut Growers Association (NNGA). He reviewed intelligence acquired about the enemy and revealed his desire to engage it in the field as a plant breeder. He noted the ability of apparently dead trees to produce sprouts from the root collar, "the region where the trunk and roots join. . . . It would seem . . . that the tissues of the root collar and of the roots as well, are more resistant to the growth of the fungus than the parts above the ground. Inoculations of the roots, and at the same time of shoots of the same diameter, have proved . . . that the growth of the fungus is much slower in the root tissues. . . . Just why the growth is slower here is not so clear." He discussed his breeding objective: "To produce a forest tree it is necessary to cross our native tall-growing and timber-producing C. dentata with the resistant Japanese and Chinese stock, on the chance that some of the off spring will inherit the timber-producing quality of one parent joined to the resistant quality of the other parent."

The fifty-year-old Graves was itching to engage the enemy. But did he have the time? "Well, I wish I wasn't quite so old. It seems that if one had time he could get this result. It is going to be a wonderful thing when it is done, and it can be done . . . and it is going to be done some day."

Graves decided he wasn't too old and in 1930 commenced his campaign to develop a blight-resistant forest-type chestnut—a mission he conducted with ever-increasing effort for thirty-two more years.

Graves decided he wasn't too old and in 1930 commenced his campaign to develop a blight-resistant forest-type chestnut—a mission he conducted with ever-increasing effort for thirty-two more years. His presentations at several NNGA annual meetings through 1949 are optimistic reports of a goal to be achieved whatever the difficulty. Nuts were planted on his plantation next to Sleeping Giant State Park and other nearby sites in Connecticut. He began by making crosses on mature Japanese chestnut on Long Island estates with pollen from American trees provided by the USDA in Washington, D.C. These hybrids were later crossed with Chinese trees and with each other. The harvest was taken to the Brooklyn Botanical Garden, where Graves was a curator. The seeds were planted in the fall and the seedlings then transplanted to Connecticut the following spring. Each was surrounded with a wire cage to protect it from rodents and deer. A copper tag identified the parentage. The breeding objective expanded to include "cold or frost resistance, resistance to insect attack, quality and quantity of fruit, precocity, and prolificness." In this regard, the genes of the European chestnut, the Allegheny chinquapin, and the dwarf Chinese chestnut were allied to the mission. The blight prevailed among surviving chestnut sprouts in the surrounding woods and provided a "passive" test for his hybrids. Graves, however, determined blight resistance by inoculating the young trees with cultures of the blight grown in his laboratory. Each tree was inoculated for three successive years. American sprouts were inoculated as checks.

The blight was the principal enemy, but drought and severe winters weakened the trees and their harvest. Canker worms devoured the newly emerging leaves in spring, followed by Japanese beetles. In midsummer aphids concentrated along the mid-veins, sucking the juice and causing the leaves to curl into a roll. Crowds of mites gave the leaves a distinctive grayish cast from the refuse of their molting. A pestilence of seventeen-year cicadas seemed to prefer chestnut for their egg laying, puncturing lengthwise slits along the outer growth. "One young American chestnut, 12' high had 14 of its branches ruined," Graves noted in 1945.

Following a drought year, squirrels made ravenous by lack of acorns gnawed off twigs bearing burs in early September, dropping them to the ground. Carrying them to a place of safety, they defied the spiny burs to devour the green nuts. Graves described his adversities but never faltered in optimism. "For it is the ultimate aim of this work to develop a race of tall, hardy, blight resistant individuals which will breed true and thus of themselves reestablish the chestnut tree in the forests of eastern North America."

In 1947 he resigned as curator for the Brooklyn Botanical Garden and applied himself full time to his chestnut campaign in cooperation with the Connecticut Agricultural Experiment Station. This was also the year that Graves began providing hybrids for test plantings of Chinese chestnut and blight-resistant hybrids in a project headed by Jesse D. Diller of the U.S. Forest Service. In 1949 Diller approved a site at the Crab Orchard National Wildlife Refuge in southwest Illinois. The USDA and Graves each contributed seedlings. In 1962 Richard A. Jaynes visited the refuge and brought news home to Graves of hybrid B-26. Although it was not one of those contributed by Graves, it was blight-free after seventeen growing seasons, forty-five feet tall, and 7.3 inches in diameter at breast height.

One of the last requests Graves made before he died, on December 31, 1962, was for scions from B-26, now well known as the "Clapper" tree. In 1989 scions from the Clapper tree, and from the 'Graves' BC_1 (a first backcross, descended from the Chinese tree 'Mahogany'), were used to provide a jump start to TACF's breeding program at Meadowview Research Farms. Measured in years, the two generations gained the program a decade.

Graves's campaign was not a failure. He never surrendered. ~

The Chestnut Plantation at Sleeping Giant: The Legacy of Arthur Graves

By Dr. Sandra L. Anagnostakis

The following originally appeared in a different form in the 53rd Annual Report of the Northern Nut Growers Association.

In 1914 Arthur Harmount Graves wrote: "The most hopeful indications for chestnut in North America in the future lie along the line of breeding experiments. . . . Work of this kind is extremely valuable and, although slow in yielding results, may eventually prove to be the only means of continuing the existence in our land of a greatly esteemed tree."

Sixteen years later, in 1930, Graves undertook such a breeding project, eventually planting more than 2,000 chestnut trees on land that he owned in Hamden, Connecticut, just north of New Haven, next to what is now Sleeping Giant State Park. He got many trees from the USDA, planting them first on the land south of his house, and many of those first trees are still alive.

When he retired as a curator at the Brooklyn Botanical Garden in 1947, Graves moved back to his native Connecticut to work full time with the Connecticut Agricultural Experiment Station on chestnut breeding. In 1949 he sold 8.3 acres of his land to the Sleeping Giant Park Association, which then gave it to the state of Connecticut, stipulating that the property was to be for the experiment station for tree-breeding experiments. Graves worked with geneticist Donald F. Jones at the experiment station, and together they supervised such notable students as Hans Nienstaedt and Richard Jaynes. In 1962 Graves reported that he and his associates had made more than 250 combinations of all the species of chestnuts, resulting in over 20,000 nuts.

Graves's plantation was not a prototype of a commercial orchard. Specimens include all the species of chestnut, plus numerous hybrids—probably the finest collection of *Castanea* in the world. I took over the chestnut breeding project in 1983 and made new labels for the trees in the planting. This breeding program is the longest-continuing chestnut breeding project in the U.S., and many people have added and removed trees from the plantation. Fortunately, they all wrote it down.

Graves divided chestnuts into twelve species and had representatives of all of them in his plantings. He released many cultivars that are still grown today for their nuts, such as 'Sleeping Giant', 'Eaton', and 'Toumey', and provided a solid basis for the continued breeding of timber chestnut trees. His hybrids and species are still used for producing orchard and timber trees with resistance to chestnut blight disease, ink disease, and Oriental chestnut gall wasp. The experiment station is also using trees at the plantation in a backcross breeding project to move resistance genes into Ozark chinquapins (*C. ozarkensis*), because that species, native to the Ozark Plateau, is now threatened by chestnut blight disease.

New trees are still being planted at the plantation, as those that don't live up to expectations are removed. I know that chestnut workers all over the world are aware of our plantation, but I continue to be surprised at the requests for cuttings and seeds that come in every year. The study of chestnut genetics is as far along as it is today because of the foresight of Arthur Graves and because the state of Connecticut chooses to support a project with a long history and great potential for the future.

The chestnut plantation at Sleeping Giant in Hamden, Connecticut, 1936. (Courtesy of Connecticut Agricultural Experiment Station.)

The Accidental Chestnut Ecologist

By Frederick Paillet

Dr. Frederick Paillet recently retired as a research scientist with the U.S. Geological Survey, where he was a principal investigator at the Hubbard Brook Experimental Forest in the White Mountain National Forest in central New Hampshire, one of the premier ecological laboratories in the country. Dr. Paillet is now Research Professor of Geology at the University of Maine, where he continues his studies in paleoecology and paleoclimate. In addition he is an artist of significant talent, constantly sketching in his notebook to visually convey the complex ecological insights his observations and researches yield, and has illustrated this essay.

My career as a chestnut scientist began by default—you could probably call me an accidental ecologist. In my early efforts to establish a career combining geology and meteorology in what we now call paleoclimatology, I noticed that American chestnut trees seemed to be out of phase with other forest trees in New England. I had a hunch that this might be related to rainfall or some other aspect of hydrology. But I ran into a blind alley: there were absolutely no modern ecological chestnut facts in the literature. Being a resourceful young scientist, I began to go out and collect my own data. And as a young scientist I proudly compiled these hard-won facts in an article for a botanical journal. You can imagine my dismay when the reviews of my submission generated a profound lack of interest. One reviewer commented that this reminded him of efforts to freeze dead bodies until a cure could be found for their disease. His final words on my submission were a resounding pronouncement that "chestnut is dead and gone—who cares!" My article was eventually published, but the editor made it clear that my contribution was something akin to a mere footnote on forest history.

My interest in chestnut continued over the years, driven by a love of the deciduous forest and a sense of wonder about a great tree that no longer graced our woodlands. The ambitious idea that my original hunch could be turned into a fully funded line of research went by the wayside. My salaried work followed other, more practical lines. Yet I made the pleasant discovery that there were other chestnut enthusiasts out there, and their encouragement helped to keep me going. With this little bit of moral support and the fact that a day in the woods can never be truly wasted, I began to really look at chestnut.

This wasn't done in a vacuum; other ecologists were beginning to ask questions about long-established ideas related to forest ecology and succession. The importance of the natural disturbance regime and the subtle effects of land-use history on plant communities were suddenly of great interest. Other researchers began to provide data showing that my hunch about chestnut growth being related to some important climate signal had a real basis in fact. Something indeed had happened about 2,500 years ago in New England that drastically rearranged the forested landscape, and chestnut definitely was a lead player in the events at the time. We had a real mystery on our hands, and ecologists suddenly did begin to care.

That's the story of how I got involved with chestnut. A second question was how one could begin to make headway in understanding the ecology of a species that is completely "dead and gone." A good starting point was the recognition that chestnut was not quite dead and certainly far from gone. For example, I noted that chestnut sprouts were virtually everywhere in some forests, and I saw the same phenomenon in compiled lists of species reported for test plots in the literature. Most of these studies were concerned with tracking the growth of future woodlands. Since chestnut was supposed to have no future, it was effectively ignored as if it was just another weed. In fact, one publication in a prestigious journal came perilously close to actually invoking the "W" word, noting that chestnut sprouts were the dominant component of regenerating biomass in the years after massive clear-cutting in the southern Appalachians (1880–1930), posing a severe complication for the regrowth of valuable hardwoods. Even in that case there was no question about how a tree that is supposedly incapacitated by blight could be such a tenacious competitor in our forests. There just had to be more to the story than dying trees "smoldering at the roots," as Robert Frost so eloquently wrote.

There was no question about how a tree that is supposedly incapacitated by blight could be such a tenacious competitor in our forests. There just had to be more to the story than dying trees "smoldering at the roots," as Robert Frost so eloquently wrote.

It seemed clear that to me as a scientist one had to apply some new statistical analysis to existing data sets to find out what was really going on with chestnut. But I was at a loss as to what specific questions to pose in an effort to extract answers from the available data. The obvious approach was to examine a few typical study sites in exhaustive detail, and then use this insight to formulate wide-ranging studies. I would identify what kinds of living sprouts were present at a location, exactly where they were located in reference to other trees and topographic features, and how they might have been related to large chestnut trees that once grew in the area.

Suburban New England was ideal for this purpose because the forest started with a clean slate about 150 years ago. At that time vast clearings for farms and pastures were abandoned and grew up with trees—first cedars and pines, and then hardwoods like oak, maple, and chestnut. Woodlots remain nicely segmented by old stone walls, forming convenient baselines for mapping the forest floor. The sawed-off stumps of former large chestnut trees or the fallen hulks of dead chestnuts that toppled under their own weight could easily be identified. Tree rings from "cookies" cut from chestnut logs, or cores extracted from oaks that suddenly increased their growth when forest-dominating chestnuts died from blight, were used to date the exact time when blight first affected the forest. These dates varied from around 1910 in south-central Connecticut to about 1925 in New Hampshire. Most important of all, the observed locations of these big old blight-killed trees could be related to the sprouts we see living in the forest today.

Within a few years a very consistent model for chestnut sprouting and survival began to emerge. Probably the most astounding observation was that most of the chestnut sprouts we see today (at least in New England) are not from the roots of former chestnut trees at all. They represent what I call "old seedlings." These sprouts were never attached to the roots of a big tree. Instead, most sprouts probably represent seedlings from nuts that have continuously sprouted, stagnated, and resprouted in the understory of a closed forest. That, coupled with the fact that there were often a hundred or more individual sprouts in an acre of forest, produced the amazing conclusion that chestnut seedling sprouts are virtually immortal. Those I studied in New England had to have been around for fifty to one hundred years since the time when chestnut seed was still being produced, and yet large numbers had survived virtually hidden on the forest floor. Most foresters now agree that our eastern deciduous forests regenerate by "advanced reproduction"—that is, big trees originate from small trees already established when logging or disease or windstorm remove the overstory. Chestnut was thus displaying a highly effective form of advanced regeneration.

A small opening under oaks in a former pasture contains a mound of rotted wood. A set of three little chestnut sprouts grows around the edge of the mound, marking the perimeter of the old chestnut stump. Although the sprouts look like seedlings, each represents a root collar sprout from what was once a large chestnut tree.

This also provided a partial answer for another great chestnut puzzle. If chestnut seed is meant for reproduction, why are there no defense mechanisms to protect the seeds such as bitter tannins or thick shells or early spring flowering, when late frosts produce occasional nut-free years to starve the squirrels who would otherwise eat the nuts? Why are chestnuts so sweet and delicious, and why do they pop out of their protective burs as soon as they ripen? Some tree species produce millions of tiny and easily windborne seeds. There is almost nothing invested in each seed, but so many are broadcast that some will find the right place to prosper. In contrast, chestnut invests lots of resources—carbohydrates and fats—in its seeds and makes them as attractive as possible for rodent disseminators. The idea is that only a very few nuts need get established because they are virtually indestructible once they get their initial start. They have the resources to make a good start and the genetic instructions to insure survival as a heavily suppressed seedling for as long as it takes to make a break for the canopy.

All of this prompted a much closer look at exactly how chestnut sprouts. Most hardwood trees sprout when cut, and many such as ash, oak, and basswood do so prolifically. These are adventitious sprouts that arise in response to the injury from the living cambium cells in the bark. Chestnut does not usually sprout in this way. Chestnut stump sprouts originate only from preformed buds perched on the root collar—the flange of tissue where the roots spread out from the base of the trunk. These buds are already formed during the first year as a seedling is established. They are almost separate growing entities, shedding bud scales every year or so. When the dominant stem on the little seedling is damaged or cut, the waiting buds emerge. They also do two other things: they cut themselves off from the old root system, and they develop their own new set of preformed basal buds. Thus, we are looking at the ultimate arboreal fountain of youth. Chestnut has a mechanism for continuously being reborn as a new seedling whenever the need arises, until natural events produce a proper place in the canopy.

But that left another puzzle. Foresters always maintained that the only way to manage chestnut as a timber crop was by stump sprouting. Chestnut seedling establishment—at least in the short term—was deemed just too unreliable. But the harvested trees could be counted on to form new sprouts and replace themselves. If that was so, why was I finding so little evidence of chestnut sprouts originating from the stumps of big, blight-killed trees? A little forensic excavation told the story. The first hint was that the few remains of large old chestnut trees that did have living sprouts still attached were always from trees cut soon after they died. It is easy to see the many sockets where the little bulblets of sprout tissue were once seated on the old root collar. When a long-dead chestnut snag finally topples over, the process pulls the base of the tree out of the ground. Any attached sprouts come out with the stump.

If the tree is cut, the stump stays in the ground. The location of root-collar buds up on the side of the root collar on such stumps posed a problem for sprouts in the development of their own root system. This difficulty was compounded by upland erosion washing soil from around old stumps that are located on hillsides. When chestnut blight appeared in Connecticut and Massachusetts shortly after 1900, most woodlots were restricted to steep hillsides and ridgetops, because level land with deep soil was still used for crops or pasture. Thus, erosion of soil from around the base of chestnut trees was a common process. But there were a few cases where debris piled up against one side of the old stump, and the sprouts could take root. If you exhume these deposits you see what seems to be a tree seedling with its roots draped over the dead wood of an old stump—just like we see hemlocks that have seeded into the mossy tops of old stumps. But here the seedling originated from the former tree. We know the old adage of mighty oaks coming from a tiny acorn. Here we have the unusual proposition of an apparent seedling developing from the tissue of a mature tree. Obviously, these are not true seedlings, but such sprouts seem to have all the attributes of juvenile growth from a true seed.

Why does the tree do all of this? Chestnut has been around as a recognizable genus for at least fifty million years, so there must be an adaptive advantage in this unusual mode of propagation. If you look at other trees in the so-called sprout hardwoods of New

England you see oaks, maples, and tulip poplars that are still attached to the stumps of trees that were cut almost a century ago. The remains of the stump persist as a hollow of dead and decaying wood penetrating the base of the regenerated trees. The sprouting process in chestnut seems designed to avoid creation of such basal hollows. Perhaps this has something to do with the fact that chestnut is intended to become a canopy-dominating forest monarch. A pronounced defect in the tree's foundation that might develop into a hollow and weakened lower trunk would be a distinct disadvantage in later life.

The elaborate design of a defect-free support system is just a part of the ecological strategy that helped American chestnut become the dominant tree in its chosen habitat. The accumulation of such chestnut facts suggests that the tree is programmed to remain virtually dormant on the forest floor for decades or even a century. This population of advanced chestnut reproduction is designed to carefully maintain a clean stem form and a root buttress in structurally perfect condition, awaiting the day when a disturbance makes an opening in the canopy. The young trees, once established as well-rooted seedlings, have carefully husbanded their resources so that they can outgrow the competition when the need arises. We see such released sprouts doing so today—much to the dismay of commercial foresters. Having a defect-free platform upon which to build the future forest giant is an important part of the program. This also explains why there are so many reports of young American chestnut trees and seedlings in woodlots where there has not been any chestnut seed for almost a century. The little trees just maintain the appearance of thrifty new seedlings throughout their cycle of stem replacement.

Base of a chestnut sprout showing typical root collar structure. The sprout often has a single large stem with enlarged burls of tissue at the base—the root collar. Some buds show signs of growth by shedding scales annually. These buds are the source of new stems when the primary stem is killed by blight or other damage.

What other ways could be used to test this theory? One thought that occurred to me was to compare the chestnut, a large, long-lived forest tree, with its southern cousin, the chinquapin. The latter grows as a bush or small understory tree. The literature indicates that chinquapin sprouts like chestnut, but surely its ecological niche must be substantially different. What did this tell me about the peculiar sprouting habit of American chestnut? My studies showed that chinquapin did "turn over" its stem population by resprouting from the base, just like chestnut. Chinquapin lives for many years as a small, suppressed clump of stems in the understory, producing few leaves and almost no fruit. Like chestnut, chinquapin responds to cutting and opening of the canopy with rapid upward growth from healthy stems, and rapid generation of sprouts from the base of damaged stems. But there were two very big differences. First, the sprouts do not come from preformed bud tissue, but from an extended region of the lower stem and from the tops of roots near the base of the tree. Second, the expanding new growth eventually stops shooting upward and begins to branch out laterally. This results in a massive crop of nuts over the next few years.

We have two sides of the same story here. Both chestnut and chinquapin are designed to survive for extended periods in the understory, and then to rapidly take advantage of canopy opening when it occurs. Chestnut is a giant forest tree with an extended apprentice period in the understory. Chinquapin is a large shrub that lives in the understory and occasionally escapes to produce a large crop of nuts when the opportunity arrives. This converges on the eternal question as to whether the tadpole is the juvenile form of the frog, or whether the frog is the reproductive system for the tadpole. Either one of these alternatives can apply to certain amphibious species. The same appears to apply to our two native *Castanea* varieties.

As a paleoecologist, I enjoy sharing yet another chestnut insight with colleagues. One of the common ways to investigate forests of the past is to drill sediment cores from ponds and bogs where pollen has been settling into the mud on the bottom for long periods of time. These cores provide a snapshot of the changing forest composition over time through the natural cycling of climate. You have to do some statistical work relating pollen proportions to forest composition. For example, my studies suggest that you have to multiply chestnut pollen by a factor of three to get an estimate of the proportion of chestnut in the forest. That's because other trees like oak and hemlock shed their pollen when the canopy is bare. Chestnut blooms in late June or early July within a leafed out canopy and is thus at a disadvantage as far as pollen dispersal goes.

Pollen studies provide a fascinating snapshot of changing forest conditions over time. One of the prominent events in pollen profiles throughout eastern North America is a sharp "notch" in the amount of hemlock pollen at 4,700 years ago. That feature appears everywhere from Georgia to Quebec at exactly the same time. This "blip" in hemlock abundance almost certainly represents some kind of disease that virtually eradicated the tree from its natural range. The notch looks narrow—perhaps a few centuries in all. And it is likely that sediment mixing on the lake floor has eroded the edges of an even narrower drop in hemlock pollen influx. The depth of the notch does go to zero, so there is no doubt that hemlock was effectively removed from the forest. If American chestnut can be restored to its natural range in the next few decades, I suspect that future generations will see a similar notch in chestnut pollen profiles.

Each of us contributing in our own small way to the chestnut restoration project will have long been forgotten by the time that pollen notch is evident. There is some small comfort that such an eternal monument to my existence will remain throughout the ages to come. ❧

Hypovirulence of Chestnut Blight

By Dennis W. Fulbright

The author is a professor of plant pathology at Michigan State University and specializes in chestnut trees.

One of the positive outcomes of the scientific process is the ability to make accurate predictions based on a certain set of facts. It took the residents of eastern North America a couple of decades to realize that there was nothing they could do to save their cherished American chestnut trees from the ravages of chestnut blight. The facts showed that an aggressive fungal pathogen had entered the continent and infected American chestnut tree bark and the certain predictable outcome was death of the aboveground portion of the tree. Hard to understand and hard to take; the pessimistic news was followed by optimistic reports of treatments and elixirs that could cure blight, and not surprisingly none of these treatments ever changed the long-term outcome of the relentless blight.

As blight moved to the European continent and began to destroy the European chestnut trees (*Castanea sativa*) in forests and orchards, a report from Italy in the 1950s, which was followed by more work in the 1960s, indicated that something had changed in the response of the European chestnut tree to blight infection. Instead of succumbing to the blight, some infected trees survived. Where the trees were surviving, the blight infections or cankers appeared to be different when compared to the cankers from trees where the outcome was certain death. In cases where the stems or tree died, the cankers were flat and the bark peeled off in sheets once the cambium died, yielding the expected and predictable lethal canker. Where trees were surviving, even recovering, the cankers show callus or wound tissue surrounding the cankers. This tissue would continue to grow in the face of chestnut blight and close the canker. The cankers could still be seen, but they were, for the most part, nonlethal cankers.

Confused, some researchers thought the trees had somehow gained resistance, while other researchers presented data suggesting the fungus had somehow changed. The latter data withstood scrutiny of the scientific process, and new facts were now emerging from the European chestnut forests. Somehow the bright orange aggressive pathogen, known then as *Endothia parasitica,* today as *Cryphonectria parasitica*, was in some cases losing its pigment while at the same time losing its aggressiveness. If that wasn't good news, the next part was better: the process was infectious. That is, chances were good that an aggressive orange strain of the pathogen would become white and less aggressive if the aggressive and less-aggressive strains touched each other while growing on trees or in culture in the laboratory. The less-aggressive strains were given a name by Jean Grente, the

French researcher who discovered the salient pieces of the process; he called them hypovirulent strains. Even before the cause and mechanism of the changes were understood, chestnut workers in Italy began a campaign of orchard and forest treatments where the white, nonaggressive—hypovirulent—strains were placed on the beloved sprouts and existing trees throughout chestnut-growing regions. Trees appeared to respond, and chestnut recovery was under way in Europe.

Most of this research was unknown to American scientists, as the research on chestnut in Europe was published in French, Italian, or German scientific journals and technical reports. Anyway, during this time American researchers had largely given up on American chestnut tree research, except for the few studies on blight resistance, and even that was beginning to wane in the 1950s and early '60s. Nothing exciting was happening to American chestnut, and interest in chestnut had been diluted by the Dutch elm disease epidemic that was striking the more well-known and costly-to-bring-down elm trees planted on city streets throughout eastern and midwestern North America.

In the 1970s researchers at the Connecticut Agricultural Experiment Station in New Haven discovered the European reports about the hypovirulent strains, and they wondered if this system might work on the American chestnut tree. They soon discovered that the hypovirulent characteristics of European strains could be transferred to American strains of the chestnut blight pathogen and that blight could be treated, as in Europe, at least on trees in the greenhouse and in small plots. These researchers also discovered other important elements about the hypovirulent strains.

It appeared a new chestnut paradigm was ready to be set in motion: chestnut trees in North America would come back from the brink based on a naturally occurring biological control found in Europe.

That hypovirulent characteristics were transmissible from one chestnut blight strain to another was well known and probably the most important factor in successfully treating chestnut blight cankers. If strains were found reduced in aggressiveness, but not capable of transmitting this characteristic to other strains, the system would be rendered practically useless. So long as something moved from the hypovirulent strain to the virulent strain, making the virulent strain into a hypovirulent strain, the system appeared to be unstoppable, and surely chestnut blight would soon be in remission and the trees would grow back. But a huge mystery remained unanswered: what was being transferred? Again, the Connecticut group came through with the answer. At first highly correlated, and since proven, the cause of hypovirulence in the chestnut blight pathogen is the genetic information encoded on double-stranded RNA (dsRNA) molecules. These molecules carried genes that were somehow involved with changing the pigment of the fungal pathogen from orange to white while reducing the aggressiveness of the pathogen. Also, these molecules would leave copies of themselves behind in the existing hypovirulent strain and move into new strains, turning the new strains into hypovirulent strains after the strains touched, forming an intimate connection known as an anastomose (fusion). It appeared a new chestnut paradigm was ready to be set in motion: chestnut trees in North America would come back from the brink based on a naturally occurring biological control found in Europe.

Naturalist's discovery

To enforce the notion that chestnuts were ready for a comeback, a series of unlikely events unfolded. Publicity scared up by the new findings in Connecticut made its way into newspapers around the country. A naturalist cross-country skiing on a golf course in western Michigan observed a small stand of naturalized American chestnuts about 150 miles outside the natural range of the tree. She not only recognized them as American chestnut when they were without their distinctive leaves, but she was able to tell that the chestnut blight infections on the stems were the abnormal, nonlethal type much like the photos she had seen in the newspaper. She took it upon herself to remove some of the stems harboring the abnormal swollen cankers and mailed them to the researchers in Connecticut. The researchers isolated the pathogen from the cankers, determined the cankers to be chestnut blight, and found that some of the strains they isolated appeared to be reduced in aggressiveness and harboring dsRNA molecules. These Michigan strains had most of the hallmarks of hypovirulent strains, except they maintained their natural orange color rather than turning white, as did the hypovirulent strains from Europe. In a matter of three to four years, North America had gone from discovering the hypovirulent research of Europe, to determining the cause of hypovirulence, to finding native hypovirulent strains just slightly outside the natural range of the American chestnut tree. Enthusiasm had returned to American chestnut tree research.

Blighted but surviving American chestnut tree at Grand Haven, Michigan. Hypovirulent strains of Cryphonectria parasitica *were isolated from cankers on trees at this site.*

The Connecticut researchers and others came to Michigan to see what was happening with American chestnut. Here they found a few people informally linked and dedicated to finding all of Michigan's chestnut trees that were scattered around the state and determining their health. Taken from small stand to stand, the researchers found the chestnut stands to be like islands of chestnut biomass surrounded by farms, towns, and native vegetation. A small stand could consist of one to one thousand trees, including mixtures of chestnut species. Most of these stands appeared to have started near old farmhouses, perhaps as a few trees planted as small orchards that had naturalized into forests. Most were in western Michigan, and the most famous and largest recovering stand was the Grand Haven stand. At the Grand Haven site, the researchers found extremely old and large American chestnuts with dead tops, victims of blight in the 1960s. But the death stopped one-third of the way down the trunk, and branches and sprouts high in the trees were growing up through the dead, gray, concretelike stems of the hundred-year-old giants. Surely, none of this would have ever been observed if not for the decay-resistance of the tree providing the infrastructure on which the new growth could live. The younger trees in the stand were also suffering from the throes of blight, but there were plenty of signs of nonlethal cankers throughout the stand. The owner of the stand, George Unger, noticed the trees were recovering, and he noticed the change in the cankers during the 1960s. Given a chance, he would speak about how the trees would fight back and about the tree where he first noticed it. He called that tree his "fighter." Unger's description was not very far off the mark. Unfortunately, we will never be able to fully appreciate what ultimately might have been, as a housing development now occupies much of the land where the recovering chestnuts once lived.

From these and other Michigan trees, Connecticut researchers isolated orange, hypovirulent strains and added them to their hypovirulent strain mixture containing European hypovirulent strains. This mixture or "cocktail" of hypovirulent strains was placed on a planting of young American chestnut trees at the Connecticut Agricultural Experiment Station. Amazingly, these trees are still alive today, with callusing and gnarled bark, right in the heart of chestnut blight country, some still on their original stems. At first, the survival of this planting was not that impressive, because after all, this is what everyone expected would happen. But with the passing of three decades, and now with a better understanding of the limitations of hypovirulence, these trees represent an unparalleled early achievement in chestnut blight research in North America. Mankind finally did something about chestnut blight on American chestnut trees that a few years previous would have been thought impossible.

Mankind finally did something about chestnut blight on American chestnut trees that a few years previous would have been thought impossible.

When the blight fungus is isolated from these trees, the strains recovered are frequently hypovirulent, contain dsRNA, and are orange, not white, perhaps indicating that the basis of biological control at that site may be from the Michigan portion of the hypovirulent strain cocktail. Such a mixture is truly complex, but it demonstrates the importance of the dsRNA in the equation. What is this dsRNA that turns the cultures hypovirulent, and is there a difference between the European and the Michigan dsRNA?

The dsRNA molecule causing hypovirulence in *C. parasitica* is the chromosome of a group of fungal viruses. Generally speaking, viruses are nonliving molecules of genetic information that hijack the genetic and biochemistry machinery of the cells they infect. All organisms on earth have viruses, and that viruses exist in *C. parasitica* is not surprising. But these viruses were different. A typical virus has a chromosome surrounded by a protein coat. The proteins that make up the coat, while made inside the hijacked cell from the cell's own molecular makeup, are placed there on orders from genes carried on the chromosome of the virus. The viruses causing hypovirulence in *C. parasitica* have no protein coat; they are naked dsRNA chromosomes. By definition, a virus had to have a protein coat. But not these. In fact, this was the first group of viruslike molecules without a protein coat to be called a virus.

Today there are three recognized viruses, now called hypoviruses, that cause hypovirulence in *C. parasitica.* Overall, these viruses possess unique aspects that unite them in the hypovirus group, such as they are composed of dsRNA, they all lack a protein coat, they have the ability to replicate and cause hypovirulence in *C. parasitica*, and they have a similar genetic organization. They are separated from each other based on the specific differences found in their genetic makeup—that is, their molecular sequences that compose the dsRNA are very different. These hypoviruses can be divided into three types based on molecular similarities and differences found among them, and it just so happens it is also based on their location of discovery. European hypovirulent strains (hypovirus 1) have been found throughout Europe and in China; a hypovirus isolated from a New Jersey strain (hypovirus 2) appears to be unique to that region; and hypoviruses isolated from Michigan strains (hypovirus 3) found in different recovering stands appear to be related to each other but different from hypoviruses 1 and 2.

There are other features of the hypoviruses of *C. parasitica* that make them different from most viruses. Hypoviruses lack the ability to physically leave the infected host and reinfect another host from the outside world. Without this ability, most of the viruses of the world would cease being scourges, as their epidemic underpinnings would be knocked away. A sneeze, cough, or handshake would no longer suffice in transferring viruses, and some viruses like the common cold would become extinct. Instead of this exit-the-cell and reenter-a-new-cell strategy, hypoviruses infect new strains by transferring from strain to strain through the natural fusions of the pathogen that occur spontaneously when the fungal strains grow together. As a filamentous fungus, *C. parasitica* grows with microscopic threads of cells. Each thread is called a hypha. When these hyphae grow together, cells making up the thread unite, and the cytoplasm of the cells can exchange and hypoviruses can transfer during this time. Once inside the thread, the hypoviruses can take over the entire network of threads that make up the organism we call *C. parasitica.* This process is better referred to as hypovirus transmissibility rather than infection, but the outcome is the same; a new strain now carries the hypovirus.

This process of strain fusion, or anastomosis, is governed by a series of genes found in the fungal chromosome termed vegetative incompatibility genes. The products of these genes can determine which strains of *C. parasitica* can unite and exchange cellular materials, including hypoviruses, and which ones cannot. There are other outcomes, too. Sometimes the genes allow a one-way transfer of hypovirus, and other times they allow for only low levels of transfer. The outcome is that these fungal genes can make the transfer of the hypoviruses problematic, and some researchers believe this may be the single most important factor in the lack of hypovirus dissemination and success in North America. Other scientists believe that this factor is important and may lead to problems, but that overall it is not the major obstacle in the biological control of chestnut blight.

Three categories

To understand hypovirulence and the biological control of chestnut blight in North America, it is important to look at simple successful systems before studying complex ones. In Michigan, as late as the mid-1990s, American chestnut trees could be put in three categories: 1) disease-free escapes; 2) dead and dying from chestnut blight; or, 3) diseased to some extent with chestnut blight but recovering due to the presence of hypovirulent strains. At the beginning of the twenty-first century, almost all the category 1 trees are gone, or at least stands of disease-free trees are gone and they have become category 2 trees. Almost all category 3 trees identified in the late 1970s or early '80s still reside in a category 3 scenario. With the loss of the Grand Haven site, another site on the county road between Manistee and Benzie counties has become the premier site in the state. This site, known as the County Line site, is a site to behold. As blight has waxed and waned at the site throughout the 1970s and '80s, today it is hard to find chestnut blight on these trees. However, it is important to note that not all trees are recovering at this site. One would hardly notice the failures, small sucker-sprouts on stems that have repeatedly died over the last twenty years, for the sight of the larger, successfully protected trees from naturally occurring hypovirulence.

Overall, there are probably twelve sites in Michigan where chestnut blight is at bay due to hypovirulence. The County Line site is the primary site, but trees are surviving elsewhere. While most of the sites where blight-recovering trees can be found are along Lake Michigan, at least one site is located in the center of the state, near Roscommon. Other sites may be represented by only a few trees. For example, on a rural route in south central Michigan, a lone American chestnut tree struggles on the shoulder of the road, squeezed between the asphalt, a weed tree, and mowed lawn. Somehow it is able to withstand assaults from drought, compaction, weeds, weed control, county salt trucks, and chestnut blight.

American chestnut trees at the County Line site, 1985, left; *and 2005,* right.

An American chestnut tree at the County Line, Michigan, site survives chestnut blight because of hypovirulence.

In this case, chestnut blight is the least of its troubles, as hypovirulent strains somehow arrived from some unknown source and somehow protect the tree.

The County Line site is today one of Michigan's most important American chestnut resources, with hundreds of trees growing on about five acres. In the 1970s there were signs of hypovirulence and recovery, but it was not obvious to visitors whether the aggressive form or the hypovirulent form of the blight would predominate. However, today it is obvious that recovery predominates in this stand, and researchers have also determined that there is enough recovery and nut production to sustain this stand and allow naturalization of the tree in this location far from its natural range.

The County Line site is today one of Michigan's most important American chestnut resources, with hundreds of trees growing on about five acres.

In the early 1980s seed was collected by the owners of the stand and planted in two orchardlike rows near the homestead about two miles away. Not surprisingly, chestnut blight infected these trees in the early 1990s. Also not surprisingly, infection in this new stand was caused by the same strain as that down the road, *sans* hypovirus. Today, those planted trees are completely devastated by blight, and some are struggling even to produce sprouts. It is obvious that little protection is granted by the genetics of the tree or the ability of the hypovirulent strains to disseminate two miles in ten years. With family members and researchers moving between the two sites, it seems natural that hypovirulent strains would have reached the secondary site from the County Line site and initiated biological control.

While natural dissemination was somewhat expected and did not occur here, hypovirulence researchers were more proactive in another stand. A well-studied hypovirulent strain of *C. parastica* from the largest Grand Haven tree was taken in 1982 to Crystal Lake in northern Michigan, where a couple thousand American chestnut trees had disseminated from an American chestnut orchard started in 1912. At this stand, naturally occurring cankers first noticed in the late 1970s were treated with the hypovirulent strain from Grand Haven. The hypovirulent strain was placed into holes made in the

Tree at Crystal Lake site with nonlethal cankers twenty years after treatment with a hypovirulent strain from the Grand Haven site.

healthy bark of the trees around the edges of the cankers incited by the aggressive Crystal Lake strains. In short time, the strains would meet within the bark, and the hypovirus of the hypovirulent strain would transfer to the aggressive strain, turning the aggressive strain into a hypovirulent strain. This haphazard procedure was done while other, more scientifically based studies were undertaken on trees in the stand. After data were collected and published on the scientific portion of the studies, the plot was abandoned for nearly two decades. A visit in the mid-1990s did not offer much hope and did not reveal the surprise that that would occur a decade later. A visit in 2006 showed a completely different story. About twenty years after treatment of the cankers ceased in the stand, it is now possible to see tree survival, nonlethal cankers, and the beginnings of recovery. Nonlethal cankers can be found on small as well as large trees, and some portion of the chestnut canopy has remained intact. It is the first time in North America that aggressive forms of the chestnut blight have been impacted by released hypovirulent forms placed in the stand for this purpose. Before this, biological control occurred only where it was found, and creating biological control in other stands had been problematic. This is the first optimistic sign that hypovirulence, when placed in a declining stand, can have a positive influence on chestnut blight. But it took more than ten years for the hypovirulent strains to show their impact.

Another test for determining the effectiveness of hypoviruses in a forest setting, better planned, conceived, and carried out than the Crystal Lake test, was set up in the early 1990s in West Salem, Wisconsin. This stand of about five thousand trees had begun to feel the impact of blight first noticed in the mid-1980s. At first, attempts were made at blight eradication, but blight continued to appear on trees. At that point researchers determined that many of the features of this infection warranted an attempt to manage the trees through the introduction of hypovirulent strains. The West Salem strain—and it was primarily a single strain of the blight responsible for causing most of the infections—was taken to the lab and infected with a Michigan hypovirus and then released in the stand. Three years later, the West Salem strain was infected with an Italian hypovirus and released in the stand. For six years, every canker on every infected tree was treated, when possible. But this treatment affected just one small portion of the thousands of trees, and soon blight had spread faster and farther than researchers could treat. Watching the aggressive form of the blight move through the trees may have been reminiscent of being in the Appalachian Mountains when chestnut blight was at its most destructive. Different attempts were made in different ways as new ideas or new data suggested better approaches. Treatments were halted and then started again a few years later when it was determined that treated trees were actually faring better than untreated trees. In other words, trees treated with hypovirulent strains appeared to be showing more nonlethal cankers than untreated trees. It was hoped that the hypovirus would not only move from canker to canker on treated trees, but also jump to other nearby untreated trees and provide protection for them. In the course of these studies, dissemination from tree to tree was not occurring as fast as dissemination within a tree.

Treatment was not the only gauge of success. Of those trees treated, many died to the base and began sprouting; but it is obvious that some have survived and have begun to show nonlethal cankers under their thick bark. Unfortunately, when the many trees that were never treated and died are added to the trees that were treated and did not recover, a resounding number of dead and dying trees (most with sucker shoots) can be found at West Salem. But some believe that subtle changes are beginning to occur at West Salem, and that these changes are starting where trees were first treated in the early 1990s. At this site, visitors will see large American chestnut trees living in spite of infection by chestnut blight.

There are still more questions than answers regarding the mysterious nature of hypovirulence and chestnut recovery.

Obviously, optimism exists for the sucker sprouts growing from the base of the dead and dying trees. These sprouts will grow in a different blight scenario from that of their parents. These sprouts are subjected to aggressive blight strains raining on them from the bark of the surrounding large infected trees, but there are hypoviruses lurking in the recesses of the nonlethal cankers. Given another ten to twenty years, the blight scenario may appear very different than it does today.

There are still more questions than answers regarding the mysterious nature of hypovirulence and chestnut recovery. For example, if vegetative incompatibility among *C. parastica* strains is the primary reason recovery has not occurred in the natural range of the chestnut forest, why have so many treated chestnut trees died in West Salem, where there is only one primary type of infection, and incompatibility was not at play? What does time have to do with treatment and recovery? For example, if it takes twenty years for hypovirulence to become established before trees begin recovery, what would a stand in the Appalachian Mountains look like when compared to Michigan? Michigan trees are not outcompeted by faster-growing trees such as yellow poplar. Overall, where hypovirulence has been naturally established, it appears to be successful in reducing the impact of chestnut blight on two continents. Where hypovirulence has been released, the outcomes have been mixed. One thing is certain: in the first part of the twentieth century, the facts showed that an aggressive fungal pathogen had entered the continent and infected American chestnut tree bark and the certain predictable outcome was death, while today the outcome is less predictable, especially when hypovirulent strains are involved. Only time will tell if hypovirulence will have a true impact on chestnut blight in North America, or if it becomes just another magic elixir with promises unfulfilled. ~

Evil Tendencies Cancel

By Robert Frost

Will the blight end the chestnut?
The farmers rather guess not.
It keeps smoldering at the roots
And sending up new shoots
Till another parasite
Shall come to end the blight.

Blighted American chestnut with chickadees and lichen. Illustration by Susan Bull Riley.

I was chasing some cows that busted out of a pasture and [I] got into conversation with a farmer. He showed me a chestnut tree [sprout]. . . . He told me about the blight that wiped out the forests all over New England. I thought it would be good to go study and do something about it.

—Fred Hebard

A row of young seedlings at The American Chestnut Foundation's Wagner Research Farm in Meadowview, southwestern Virginia.

THE FOUNDATION AND BEYOND

My hope is to see Appalachian mountainsides look snow-covered on the Fourth of July.

—Fred Hebard

Meadowview Dream

By James Ulring

On a beautiful fall day in 1991 I made my first trip to the Chestnut Foundation's "new" farm. Fred Hebard had spent the last two years trying to make plantings on the old pastured clay hill near the interstate. I could see Phil Rutter's vision as we surveyed the landscape with the view of Mount Rogers to the south and the rolling highlands of the Cumberland north and west. Fred faithfully drove his rusty 1952 8N Ford tractor up and down the hillsides, pulling his broken boom sprayer and his 200-gallon watering device made from an old milk holding tank salvaged from an abandoned farm.

Fred scowled and grumbled, though his eyes twinkled while he told me of his dreams for this brushy hillside. We walked down to his leaky hundred-year-old barn, the siding boards so wide apart that the barn swallows could fly between them in places, busy feeding their young, rather than through the old barn door. As we stood outside that barn Fred told of a small piece of his vision for Meadowview and TACF. He also tried to explain some details of breeding, but the only part I remember is him telling about walking up high on the side of Mount Rogers where the chestnut stumps litter the mountainside. He searched for seedlings to cross with his early plantings. Leaving that little farm the first time I came away enchanted with that little clay hill and that twinkle in the eye of one dedicated scientist and his dream for TACF.

Two years later I returned to that place to find a newer used tractor parked at the farm. A weathered sign announced to the world our vision. A small group of chestnut dreamers gathered for our annual meeting. My wife sold the first chestnut T-shirts and coffee mugs, and the foundation was excited about our $200 profit.

Hundreds and hundreds of magic little trees were covering the brushy clay hillside.

Fred had worked miracles. Hundreds and hundreds of magic little trees were covering the brushy clay hillside. Fred's victories and defeats were enthusiastically described as we tromped over the ground. Fred grumbled and lamented about his antiquated equipment and the dirt-poor situation of TACF. But that twinkle in his eye seemed brighter as he told his story to the new chestnut enthusiasts. The dream had grown, and even though he had told the story countless times, I relished hearing it again. We walked back down that hill admiring those beautiful little trees. The sun broke through on the top of Mount Rogers, giving us an afternoon show as the low-angle light glowed with the red and oranges of the fall.

Now when I travel to Fred's four farms, I laugh at those early days. I smile when I recall some of Fred's frantic calls. The time we argued over that last $1,000 for Fred's first real tractor and again when he convinced me that the Price Farm would work for our mutual dream. I told him the foundation couldn't afford his dreams but agreed we had to have the land. It took many calls and visits to cobble together enough land so Fred could continue his science. Those many trips made me fall in love with the beautiful Cumberland highland. And I am so thankful this place chose us for the birth of the chestnut's future.

The chestnut people have seen the twinkle in Fred's eye. The tough farmer/scientist has brought the dreams of thousands of chestnut lovers to life on one hundred acres at the base of Mount Rogers. I think if the mountains were alive as the Cherokee believe, they smile every day at his accomplishment.

A crop of chestnut seedlings at Meadowview.

Burnham Relights the Torch

Charles Burnham: His Breeding Program and The American Chestnut Foundation

By William Lord

According to those who knew him, Charles R. Burnham was an inveterate investigator. When not problem-solving with colleagues, he was absorbed like Archimedes in silent conversations with his brain. Born in 1904 on a farm in Wisconsin, he had enough of the rural grind by the time he reached his teens and prepared instead for the more stimulating realm of teaching and research. He earned all his degrees, including his doctorate, at the University of Wisconsin, majoring in genetics with a minor in plant pathology. His academic assignments took him to Cornell, Harvard, the University of Missouri, West Virginia University, and the California Institute of Technology. In 1938 he became a staff member of the Department of Agronomy and Plant Genetics at the University of Minnesota, where he remained for most of his career, up to and beyond his retirement in 1972. During his lifetime he developed improved varieties of corn, beans, flax, wheat, barley, and tomatoes and published over sixty scientific articles on such botanical subjects as disease resistance, male sterility, gene mapping, and breeding.

Retirement with a pipe and a TV set was something no one would dare suggest. Burnham had too much going and couldn't let go. In recognition of his achievements and his current studies, the university gave him an office to employ his energy free of administrative duties. This was his kind of retirement. He could chat with former students dropping by and keep tabs on his one-and-a-half-acre summer corn nursery. And he could also go into the lobby and check what was new on the bulletin board. This he did one day in December 1980, when an article caught his interest. It was entitled, "Prospects for the American Chestnut in the Upper Mississippi Valley."

He took the article home to read over the holidays. He learned that the breeding program of the United States Department of Agriculture had not been successful in producing a blight-resistant American chestnut. In his own words, "Why not? What happened?"

The federal program had ceased around 1960, but Burnham managed to gather information from government records and from persons who had worked on the endeavor. Lack of success had not been due to lack of effort. Starting in 1911 at the National Agricultural Research Center northeast of Washington, thousands of hybrid crosses had been made between the different species of chestnut, primarily the Japanese, the Chinese, and the American. The Japanese and Chinese trees were resistant to the blight but did not grow tall enough to produce timber. The American was a timber tree, but it was susceptible to the blight. The researchers' goal had not been to produce a blight-resistant American chestnut, but rather to develop, using any combination of chestnut species, a tree that would be blight resistant and also be a timber-type tree. A similar program had been begun in 1929 by Arthur H. Graves in Connecticut. Unfortunately, not one tree was produced with the desired characteristics.

In developing improved varieties of food crops, Burnham had applied with great success a system of plant breeding known as backcrossing; the method is used to transfer a single hereditary trait among interbreeding species. Burnham and a cadre of chestnut devotees commenced to put a backcross plan to work on the American chestnut.

The backcross method is actually fairly straightforward. As presented by Burnham, it involves a minimum of six generations and begins by pollinating the female flowers of a blight-resistant Chinese chestnut with the pollen from a blight-susceptible American chestnut. This produces a hybrid (termed F_1, the first-generation hybrid) with half its genes from the Chinese parent and half from the American parent. Blight resistance in the hybrid is intermediate between that of the two parent trees.

All trees are hand pollinated and bagged to guarantee the identity of the progeny.

In the next step, the Chinese-American hybrid is crossed with pollen from an American chestnut—thus a cross "back" (backcross) to the American. This will increase the percentage of American chestnut genes in the second generation. The blight resistance in the second-generation trees ranges from the intermediate resistance of the first-generation hybrid to the lack of resistance of the American. When trees of this first backcross (BC_1) grow sufficiently, usually in about five years, they are intentionally infected with the blight, and only the most resistant are selected. Trees are also selected that promise to grow straight and tall like the timber-producing American.

After the first hybrid generation, the backcross breeding procedure is conducted for a total of three additional generations, producing trees with intermediate resistance and greatly increased American chestnut traits. Pollen from a variety of American chestnut trees is used to prevent inbreeding.

Charles Burnham, upper left, was a postdoctoral student in his mid-twenties studying corn cytogenetics when this photo was taken at Cornell University in 1929. Marcus Rhoades, standing next to Burnham, and George Beadle (with dog), were graduate students of Dr. R. A. Emerson (in cap), head of the Cornell Department of Plant Breeding and Genetics. At right is Barbara McClintock, who taught Burnham, Rhoades, and Beadle how to work with chromosomes. McClintock and Beadle both won a Nobel Prize in Medicine. (Courtesy of Richard Zeyen, University of Minnesota.)

Trees of the third backcross are then interpollinated, producing the fifth generation. A small percentage of the fifth generation will have the blight resistance of the original Chinese ancestor and the tall, timber production of the American.

Trees of the fifth generation are intercrossed and, according to plan, will produce an abundance of blight-resistant, timber-type chestnut. The trees will be almost pure American.

Burnham traveled the country seeking suitable trees to begin his project. He acquired pollen from Chinese-American hybrids in Indiana and Tennessee and crossed them with American chestnut at the University of Minnesota. His associate, Philip Rutter, used the pollen on isolated American chestnut in northern Iowa. Nuts from these crosses were planted at Oberlin College, Ohio. Hopes that this site would be an excellent proving ground for the backcross method were dashed when the college removed the trees to install a parking lot.

Fortunately, Burnham was pursuing other sources. He contacted Richard Jaynes at the Connecticut Agricultural Experiment Station. Jaynes, at the beginning of his career in plant breeding, had worked at the station with Arthur Graves (1879–1962), with whom he coauthored the 1963 bulletin "Connecticut Chestnut Hybrids and their Culture."

Burnham was on the trail of the famous Clapper tree. It was produced by pollinating a Chinese-American hybrid with pollen from an American chestnut. It was, therefore, a first backcross and a tree of the second of Burnham's required six generations. It was one of many thousand hopefuls bred by Russell B. Clapper of the USDA in 1946. It was transplanted with a group of other seedling hopefuls in the Crab Orchard National Wildlife Refuge in southern Illinois in 1949. For a time it promised to be a prototype for a blight-resistant timber-type tree. However, blight was first noted on it in 1968, and the tree died in 1977. Jaynes had acquired scions of the Clapper in 1963 and grafted them to Chinese trees in Connecticut. Three grafts were viable and producing pollen. Clapper pollen was used by several participating breeders at locations in Minnesota, Iowa, Virginia, and West Virginia.

Trees of the fifth generation are intercrossed and, according to plan, will produce an abundance of blight-resistant, timber-type chestnut. The trees will be almost pure American.

As their work progressed, the vexing but necessary need for adequate funding had to be addressed. Rutter proposed that a chestnut foundation be established. With the help of Donald Willeke, a Minneapolis lawyer with an active interest in trees and the chestnut, The American Chestnut Foundation was established in 1983 in Washington, D.C.

In 1989 Fred Hebard, the foundation's newly hired pathologist, visited the Connecticut Agricultural Experiment Station and obtained scions and pollen from the Clapper and from the Mahogany, also a first-generation backcross, developed by Arthur Graves. Hebard benefited from the help and cooperation of Sandra Anagnostakis, who currently heads the Connecticut station's science program, continuing the tradition of Graves and Jaynes.

The Clapper and Mahogany trees provided a jump start to the breeding program initiated at the Wagner farm in Meadowview, Virginia, in 1989. ∾

Some Advice for Breeding Blight Resistance into American Chestnuts

By Norman E. Borlaug

As a farm boy in Iowa, born in 1914, Norman E. Borlaug learned firsthand what disease and drought can do to crops, sparking an early interest in agricultural improvement. From the one-room rural school that his father and grandfather had attended, he went on to flunk the entrance exam at the University of Minnesota. After remedial work at the University's General College, Borlaug received degrees in forestry and plant pathology as well as awards in wrestling (he was inducted into the National Collegiate Wrestling Hall of Fame in 1993).

In 1944 Dr. Borlaug went to Mexico, where he started Mexico's first Little League to entertain his two children while he worked on wheat. His aim was to increase and improve the world's food supply so that "no one shall lack bread." At that time the average annual wheat yield in Mexico was 11.25 bushels per acre and Mexico imported some ten million more bushels to feed its people. In 1961, after Dr. Borlaug had bred a high-yield wheat variety resistant to rust and adapted to arid soils, the average yield was 28.5 bushels per acre and Mexico was self-sufficient in wheat. India, Pakistan, and other developing countries soon followed Mexico's—and Dr. Borlaug's—example.

The results of Dr. Borlaug's work are known as the "Green Revolution." Although some environmentalists decry its dependence on irrigation and petroleum-based fertilizers, few dispute that the Green Revolution has saved, by some estimates, as many as a billion people from starving to death. Dr. Borlaug has received innumerable honors, including the Nobel Peace Prize in 1970.

The following short essay includes technical advice on backcrossing chestnut trees that was not written with the lay reader in mind, but Dr. Borlaug's hard-won expertise and unflagging optimism come through clearly.

During the Great Depression of the 1930s, I would periodically leave my university studies to work and earn money to finance my education. In 1935 I was working in Massachusetts for the U.S. Forest Service, supervising some men in the Civilian Conservation Corps, the federal program to employ destitute young men on national forest projects. Many of the people who came to work were starving. I saw how food changed them, and it left scars on me. It was the beginning of my understanding that the first essential component of social justice is adequate food, an understanding that has been fortified by more than half a century of experience in some of the poorest, hungriest areas of the world.

In 1936, again in Massachusetts, I was in charge of mapping and taking the registration inventory on the Hopkins Memorial Forest of the Northeastern Forest Experiment Station (now a field station for Williams College's Center for Environmental Studies). The blight was killing the last chestnuts, and I saw some of them dying, but was too young and inexperienced at that time to really understand the implications. But as I continued my studies in the 1940s, and especially when I studied forest pathology and later plant pathology, I came to realize what a disaster I had witnessed in those early years. In some ways, chestnuts had been nearly as important as grain to poor people in American rural areas and represented a significant amount of food security.

After shifting my career from forestry to genetics and plant pathology, I have spent most of my career breeding wheat, for high grain yield, broad ecological adaptation and resistance to diseases—especially against the rust fungi (three species of *Puccinia*). Having worked in innumerable countries around the world, I have come to appreciate the great genetic variation in pathogens that attack our crops and forest trees. For that reason, I am especially fascinated by the work TACF is doing.

In some ways, chestnuts had been nearly as important as grain to poor people in American rural areas and represented a significant amount of food security.

I would like to make a few comments on the TACF breeding program that I hope might be helpful. Based on my long experience in backcrossing to control various diseases of wheat, while at the same time trying to improve grain yield and agronomic characteristics such as adaptability to soil and climate, I have come to realize that by growing a large population of F_1 plants of the second backcross (BC_2), and selecting vigorously in the progeny for the morphologic phenotype of the recurrent commercial parent with resistance to the disease you are breeding for, you can skew the selection more rapidly back towards the morphologic phenotype of the recurrent parent than if it is done at random, in which case you will probably need to use BC_3 or BC_4.

If this procedure is followed, and if a large number of F_1 seeds of the second backcross are used, I think that you can greatly save on the land required for "out-plantings" and at the same time make more rapid progress in obtaining good blight resistance in forest phenotypes similar to those of the native American chestnut. If this procedure is followed in the BC_2 generation, rather than carried on to BC_3 and BC_4, a large percentage of those seedlings in the last backcross (BC_2) will be within the acceptable morphologic traits of the native American chestnut.

I would urge that you inoculate aggressively all segregating populations with *Cryphonectria parasitica* (the chestnut blight) inoculum taken from infected sprouts from as many different parts of the range of the American chestnut as possible. Incorporating the genetic variation within the pathogen itself into your program will help you build a more long-lasting resistance to the possibility of mutations within the blight organism.

Since your breeding program is using more than one species as a source of resistance—Japanese and possibly European chestnut as well as Chinese—I suggest you attempt to make a few crosses between the different F_1 single crosses.

Norman Borlaug, father of the Green Revolution and winner of the Nobel Peace Prize. (Photo courtesy of the family.)

The second point which I would like to make is that once you have a few outstanding seedlings identified in the second backcross (BC_2) with good resistance to *Cryphonectria* in acceptable morphologic makeup, I would suggest that some vegetative cuttings or clones be tested for their scope of resistance in the several areas of the original home of the chestnut blight pathogens, namely China or Korea. That will be where the greatest variation of the pathogen exists.

I feel quite confident if a concerted effort is made that satisfactory arrangements can be made for such testing in the People's Republic of China, where you are likely to have good collaboration. If you encounter problems in making arrangements for such testing, perhaps I can serve as an intermediary, since I have been working in cereal production and disease problems in the People's Republic of China for more than twenty-five years.

When the Nobel Peace Prize Committee designated me the recipient of the 1970 award for my contribution to the "green revolution," they were in effect, I believe, selecting an individual to symbolize the vital role of agriculture and food production in a world that is hungry, both for bread and for peace. I was but one member of a vast team made up of many organizations, officials, thousands of scientists, and millions of farmers. Similarly, I expect that there are many people from many different backgrounds that are collaborating with you in this adventure. All are to be congratulated for the progress that has been achieved and for the continuing vision of full success. ❧

The Creation of The American Chestnut Foundation

By Donald C. Willeke

Donald Willeke is the founding director, first vice president for science, secretary, and general counsel of The American Chestnut Foundation.

The American Chestnut Foundation formally began when its articles of incorporation were signed in Minneapolis, Minnesota, on June 22, 1983 (a date that one of its founding directors and general counsel remembers, because it is his birthday), but it existed in spirit before that. The foundation was essentially a Minnesota creation, like so many other progressive efforts in the United States. Over the years, the foundation has matured and largely moved back into the original range of the American chestnut, but it should never be forgotten that it was Minnesota visionaries who created the foundation.

The effort was started by Dr. Charles Burnham, retired University of Minnesota professor of agronomy and plant genetics, a corn geneticist who participated in the development of hybrid corn in the 1920s. Burnham had been interested in chestnuts for years as a part of his larger work in breeding crop plants. On his own, he had done some limited breeding of chestnut trees, and some of the specially bred nuts he produced had been planted out at several college sites. One of Burnham's former students was Dr. Norman Borlaug, who received the Nobel Peace Prize in 1970—probably the world's most prestigious award—for his work in creating the movement known as the Green Revolution. Using improved crop seeds and farming methods developed by Borlaug, China, India and other areas of the world greatly increased their agricultural production and nearly eradicated famines. Burnham and Borlaug met one day in the 1970s and were reviewing technical literature on the work done by the U.S. Department of Agriculture in the 1920s and 1930s to try to develop a blight-resistant American chestnut. The USDA scientists had crossed American and Chinese trees, and upon observing that the 50-50 offspring were not as blight resistant as their Chinese parents, they recrossed the offspring to Chinese. Predictably, they ended up with a tree that was 75 percent or more "Chinese," and thus it grew like the shorter Chinese trees, not like the majestic, rapid-growing American chestnut trees.

The effort was started by Dr. Charles Burnham, retired University of Minnesota professor of agronomy and plant genetics, a corn geneticist who participated in the development of hybrid corn in the 1920s.

Burnham and Borlaug, in working with grain plants with desirable characteristics but also a fatal flaw, had learned to proceed differently. They would "outcross" once to a related plant without the flaw and then repeatedly "backcross" to the desirable plant, while in each generation choosing only those progeny that clearly had the desirable genetic material. That way, after selecting the best plants from several successive generations of backcrosses, they would have plants with most of the characteristics of the desirable but flawed plant while also incorporating genetic material that eliminated or defeated the fatal flaw. These plants—of the third or higher backcross generations—would then be crossed with one another to produce even higher levels of genetic protection against the fatal flaw, and the two saw no reason that chestnut plants should not be treated in the same manner; indeed, Borlaug noted, the American chestnut is the grain that grows on trees, because of its huge production of grainlike starchy nuts.

Philip Rutter, a tree genetics researcher in southern Minnesota, had also been a student and friend of Dr. Burnham's, and they worked together to make a number of crosses of Chinese-American hybrids back to pure American trees, and outplanted these trees on various sites at several universities and parklands. Unfortunately, many of these plantings were lost over the years because the land belonged to others, who had no special interest in the American chestnut.

By 1982 Burnham had been retired from the University of Minnesota for years and was in his eighties, although still extremely active. Borlaug was busy with the operation and management of the International Wheat and Maize Institute in Mexico, and Rutter was involved in the running of his research company. But all three were concerned that work go forward on the American chestnut tree in line with the conclusions they had reached and were worried that traditional university and governmental research facilities were not suited to undertake long-term tree-breeding projects. So Rutter asked several other distinguished Minnesota-based scientists to meet with him and Burnham to discuss what could be done to provide a "lasting framework" for chestnut breeding.

The group concluded that the American chestnut could be restored, but that any approach had to be long-term.

The Minnesota scientists began meeting at the St. Paul campus of the University of Minnesota to talk about a larger vision of restoring the American chestnut to its position of primacy in the forests of the eastern United States of America. In addition to Burnham and Rutter, the founding group included Dr. David French, the chairman of the Department of Plant Pathology at the university; Dr. Ronald Phillips, professor of agronomy and plant genetics at the university (and later senior scientific adviser to the U.S. Department of Agriculture); Dr. H. B. "Budd" Tordoff, head of the university's Bell Museum of Natural History; Dr. Harold Pellet of the Minnesota Landscape Arboretum; and Minneapolis attorney Donald C. Willeke, who served as chair of the National and Minnesota Urban Forest Councils and as president of American Forests.

The group concluded that the American chestnut could be restored, but that any approach had to be long-term. After conferring with Rutter, Willeke suggested the creation of a nonprofit corporation with perpetual existence; such a corporation could acquire funding, purchase or lease land for research, and carry on chestnut breeding and reintroduction into the nation's forests over the time span of a century or more needed to produce lasting results. Rutter suggested that a nonprofit organization could seek "citizen members"—Willeke became the first nonscientist member—who would not only care about restoring the American chestnut but could help finance it.

In these meetings, Rutter and Burnham initially projected that it might take from 1982 to about 2040 to get to the point of intercrossing the best of the third backcross generations. As it turned out, Rutter and his successors were able to compress the time frame to the point where the intercrosses of the third backcross generations were being made in 2005 and thereafter. They accomplished this remarkable and happy success by getting trees in the breeding program to flower at a very young age, especially when grown in full sun on fertile soil.

The American Chestnut Foundation was incorporated with the stated goal of "restoration of the American chestnut" and with the following original board of directors in addition to Rutter, Willeke, and Drs. Burnham, Borlaug, French, Pellet, Phillips, and Tordoff: Dr. R. A. Blanchette, University of Minnesota forest pathologist; Dr. Richard Jaynes, horticulturist at the Connecticut Agricultural Experiment Station; Dr. S. Kirkwood, University of Minnesota biochemist; Dr. D. J. Merrell, University of Minnesota ecologist and behavioral biologist; Dr. Carl A. Mohn, University of Minnesota forest geneticist; and Geoffrey Barnard, director of the Minnesota Nature Conservancy.

At its first meeting, the foundation's board elected Rutter president, Burnham vice president, Willeke secretary, and French treasurer. Burnham contributed $5,000 of his own money to commence the operation, and Rutter undertook the grueling multiple roles of chief plant breeder, administrator, fund-raiser, and seeker of additional supporting members. Burnham was elected senior scientific adviser and chair of the scientific steering committee.

The foundation's board met throughout 1983 and 1984 and struggled with every foundation's problem of raising funds. Rutter and Burnham continued their backcross breeding efforts, in some cases using material that Jaynes and others had previously created. In April 1984 Dr. Paul Read of the University of Minnesota was added to the board (and became president of the foundation some years later), as was Dr. Cameron Gundersen, M.D., of the Gundersen Clinic in La Crosse, Wisconsin.

The foundation's first annual meeting was held at the Minnesota Landscape Arboretum on September 22, 1984. The meeting featured an address by Burnham on his theories for "establishing the genetic material for blight resistance in a hybrid tree which otherwise has substantially all of the characteristics of the American chestnut," and Pellett conducted a tour of the American chestnut plantings at the arboretum. The minutes record that "such was the enthusiasm of the participants in the tour that a substantial downpour did not prevent them from examining the Arboretum's chestnut trees." Also at that meeting, Dr. William MacDonald of the University of West Virginia, an authority on the hypovirulence phenomenon that can debilitate the chestnut blight fungus, was added to the board. MacDonald later served faithfully for about twenty years as the foundation's treasurer.

Rutter proposed the establishment of state chapters at the foundation's board meeting on November 16, 1984. But the foundation's scientific and financial reach in those earlier days clearly exceeded its grasp, as French's treasurer's report from April 19, 1985, showed: the balance of funds was $4,148.12.

In September 1985 Dr. Albert Ellingboe of the University of Wisconsin was added to the board, and when Burnham retired as senior scientific adviser, Ellingboe was elected to succeed him and has served in that position to the present time. Dr. Borlaug addressed the 1985 annual meeting on the subject of "Tree Breeding–Challenges and Opportunities."

The year 1986 saw the creation of the *Journal of The American Chestnut Foundation*, and the first several issues were typed by hand by the foundation's secretary and general counsel. By that year the foundation's budget had grown to $26,400, with $11,200 of that designated for funding scientific research. But the directors that year received a report that the foundation's plantings at Oberlin College in Ohio "can only be termed a disaster," so they searched for ways that the foundation could own and control its own planting sites. Also in 1986, visits by President Rutter, Secretary Willeke, and Director Gundersen were made to what the directors' minutes record as the "very remarkable West Salem, Wisconsin, site, where a large quantity of blight-free American chestnuts of every size . . . are growing in an ecosystem which is obviously expanding and covering more than a square mile in area." Finally, in 1986, Dr. Dennis Fulbright of Michigan State University, like MacDonald an expert on hypovirulence, was added to the board, and so was Dr. Mark Widrlechner, a plant geneticist at Iowa State University.

A historic action was taken by the board at its meeting in February 1987, when it resolved "that The American Chestnut Foundation adopt as a long range goal the establishment of a National Chestnut Research Center, to be located within the central part of the old range of the American chestnut, with facilities for research, preservation of chestnut genetic material, and a library of . . . material relating to chestnuts."

Field work at Meadowview.

Planting time at TACF's Price Farm in Meadowview. (Photo by Fred Hebard.)

But that same year the board received a report from President Rutter that chestnut blight had been found in the remarkable West Salem, Wisconsin, stand.

In 1988, through the hard work of Rutter, and through his multiple contacts, Jennifer and Cheri Wagner and Jennifer's husband, General Robert Vessey (former chairman of the Joint Chiefs of Staff and a Minnesota native), offered the foundation a long-term lease on their family farm in Meadowview, Virginia, to serve as the foundation's research center and to be a memorial to the Wagners' mother. The thirty-year lease on the Wagner Research Farm was signed early in 1989 and contained an option to purchase the land. But even before that, in November 1988, a young scientist from the Department of Plant Pathology of the University of Kentucky, Dr. Fred Hebard, heard about the agreement and wrote a letter applying to be the foundation's "resident researcher" so that he could continue his work of fifteen years' standing on chestnut blight and chestnut breeding. The foundation agreed to hire him at a "half time" rate, although his pay was considerably less than half time; and Hebard, like Rutter, made great sacrifices for the foundation in its early years.

In April 1989 Rutter drove from Minnesota to the Wagner Research Farm and brought with him many young chestnut trees for planting. Cold weather forced him to bring the plants into his motel room on the journey, but they arrived safely, and research on breeding a blight-resistant chestnut began in earnest in Meadowview. The official groundbreaking occurred on April 15, and, as the saying goes, the rest is history.

So . . . from 1989 onward, the Minnesota origins of the foundation slowly gave way to the foundation's robust and productive growth within the original range of the American chestnut. But the vision of the Minnesota founders of The American Chestnut Foundation still nurtures the foundation's strong Minnesota roots, and those roots are sure to be the basis for glorious harvests in the years to come. ~

The Beginnings of TACF

By Philip A. Rutter

The author is the founding president of The American Chestnut Foundation.

Origins are fascinating to me. As an evolutionary ecologist, though, I have to tell you I usually also find them complex and confused. Where is the beginning of this thread? Pull a little, and it usually just gets longer. With knots and tangles in it.

The furthest back I can trace the origin of the foundation is to my own first experience with gigantic trees. That was Muir Woods—a stand of primordial coast redwoods just north of San Francisco, and a National Monument. I was about eight years old. I was given some time to be entirely alone with them—to look, and to climb inside some of the fire-hollowed creatures. That they were alive, just like me, was completely obvious to me. I was awed, and made permanently aware of the intense life, and majesty, of great trees.

The next knot in the thread came only a little later, while visiting my uncle Homer and aunt Ruth on the shores of Lake Erie. The new farmhouse they'd built, solid and idiosyncratic, had a huge living room, with my aunt's baby grand piano seeming tiny in one corner. It was entirely paneled with this weird but beautiful wood, full of wormholes. Acres of wormy chestnut paneling, it seemed. I asked, and my uncle told me the story for the first time. I was nine years old, I think, and all that paneling had come from logs killed in the blight decades earlier, but taken from this farm to the mill only the year before. More awe, and I knew my father had grown up here, had seen these trees still alive, and seen them die. More permanent awareness, and a new permanent sense of loss.

Next knot: college, and the serious study of ecology, and evolution, and their slow, complex interactions. This was a field that was just emerging at the time, "hot," and fascinating. What I learned about how species respond to disasters, or "evolutionary bottlenecks"—a disease or other catastrophe so dire that it threatens the continuance of the species—made me aware that something in the American chestnut story did not add up. What we knew almost had to be a wrong answer. For a species so strong, so abundant, to be driven to extinction by a fungal pathogen—*should not happen.* All kinds of organisms, from bacteria to bats, have ways of dealing evolutionarily with disaster. All the species alive on the face of the Earth *have* coped successfully with many similar challenges to their existence. If they hadn't, we'd be sitting on an empty planet. An event like the chestnut blight, where a population of four billion robust individuals could not answer a simple fungus, is not impossible; but it should be incredibly rare. Maybe it could happen once in a million years. That rare. The power of evolution to answer such threats is enormous—complex and layered, and *virtually always* successful, given time for the processes to work. The probabilities, then, were: either we've just witnessed an astonishingly rare event, or something in our understanding of the problem was very, very wrong. For me, the problem did not go away. The chestnut was already too personal a disaster. The inconsistencies sat in the back of my brain, and nagged.

Then there is a long stretch of smooth thread. The next tangle in it finds me on my knees in my garden, looking up at my longtime friend, teacher, adviser—intellectual soul mate—Dr. Philip Regal. At this point in my life I'd decided that the university was not for me. Though I was within a year of receiving my PhD—all the course work done, or doubly done—my wife and I had both come to the conclusion that being professors was not what we wanted. We both left our PhDs and the University of Minnesota and came to our farm in the southeast corner of the state to figure out what happened next in our lives. We weren't very sure.

I was starting, in 1978, to come to the conclusion that what I wanted to do was attempt to pick up the work of J. Russell Smith, author of *Tree Crops: A Permanent Agriculture*. That book was among the most important foundations of "agroforestry"; I've met few scientists in the field who didn't get their inspiration there. Smith was a brilliant and keen observer, and a powerful writer. But he was not a biologist, at all. He was a geographer, and a self-taught anthropologist. Most of his work was done in the first years of the twentieth century, before the blossoming of biology brought on by Darwin and Mendel. Reading his book excited me. I could see possibilities he never had, because of the difference in our perspectives. Those possibilities looked enormously promising to me, and they are what I work on now.

Back to that row in my garden. I was already growing hybrid chestnut trees; not particularly attempting to breed blight-resistant American chestnuts, but to breed chestnut trees that were cold-hardy and productive, and useful in North America. Of course they had American genes in them. My own analysis of the genetics of the situation had led me to believe that such a project might be difficult but was certainly not impossible—and I'd made a start.

Regal was standing, looking down. I was kneeling, automatically pulling some weeds in the row, and we were looking at a couple of rows of young hybrid chestnut seedlings, probably about five hundred or so. He was just down from the university for a visit, keeping track of me. He didn't recognize the tree at all and asked, "So what the heck are these, then?"

"Hybrid chestnuts," I said.

"Why?"

That opened the whole can of worms, and I told him my thoughts on chestnut blight resistance genetics.

He said, fairly quickly, "This is crazy! You're not going to believe this, but I know someone else who is working on this problem!" Working on chestnut blight resistance was far from a common enterprise at that time.

Charles Burnham. (Photo courtesy of Richard Zeyen, University of Minnesota.)

Strange and wonderful connections: Regal had once been a roommate, during his grad school days, of Charles Burnham's daughter's future husband. If you can follow that. So although Regal and Burnham mostly resided on different campuses of the U of M at that time, they'd wound up at several informal gatherings together. Both were serious thinkers, genuine scholars—I can see them gravitating toward each other in any crowd. Destiny can be amusingly convoluted. Regal explained to me that Burnham was writing letters about chestnut blight genetics and would talk to whoever would listen. "You wanna talk with him?"

"Of course."

Regal gave Burnham my phone number, and he called. And my life changed. Burnham opened my eyes to an error in the literature: Blight resistance in Chinese trees was stated to be "recessive," but the data in fact showed it was not. Studentlike, I had been accepting their statements; Charles kicked me out of student thought mode forever. We joined forces, finding each other more than congenial, more than compatible. Even if blight resistance had been recessive, breeding could have been done, and I thought the effort would have been worthwhile. But if it were not recessive, then working with it would be much easier.

Where did Charles's own thread start? He was born Russell Charles Burnham, on a farm in Wisconsin. He hated the name Russell, after having his father yell it at him throughout his youth; he would grind the name between his teeth in imitation of his father's bellows. He changed it as soon as he could, swapping first and middle names around. Another legacy of his farm upbringing was his dislike of the name "Charley." "Every old horse in the county is called *Charr-ley*," he would snort. But he never corrected colleagues. I learned because I asked: "What should I call you? It's going to be hard to work this close, eat your food, sleep on your roll-away, cook your lunch, and keep calling you Dr. Burnham."

Most important for the thread: he knew intimately how hard life on an old-fashioned farm could be, and grew up wanting to lighten that load for others. The farm also gave him a keen sense of simple responsibility. You don't shirk the job right in front of you. We shared that principle.

He left Wisconsin for graduate school at Cornell, doing cutting-edge work in the new field of cytogenetics. After that, at one point he had a job in West Virginia, at a time when the chestnut catastrophe was still fresh, still a topic of conversation. He was interested as a scientist, mostly, and somehow was reassured that the USDA had the genetics of breeding a blight-resistant tree well in hand. He moved on.

When he retired, he looked around to see what he might have been missing while focused on corn for so long, and he learned that the chestnut tree had been declared a lost cause. That wasn't right. A wrong answer. He dug deeper, learned some of the details, and was enraged. "What the *&%@ were these #!%& guys DOING all this time! This is a straightforward breeding problem!" It was fun to listen to him rant. He was passionate about the conduct of science, another thing we shared; and it infuriated him to see what he regarded as gross incompetence. And negligence. Charles was a tremendous humanist, as well as a geneticist—something unknown to most people. During all those intense days together, our conversations ranged over all philosophy, I think, and all human problems. It also enraged him that this wonderful tree had been lost—neglected and abandoned without anyone really looking with full scientific rigor at the problem. I miss him.

It was fun to listen to him rant. He was passionate about the conduct of science, another thing we shared; and it infuriated him to see what he regarded as gross incompetence.

We spent more than a year and a half checking the data, the history. I'd steal a few days in a row, come and have a three-day weekend with him, and we'd spend every minute together. We dug through all the libraries in the U of Minnesota; they are vast, diverse, and scattered, and were not computerized at that time. We would split up—"You find this; I'll dig that out." Card files, and brilliant librarians. Then we'd bring each other the gleanings. With his position as an honored professor emeritus, he had access to libraries I could never have gotten into otherwise. At his request, the USDA shipped us all the original plant introduction records on chestnut, and I went through them, card by card, matching old Chinese place names to new ones, mapping them out (tons of complex importations, a tiny percentage of which survived the trip to the U.S.A.). He also had the original plant-breeding records from the USDA chestnut program transferred to us, and we dug through the handwritten notebooks for clues. "Look at this! The @&*$ thing is in CODE, and there's no #*%^ key I can find!" And more calmly the next week: "Did you ever find a key for that section?" No. Much was lost, but we put together what we could.

The day came. We were looking at each other over his tiny kitchen table, in his home. Lunch. Toasted cheese sandwiches, I think. At some point, our eyes met, and we both saw—certainty. For the first time. Believe me, I remember that moment. "We're not crazy." I don't remember which one of us said it. "No, we're not. This could be done." "They messed up. They didn't understand it."

"We could have the chestnut back."

The next knot in the thread came right then. "What now?" "Who's going to *do* this?" And we both thought about it. Charles's first suggestion was, "We could take this to the USDA Forest Service—"

No offense intended to the Forest Service—truly—but I'm afraid I actually laughed at him, right over the toasted cheese. "Charles, you know how much they hate to talk about chestnut. They hate to listen even more. We could have this thing *done* by the time we could get the bureaucracy convinced to fund this. And it's going to take decades, anyway."

He only had to think a moment to admit it; he'd had plenty of run-ins with monolithic bureaucracies. "What, then?" he asked.

In fact, I was prepared for the question. "We have to have an independent organization; one that will survive to do the work; one that will go on working when we're both dead and gone." It didn't take that much convincing, but he was thorough in the thinking process. One of the clinchers was . . . the Pentagon. Yes, the big military office building. It used to be the biggest single building in the world—may still be. Something I learned, while digging around in the old chestnut planting records, was that the Pentagon sits right on top of the first USDA horticultural research station. Decades worth of work; thousands of fruit and nut trees, including chestnuts, were abandoned or "moved" when the government decided they needed a new office building. "Let's put it right here," I'm sure they said. "There's nothing here, just some dumb fruit trees." That has been the absolutely consistent behavior of both government and university administrators, in many places. Long-term tree research has a tendency to result in new buildings—new stadiums, new dorms. But no trees.

Long-term tree research has a tendency to result in new buildings—new stadiums, new dorms. But no trees.

"OK. How?" The first thing we needed was scientific credibility. Charles had that, in spades; but we needed much more if we were to persuade anyone to fund this. "Can you get some top-notch scientists together to talk about this?" I said.

A slow nod; "I can do that."

I'm not sure we'll ever be able to reconstruct the first meeting. No one took minutes, and I was wildly distracted. The meeting was in the private conference rooms of Dr. David French, chairman of the Plant Pathology Department at the University of Minnesota—a heavyweight scientist. He was a stranger to me, and I was pretty intimidated. I honestly cannot remember who else was there—at least two, and perhaps three others. Not more. The others were pretty prominent scientists, too. Dr. Bud Tordoff is one possibility—ecologist, ornithologist, conservationist; Dr. David Merrell, my ecological genetics professor; Dr. Paul Read, horticulturist; Dr. Carl Mohn, forestry. If those folks weren't at the first meeting, they were all at the second. What really threw me was sitting there, in all these august presences, feeling like a student, because half these professors had actually been my teachers.

"Everybody here?" French asked.

"Looks like," Charles said.

Silence.

I'm looking at Charles. He's looking at me. "This is your meeting, Phil." he said.

That was the first I'd heard of it. I'd assumed he would make the pitch to these towering professors. But it was my idea—and no one on earth was ever more careful about honoring such things than Charles. I gulped. Literally. I had no notes, no agenda. But I did have the passion, and the history. I'd sold Charles before, and he let them know it. I talked for half an hour; then there were questions for both Charles and me for another half hour.

I remember it was dark outside the windows when we finished. Minnesota winter, I think. Everyone was interested. And as I would come to learn repeatedly in future board meetings, no one had committed to anything. Time was up; folks were standing up to go home, reaching for coats, and we had no decision. It was reflex on my part, not training, but I couldn't let that happen. Charles had spent a lot of personal capital to get these folks together; we needed a decision.

"Wait a minute, gentlemen. We need to decide—now. If we don't do this, no one will." My words, popping out.

Silence.

"Are we going to *do* this, or not?"

Silence.

Dave French, the department head, finally made the leap, quietly. "We can give it a try."

I seem to remember Charles and I holding hands and skipping down the sidewalk afterward; but I don't think that really happened. I know we felt that way. We celebrated with fried crappies we'd caught together, and canned corn from my farm—Charles was a corn snob, and appreciated my sh2 corn.

Then—getting down to work. ∾

The West Salem, Wisconsin, Chestnut Stand

By William Lord

In 1980 Charles Burnham, a corn geneticist at the University of Minnesota, just happened to scan the bulletin board and noted an article about chestnut trees to read over the holidays. In that same year, Dr. Cameron Gundersen of La Crosse, Wisconsin, just happened to hear about a sizable timber cutting of chestnut. This news came in a roundabout way. Gundersen and an associate had applied their expertise in curing the persistent and painful ear infection of a young girl. By chance Gundersen happened to meet the appreciative father, Ken Smith, while walking about town. Smith gave his sincere thanks and, knowing of the doctor's interest in the chestnut, also had something special to tell him. Smith had cut some timber in nearby West Salem in 1972 and didn't know it was chestnut until recently, when the county forester had identified it.

This was big news. Chestnut was presumed by almost everyone to be a goner. Wisconsin was far beyond the tree's natural range. Gundersen made a hopeful visit to the site and was amazed and delighted to see a fifty-acre woodlot of thriving chestnuts. They dominated the associated hardwoods with a procession of seedlings, pole-straight young trees, and wide-spreading, century-old monarchs.

An original line of a dozen or so trees had been planted along a fencerow sometime during the mid to late 1800s by farmers emigrating from Pennsylvania.

An original line of a dozen or so trees had been planted along a fencerow sometime during the mid to late 1800s by farmers emigrating from Pennsylvania. The farmers had brought whatever they could transport to help them get started, and this included sweet-tasting chestnuts. The fifty-acre area had been cleared for farmland and later allowed to return to woods. It proved to be a microenvironment well suited to chestnut trees.

The trees, however, had no apparent resistance to the blight. In 1986 Philip Rutter and Frederick Paillet, two members of the newly formed American Chestnut Foundation, discovered the presence of the blight in a few trees. Attempts to eradicate it by cutting down and burying the diseased trees were unsuccessful. This unwelcome news prompted action by a cadre of TACF scientist-members doing research with hypovirulence: Jane Cummings-Carlson of the Wisconsin Department of Natural Resources, Dennis Fulbright of Michigan State University, William MacDonald of West Virginia University, and Michael Milgroom of Cornell University.

Hypovirulence, or lessened virulence, refers to the weakening of the blight, caused by a hypovirus—in effect, a disease of a disease. This biological control phenomenon had been observed in several areas in Michigan beginning in the 1970s. Chestnut trees with hypovirulent cankers were surviving. Team members were optimistic that they had an effective means to restrain the blight, and they acquired the willing consent of the landowners, Ron and Susan Bockenhauer, Delores and Karl Rhyme, and Scott and Linda

Schomberg, to apply their research. They also secured the cooperation of several state and federal agencies.

Work commenced in 1991. The team initially was surprised and encouraged to find that only one strain of the blight fungus existed in the stand. The life cycle of the fungus typically involves two breeding types, designated as type "A" and type "a." The types function as male and female to produce the sexual spores (ascospores). When only one strain, and therefore one type, is present in an area, only asexual spores, or conidia, are produced. Although cankers produced by conidia are just as lethal as those caused by ascospores, conidia are responsible for a localized spread, compared to the much more extensive wind-borne spread of the ascospores.

This comparative stalemate presented an excellent opportunity for the scientists to infect the single existing strain with a hypovirus, in an effort to initiate biological control of the blight.

Alas, life is rarely without complications. The life cycle of the blight fungus also involves a complicated survival mechanism called incompatibility. It results from the almost unlimited arrangement of hereditary traits (genes) that occur with sexual reproduction. The result is that some strains of the blight fungus cannot mate with each other. They are incompatible. The trick, therefore, is to predetermine whether any pair of strains is compatible or incompatible.

This is done in a laboratory by growing two strains in a petri dish that contains a nutrient gel on which the fungi grow. Labs contain a "library" of the many strains of the blight fungus. When placed on the flat surface of the nutrient gel, the two strains grow toward each other. If they come together and fuse and grow as a single strain, they are compatible. If the two strains reject each other, incompatibility is evidenced by a dark line of destroyed tissue along the line of

An American chestnut tree in West Salem, Wisconsin, planted outside the chestnut's natural range in the early 1900s by settlers from the east. Under the tree are, from left: TACF president Marshal Case, Dr. Cameron Gundersen, and Bruce Gabel. (Photo courtesy of Daphne Van Schaick.)

contact. By means of such pairings the various strains are identified in the "library" for compatibility.

When two compatible strains grow together, there is an interchange of cellular contents, and by this means a diseased or hypovirulent strain can infect the "wild" virulent fungus that causes a lethal canker.

Our scientists matched a Michigan hypovirulent strain with the West Salem strain in the laboratory and successfully transferred the infection of hypovirulence. The team was optimistic that they had an effective biological control to apply in the field.

However, the Michigan hypovirus was apparently too debilitating to the West Salem fungus. It was effective in reducing or stopping further canker growth, but produced spores diminished in number and ability to spread hypovirulence. Only 2 percent of the conidia transmitted the hypovirus.

Perhaps introducing a less debilitating hypovirulent strain would yield better results. This was done in 1995, the same year that TACF's national meeting was held in La Crosse in October and attendees visited the West Salem stand amid a grand display of autumn gold. An aura of hope pervaded when attendees walked the chestnut woods with Bill MacDonald and his cohorts as they pointed out cankers in remission. However, shortly after the meeting, a second center of infection was detected on six chestnut trees a quarter of a mile from the West Salem stand. Analysis showed that it was a strain capable of mating with the West Salem strain and thus could produce the faster-spreading, wind-blown ascospores. The following year several more strains were discovered in the vicinity.

A chestnut tree in the West Salem stand. (Photo by Frederick Paillet.)

Although it would seem inevitable that the above events would result in an increase of the number of blight fungus strains in the West Salem stand, as of 2007 this has not happened. There remains only one primary type of infection, a fact that can only be a help to our scientists.

Initial results were encouraging. Cankers were treated with a milder strain of the West Salem fungus infected with a hypovirus from Italy, which was transmitted to more than 95 percent of the asexual spores:

> As of June 1997, 600 cankers, occurring on 132 of the 2,600 trees in the stand have been tested. Two hundred new infections were discovered in 1997. The European hypovirus has become the most commonly identi-

> fied hypovirus, being retrieved from over 38% of the bark plug samples analyzed in 1997. The Michigan hypovirus also continued to spread and in 1997 was retrieved from 15% of the bark samples. This means that slightly more than half of bark samples removed are hypovirus infected.

It appeared that hypovirulence could make a difference, achieving in time results at least as encouraging as the natural infections occurring in Michigan. However, it was noted that "unfortunately, some infections may be unaffected by the treatment."

TACF again held its annual meeting in La Crosse in 2002. Quite a few of the attendees had been there in 1995 when cankers in transmission were pointed out. Now, at the host Bockenhauer farm, they saw bushels of plump nuts on display. A walk through the woods was reassuringly familiar. The trees had yielded a heavy harvest for our hosts and for the denizen deer, squirrels, and blue jays; just brushing away the fallen leaves revealed a pocketful in easy reach. The woods seemed a little bit more open where a blight-killed tree had been removed, but overall this omen was missed amid an abundance of apparently healthy trees. But it was indeed an omen. The most recent years have not been kind, and the blight was seemingly having its way.

Yet, even now the scientists are in the laboratory and in the field, testing and applying new strategies. As of 2006 the disease has continued to spread, but a more intensive application of hypovirulence is having a positive impact. In addition to transmitting the hypovirus directly to a canker, "scratch-initiated wounds" of hypovirus in the bark are increasing the production and spread of hypovirulent spores. "Hypovirulent treatment appears to increase tree longevity; sixty-seven percent of the trees in the Disease Center that initially were treated with hypovirulent strains from 1992-97 were alive in 2006. In contrast, 52% of the trees infected between 1998-2002, in the absence of hypovirus treatment, remain alive."

The trees had yielded a heavy harvest for our hosts and for the denizen deer, squirrels, and blue jays; just brushing away the fallen leaves revealed a pocketful in easy reach.

The year 2006 revealed another reversal of fortune, this time at the Crystal Lake stand in northern Michigan containing an estimated two thousand trees from an American chestnut orchard started in 1912. Virulent cankers first noted in the late 1970s had been treated with a hypovirulent strain by Dennis Fulbright in 1982. During the ensuing years, scientists had concentrated their efforts on the West Salem stand, and a visit to Crystal Lake in the mid 1990s "did not offer much hope." However, something was afoot, and it became dramatically apparent in 2006. Fulbright was elated to witness the successful transmission of hypovirulence and control of the blight. "Non-lethal cankers can be found on small as well as large trees, and some portion of the chestnut canopy has remained intact. . . . This is the first optimistic sign that hypovirulence, when placed in a declining stand, can have a positive influence on chestnut blight."

The positive, though delayed, results evident at Crystal Lake may even now be repeating themselves in some form in nature's laboratory, to the benefit of our scientific endeavor at West Salem. ~

Long Live the King: Continuing the Dynasty of the Shaftsbury Line

The king is dead, long live the king. The Shaftsbury tree, a solitary ninety-foot American chestnut amid a stand of sugar maple, was cut down and removed October 5, 2004, the victim of an overwhelming attack by the blight. The tree was discovered in 1998 by our president, Marshal Case, who named it for its location in the town of Shaftsbury, a rural retreat on the slopes of the Taconic Mountains in southwestern Vermont.

This July the tree was in copious bloom. The chestnut does not self-pollinate, and no other flowering chestnuts grow locally. Therefore, to produce a nut crop, skilled climbers adept with rope technique ascended into the canopy to hand-pollinate and enclose the fertilized flowers in bags. On the first exploratory climb, a pollinator was chagrined to find a sizable chestnut blight canker sixty feet up, ten inches in length, encircling 80 percent of the trunk. In a term of the field, the canker was "cooked," with dark, sunken wood. A swollen, as opposed to sunken, canker would indicate a degree of resistance by the tree. Other similar cankers were identified. The Shaftsbury tree apparently had no blight resistance and had escaped the blight because of its isolation among the sugar maples.

The blight fungus spreads from tree to tree by producing two kinds of microscopic spores—sexually produced ascospores carried off by the wind, and asexually produced conidia spores that extrude out onto the bark in minute, sticky tendrils. The latter can adhere, for example, to birds, who then transmit the infectious spores to other chestnut trees. A major suspect in this regard is the yellow-bellied sapsucker, a member of the woodpecker family.

The Shaftsbury tree, in southwestern Vermont.

Within the cankered area of the Shaftsbury tree, the knowing eye of the pollinator perceived two horizontal rows of small, squarish holes, a signature of the sapsucker. Blight spores typically gain entrance by way of wounds in the bark. The sapsucker is an obvious vector, transporting the sticky spores from a canker and enabling their access into the holes it drills into the bark of other chestnut trees. An implanted spore can then germinate and do its lethal work by girdling and destroying the thin but life-essential cambium layer

The pollinator noted that the holes were dry, confirming that the cankered wood was dead and that the sapsucker had drilled them at least one year ago. The evidence at hand tellingly implicates the sapsucker as the vector for the tree's demise.

But life prevails. A total of one hundred nuts were harvested from the July pollination to perpetuate the lineage of the Shaftsbury tree. The king is dead. Long live the king.

William Lord

A Tree by Any Other Name

The Future for Chestnuts in the United States

By Sandra L. Anagnostakis

As a plant pathologist at the Connecticut Agricultural Experiment Station since 1966, Dr. Sandra L. Anagnostakis has researched the genetics of corn smut disease, Dutch elm disease, and Nectria canker of birch, but her most famous work has been on chestnut blight disease. In 1972 she became the first scientist to import hypovirulent (virus-containing) strains of Cryphonectria parasitica *from France and demonstrate that such viruses weakened the blight's killing power enough to provide a potential biological control against the disease in the United States. In her essay here, Dr. Anagnostakis describes a genetic conundrum of chestnut restoration: are these backcross trees going to be American chestnuts?*

In 1900 there were about 130 million American chestnut trees in the state of Connecticut. They were an important part of the mixed hardwood forests of the eastern United States, but all of our native *Castanea*—chestnuts and chinquapins—are susceptible to the two major pathogens that were imported into the country in the 1800s. Ink disease, caused by *Phytophthora cinnamomi*, killed chestnuts and chinquapins in the southern United States but could not survive the winters in the colder, northern climates. Chestnut blight disease, caused by the fungus *Cryphonectria parasitica*, spread throughout the range of native *Castanea* and persists today. Trees killed by ink disease are totally dead, roots and all. Chestnut blight disease does not infect the root collar or root system, so trees killed by this pathogen are able to sprout from the root collar and grow for several years before becoming infected and starting the cycle all over again.

These sprouts have given hope that chestnuts might again be able to take their place in the United States as usable timber trees and important sources of food for wildlife in places where ink disease is not present. Breeding programs were begun by the USDA and by the Connecticut Agricultural Experiment Station in 1930 to try to produce trees with both timber form (tall, straight, slow to begin flowering, and putting all energy into vertical growth) and orchard form (short, spreading, producing nuts soon after planting, and putting most energy into nut production). After the USDA's breeding program was terminated in 1949, the Connecticut program continued and was joined in 1983 by The American Chestnut Foundation's privately funded venture.

Both the current programs use a method called backcross breeding, advocated by Charles Burnham. In this scheme, native chestnuts and chinquapins are first crossed with resistant Asian chestnut trees. The resulting hybrids (with intermediate resistance to chestnut blight disease) are selected for form. These are then crossed again to native chestnuts. Dr. Frederick V. Hebard of TACF has found that, on average, one out of eight of the offspring have intermediate resistance. These numbers suggest that at least three genes are controlling the resistance. Using this information, we can calculate how many fully resistant trees would result if we crossed two of the trees with intermediate resistance with each other. If full resistance is conferred only by the presence of two copies of the three resistance genes, approximately one out of sixty-four of the offspring will have the right combination.

By crossing trees with intermediate resistance back to native trees (hence "backcrossing"), the percentage of native genes in the offspring will be increased. At each step, selections must be made for the kind of tree desired. By the time the seedlings are five years old, they will exhibit either spreading, orchard form or straight, timber form. They can also be selected for their resistance to chestnut blight disease or ink disease, and for other desirable characteristics such as hardiness. These trees will not be *Castanea dentata*, but what should we call them? And what is happening to the chestnuts that are not being manipulated by scientists?

The Europeans who first came to this country certainly used the chestnuts and chinquapins that they found here, but then they started planting C. sativa *nuts from Europe.*

It is easy to forget that there are several different kinds of native chestnuts in the United States. Many sites in the U.S. have been examined for plant pollen deposited since 20,000 years ago. As the ice receded after the last ice age, there was chestnut pollen deposited in sites near Winston-Salem, North Carolina, that has been dated to about 13,000 years ago. As the temperatures continued to warm, chestnuts became established in more and more northern locations, until they were found throughout the Appalachian Mountain range. The trees called American chestnut are *Castanea dentata* and have three nuts in each bur. The many types of chinquapin, with a single nut in each bur, may be one species (*Castanea pumila*) with several subspecies, or may be three species (*C. pumila* Miller, *C. alnifolia* Nuttall, and *C. ozarkensis* Ashe), depending on which taxonomist you favor. Careful DNA studies will be needed to resolve this. Whatever they are, they are all able to cross with each other and with American chestnuts and produce viable nuts. In fact, all species of *Castanea* that have been used in crosses will cross with each other. Often the resulting offspring are not able to form viable pollen, but this seems to be the only detrimental effect of an interspecies cross.

The Europeans who first came to this country certainly used the chestnuts and chinquapins that they found here, but then they started planting *C. sativa* nuts from Europe. Around 1800 E. I. du Pont de Nemours wrote that he was bringing many chestnut seeds and plants from France for planting in the Wilmington, Delaware, area. A Delaware College Agricultural Experiment Station report in 1900 noted, "To many of his friends he sent nuts and cions [*sic*] from his famous French Marrons, and from these chestnuts a multitude of seedlings sprang up and are still standing along the fence rows or in the gardens."

Trees that were presumed to be European-American hybrids were also grown for their nuts. Ernest Sterling was a forester charged, in 1903, with visiting chestnut orchards in New Jersey and Pennsylvania and reporting his findings to the state of New York. He traveled about 1,050 miles in two weeks to collect his information and wrote that Pennsylvania nut grower C. K. Sober had 75,000 grafted trees of the cultivar 'Paragon'. Sober also sold grafted 'Paragon' trees, shipping boxcar-loads of them all over the country. Sterling refers to other growers in Pennsylvania and New Jersey with European and hybrid chestnut trees, totaling about 45,000 trees. The Moon Nursery in Pennsylvania and Parry Brothers' Nursery in New Jersey also sold grafted European trees in large numbers. Unfortunately, the European chestnuts and hybrids were susceptible to both ink disease and chestnut blight disease, and Sober's orchard succumbed, as did all the others. European trees sold by mail order are often found today, planted outside the native range of chestnut where ink disease and chestnut blight disease have not yet been found.

Our first record of Asian chestnuts being imported into the United States is from 1876, when Connecticut resident S. B. Parsons got seed of Japanese chestnuts that were accidentally included with lily bulbs from Japan. These *C. crenata* thrived in his garden, were more spreading than *C. dentata* or *C. sativa*, and bore nuts much earlier. The Japanese chestnuts were given to many friends, starting a demand for more importations. Chestnut blight disease must have come in with some of these imported Japanese chestnut trees, possibly on those grafted with superior nut cultivars. Infections on *C. crenata* are not easily recognized and do little damage to the trees, so the trees shipped by mail order and planted all up and down the East Coast could carry the disease to places where it could spread to susceptible, native *Castanea*.

After the Boxer Rebellion in 1900, China was opened to exploration by botanists from Europe and the United States, and chestnuts of the species *C. mollissima* (Chinese chestnut), *C. seguinii* (dwarf Chinese chestnut), and *C. henryi* (the Chinese chinquapin) were imported and planted in large numbers. All have resistance to chestnut blight disease and ink disease, and many attempts were made to replace dead American chestnut trees with Asian chestnuts. Unfortunately, they rarely grow taller than sixty feet and are quickly overtopped by oaks and maples in a forest, so they failed to thrive.

A very large number of these other *Castanea* species are now found in our forests, parks, and backyards, where they freely hybridize with any American chestnuts or chinquapins that survive long enough to flower. The resulting hybrids often have more resistance to the diseases that kill our native species, and if we were willing to wait several hundred years for natural selection to operate, we would probably see chestnuts that could compete in our forests and have good resistance to the diseases. American chestnuts rarely flower before they are ten years old, and chestnuts must be cross-pollinated to produce nuts. The chances of two trees in the wild surviving to maturity at the same time and producing a nut crop are usually slim. The exceptions are in clear-cut areas, where the chestnuts sprout and grow rapidly, and frequently produce one crop of nuts before they are killed by chestnut blight disease.

A biological control for this disease, called hypovirulence and caused by a virus that weakens the fungus, can keep American chestnuts alive, but the heavily cankered trees cannot be used for timber. However, the use of this biological control can greatly help in the breeding efforts to develop resistant hybrids.

What will happen next? Since many of us are too impatient to wait for natural selection, we will continue to breed trees for resistance to each new pest and pathogen that people import into the country. If resistant trees are planted out into the forests where sprouts of native trees persist, and if our biological control for chestnut blight disease keeps those native trees alive, the next generation of seedlings formed will be intermediate in resistance but will incorporate all the diversity that evolved in that native population. The biocontrol will help keep these trees alive to cross with each other, and soon fully resistant, well-adapted chestnut trees will start to reclaim the "chestnut niche" in the forest.

Will they be American chestnut trees? They were, after all, born in the U.S.A. Distinctions between species have already begun to blur, and only sophisticated molecular techniques can determine what species a hybrid has been derived from. The resulting hybrids will not be *Castanea dentata*, but we hope that they will have most of the characteristics that made *C. dentata* such an important part of the American forest.

Male American chestnut flower at Quabbin Reservoir in Massachusetts. (Photo by Brad Smith.)

Man with a Chestnut Mission

Chestnuts as Slow Food: The American Chestnut Foundation Award

By Corby Kummer

The Slow Food Foundation is an international nonprofit group established in Italy in 1986 to counteract the fast food industry. With some 75,000 members worldwide, it advocates education, land stewardship, ecologically sound food production, and the revival of community and culture through traditional foods. Every year Slow Food presents Awards for the Protection of Biodiversity to help "arrest the degradation of the plant and animal heritage which makes up the gastronomic culture of a country and to maintain an ecological balance on our planet." In 2002 TACF won the Slow Food award. Corby Kummer, noted food writer and senior editor of the Atlantic Monthly *magazine, wrote the following article for the Slow Food announcement of the prize.*

Fred Hebard was born in 1948 in Chestnut Hill, Pennsylvania, a prosperous Philadelphia suburb whose name would prove fateful. A lively curiosity about nature ran in his family, especially about birds and insects: his father, a lawyer, was, he says, an "advanced amateur ornithologist," a habit his understanding mother indulged, and his first cousin an "advanced amateur entomologist." His great-great-grandfather had left the small Connecticut town of Lebanon to become an industrial logger, and the family maintained its ties to the forestry business.

Hebard started college studying history and English, but then the Army drafted him, and he served briefly in Vietnam in 1968. He worked for a time at United Press International before returning to school. Then, in 1970, he spent a summer working on a dairy farm in the same small Connecticut town his forebear had left to make his fortune. There his life changed course decisively.

"I was chasing some cows that busted out of a pasture," he says, "and [I] got into conversation with a farmer. He showed me a chestnut tree"—or rather a small, struggling sprout that would never grow to its full size. "He told me about the blight that wiped out the forests all over New England. I thought it would be good to go study and do something about it."

Hebard went back to school with a mission—a dream that had driven previous generations of botanists practically to madness, and one that had mostly died. He earned a master's degree in botany and a doctorate in plant pathology. Today Hebard is the lead scientist of The American Chestnut Foundation, a movement gathering force and momentum—and growing more and more American chestnut trees—every year.

King of the forest

Chestnut trees were for millennia important to every part of North American life. The oak-like trees, often 100 feet tall and more than six feet in diameter, dominated the 200 million acres of their natural range—the central Appalachian Mountains stretching from Connecticut and Massachusetts south and westward through Pennsylvania, Virginia, and Tennessee. Chestnuts covered fully a quarter of forested land.

The trees were beautiful: in midsummer the hillsides they favored were creamy white with chestnut flowers, in winter the gray wood glinted silver in the sun. They were useful to man and nature alike. The nuts were sweet enough to eat fresh, raw or roasted, and easy to dry and store for the winter. Members of Iroquois tribes drank a hot, coffee-like drink of roasted chestnuts. Settlers ground the nuts with a wooden mallet (they were too soft for a normal flour mill) and used them for stuffings or mixed them with wheat flour to make "nut bread." Farmers bought mountainside land knowing they could fatten their hogs on chestnuts, and command a premium price for the tasty ham that would result. Bees thrived on the flowers' nectar, and chestnut honey was both plentiful and prized. Dozens of birds and animals, from bears to deer to turkeys, depended on chestnuts as their chief food source.

Chestnuts provided extra income for farmers, who often relied on them to raise enough money to cover their taxes, and itinerant foragers, who would barter chestnuts for shoes and staples like sugar, flour, and coffee to see them through the winter. In October, the prime harvest month, families would get to the woods early—"to beat the hogs," as one old-timer still remembers—and fill sacks with chestnuts to bring to the market. Or they would wait for the merchants who passed through in the fall. Men on horseback would ride through first, telling the gleaners to get their sacks ready. Chestnuts were a far more reliable source of rural Appalachian income than moonshine.

Fred Hebard at work.

The tree's main economic value was as lumber. Chestnut is exceptionally rot resistant, and lasts for decades. Because trees were strong, straight, tall, and fast-growing, they were a ready source of framing timber and telephone poles. Furniture makers, too, sought out chestnut for the fineness of the grain, the ease of working it, and the confidence they could have that the wood wouldn't warp, split, or rot.

By the 1870s, a cataclysm had come in, quietly and inadvertently, on imported Asian seedlings: a fungus that causes cankers that reach into the stem and cut the flow of nutrients up and down the trunk. Asian chestnuts had long ago acquired immunity. American chestnuts were defenseless. The blight was identified in 1904 at the New York Zoological Gardens, in Bronx, New York. By then it was far too late to stop the blight's terrible progress. The blight advanced through American forests at up to fifty miles a year, leaving millions of gray carcasses—"ghosts," devastated onlookers called them. By 1950 perhaps fifty to one hundred trees remained of the 4 billion that had covered the Appalachians at the turn of the century.

Emergency response

No one was content, of course, to stand by and watch a quarter of the forest be destroyed, and wildlife populations vanish along with them—not to mention the ruined rural economies that forced people to move to cities. From the 1920s onward, the United States Department of Agriculture and botanists at agricultural research stations intensively tried to breed a blight-resistant chestnut.

The obvious method was to cross a blight-resistant Chinese or Japanese chestnut with an American tree. This didn't work. One large problem was the constant risk that a gene for blight susceptibility would be passed to the next generation. Also, Asian chestnut trees grow much shorter than American ones.

The chances of finding a resistant cross that looked and grew like an American chestnut seemed impossibly small. A new generation would seem to be resistant, and then fail the "challenge" of being inoculated with fungus. Yet more painful to breeders was to nurture an apparently successful, blight-resistant tree over 20 healthy years, proudly watching it grow to 40 feet—only to see it stop growing, because of its high quotient of Asian genes. By the 1960s, most scientists had abandoned hope. The amount of money and scientific talent given the chestnut dwindled to practically nothing.

Just when Hebard wanted to join the battle, a new discovery revived interest. It involved the European chestnut, which is closer to American than to Asian species. Even though the Asian fungus did establish itself in European forests, in the 1930s, after 15 years of struggle the European trees revived in healthy and large populations. No one knew quite how.

In the early 1970s, a plant pathologist named Jean Grente, working at a large chestnut breeding station that was part of INRA, the French national agronomic research institute, announced that he had found the savior. It was not just plucky European savoir faire but a virus—a secondary pathogen that attacked the blight fungus itself. The virus did not actually kill the fungus, but weakened it enough to disarm it from killing trees. (The phenomenon is called hypovirulence, for the lowered virulence of the primary pathogen.)

In 1973, *Science* magazine published a study replicating and confirming Grente's work, and stirred up new excitement. Molecular analysis was at the time cutting-edge. First-rank scientists rejoined the ranks of chestnut warriors. But as research progressed, problems became clear. The virus can move easily within strains of fungus, but not among them. Europe had few strains of blight, America many. Attempting to introduce attack viruses into American forests, then, seemed a difficult if not futile effort.

The great leap forward came about not by looking through a sexy electron microscope but by thinking in a new way about boring old breeding. In 1980 Charles Burnham, a Minnesota plant geneticist who had made important advances in corn genetics, hypothesized that to breed blight resistance into the American chestnut, each new generation should be bred back to an American parent—not to an Asian parent, which for decades was the prevailing assumption. The goal would be a tree that was 15/16ths American, yet with hardy blight resistance from its Chinese ancestor.

A new foundation for a new idea

In 1983, several colleagues and friends who agreed with Burnham formed The American Chestnut Foundation. Their aim was as simple as it was lofty: to restore the chestnut to the eastern forest and its rightful place in the ecosystem.

The founders guessed that three backcrosses would be necessary, which meant at least eighteen years of hard labor and anxious waiting. There would be one more crucial intermediate step—an intercrossing of progeny of the third backcrossed generation, to eliminate the possibility that any genes for susceptibility would be passed along with genes for resistance. This step alone would add three more years.

Their aim was as simple as it was lofty: to restore the chestnut to the eastern forest and its rightful place in the ecosystem.

The government had washed its hands of long-range chestnut breeding, the new foundation said, and would never fund breeding and growing on the scale they envisioned. Breeding experiments would have to take place in many states at once, to ensure that each generation had the genetic diversity to withstand varying climates. The foundation raised money on hope.

In 1989 the directors convinced Hebard to devote his time to their efforts. It wasn't hard, even though it meant he would have to move from the University of Kentucky to Meadowview, Virginia, in the heart of the American chestnut's original range. Two sisters, Jennifer and Cheri Wagner, and their mother, Anna Belle, had just given the foundation a long lease on 20 acres of land there, hoping it would be used for agricultural research and not a new McDonald's. "I'd really wanted to breed chestnuts since 1980," Hebard says simply. "I still do." He in turn managed to persuade his wife, Dayle Zanzinger, a fellow plant pathologist, to move with their two young girls, aged 9 months and two years. In order to find a job, Dayle trained as a nurse practitioner, sacrificing many years of schooling.

Hebard immediately set to work testing the new backcross-intercross hypothesis. Within two years he had 1,000 healthy trees, and soon enough 3,000. By 1993, Hebard could show several highly blight-resistant members of two intercrossed generations. Burnham's hypothesis had passed its most stringent test.

The foundation could start selling more than hope. New state chapters were formed, and volunteers planted seedlings sent from Meadowview. A whole subculture evolved, with members exchanging photographs and news by e-mail, inviting each other to witness Pollination Day—the most important and exciting moment of the year.

Today The American Chestnut Foundation counts 5,000 members in every state (except North Dakota), and nine state chapters [fifteen as of 2007] within the chestnut's original range, where members actively plant trees and report news back to headquarters. The foundation is almost entirely funded by its members, and is always hunting for new sources of funding to keep its research and activities alive.

Every year the goal comes closer. Hebard managed to speed up the time it takes chestnuts to flower (from between six and ten years to between two and four), and thus the pace for proving resistance. He now oversees 17,000 trees on 70 acres at the three research farms [now four] in Meadowview. There are setbacks, of course. In 1997, more than half the nuts from the best harvest ever froze to death in an overenthusiastic refrigerator. And there are enormous long-range questions: Will the new trees adapt to the diverse environmental challenges they will face? Will they really look and grow like American chestnuts of old? Will the many strains of Asian fungus that have established themselves in American forests overcome the supposedly resistant new tree—and obliterate decades of hard work?

The final answers will take hundreds of years. But the first ones will come sooner than anyone could have imagined just nineteen years ago. Hebard began planting the final intercross generation last year, and expects to begin harvesting nuts suitable for reforestation around 2005 or 2006. After a few tantalizing years of final testing, the foundation will distribute seeds to its eager members, and then to the public.

The dream, certainly, is thriving. Hebard himself thinks he might see what seemed unthinkable when he first chased a cow into a Connecticut woodland. "My hope is to see Appalachian mountainsides look snow-covered on the Fourth of July," he says. "Will I see it in my lifetime? Yeah, it's possible." ∾

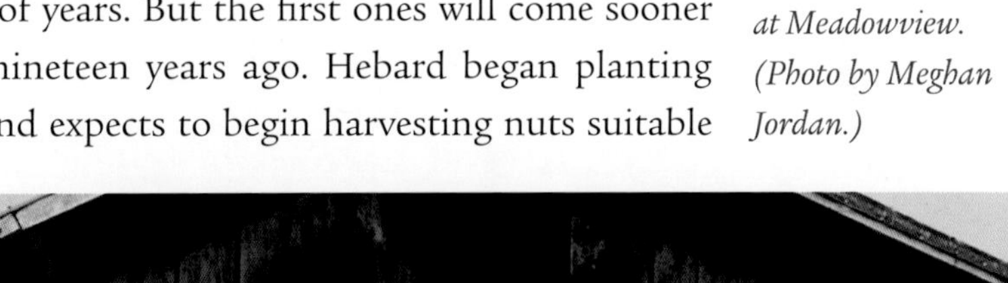

TACF barn at Meadowview. (Photo by Meghan Jordan.)

Charles E. Burchfield (1893–1967), Summer Solstice (In Memory of the American Chestnut), *1961–66, watercolor on paper, 54 by 60 inches. Reproduced with permission of the Charles E. Burchfield Foundation, Burchfield-Penny Art Museum, Buffalo, New York.*

THE VISIONARIES

1986, I

Slowly, slowly, they return
To the small woodland let alone:
Great trees, outspreading and upright,
Apostles of the living light.

Patient as stars, they build in air
Tier after tier a timbered choir,
Stout beams upholding weightless grace
Of song, a blessing on this place.

They stand in waiting all around,
Uprisings of their native ground,
Downcomings of the distant light;
They are the advent they await.

Receiving sun and giving shade,
Their life's a benefaction made,
And is a benediction said
Over the living and the dead.

In fall their brightened leaves, released,
Fly down the wind, and we are pleased
To walk on radiance, amazed.
O light come down to earth, be praised!

Excerpted from *A Timbered Choir: The Sabbath Poems 1979–1997*, by Wendell Berry. Reprinted by permission of the author.

No More Work and Royalties Forever

By Bill Owens

Born in 1935 in the Great Smoky Mountains near Pigeon Forge, Tennessee, Billy Earl Owens was ten years older than his niece Dolly Parton. Both grew up in the traditional rural Appalachian lifestyle: poor in money, but rich in family love, skills of self-sufficiency, and music. Owens heard Dolly singing as a child and knew she was gifted. He was her first manager and co-wrote her first hit songs. In her 1994 autobiography, Dolly: My Life and Other Unfinished Business, *Parton wrote, "Uncle Bill was a great visionary and really thought I had potential. . . . He was my first and special angel of that kind. He was willing to work hard, sacrifice, whatever it took to follow [our] dream."*

Owens still performs regularly at Dollywood, the 125-acre heritage-themed amusement park that Parton began developing in 1986. Uncle Bill's Music in the Valley Shop there is named for him. Today, with a staff of some 2,000, Dollywood is the largest employer as well as the favorite tourist destination in Sevier County, Tennessee. Because of Owens's dedication and effort, Dollywood also hosts a chestnut tree plantation and supports graduate students in chestnut research.

I've always loved trees. My grandpa was an orchard man who knew how to graft and he could take old trees that weren't any good and graft better species onto them. And so I grew up around that and I've always thought about it. And then I read a book by J. Russell Smith called *Tree Crops: A Permanent Agriculture.* Smith went all over the world, China and everywhere, and documented what happens when you cut all the trees down. All the soil washes away. And his idea was to plant trees back to hold the soil, but make sure you plant the kind of trees that would feed your livestock and maybe yourself at the same time.

These mountains were not made to clear the trees off, because it can rain five inches in half an hour here, in a good thunderstorm. My daddy said one time they cleared up what they called a new ground, a cornfield, you've got to cut everything down, and then you've got to dig the roots out. And he said they got it all ready to plant one time and then came a thunderstorm and in half an hour the topsoil was all down in the creek. It washed away faster than they could clear it. And that's what happened a lot to this area. Back in the 1930s, the Tennessee Valley Authority built all these dams, and they were for flood prevention as much as anything else. Because when everybody logged all the hills off there was nothing to slow the water down and it started flooding everywhere.

I remember back in these mountains, especially back in Daddy's time, when they'd turn all the hogs out in the woods. They'd mark them on the ears, everyone had their own mark and they'd turn those hogs loose to go out and eat acorns and the chest-

Bill Owens at his Dollywood American chestnut plantation. (Photo by Chris Bolgiano.)

nuts—at that time the chestnuts were very, very plentiful. And they'd eat honey locust pods and persimmons and hickory nuts too. J. Russell Smith's idea was to pick out the best of all those kinds of trees and start planting them on your place. Then you've got a permanent agriculture, no more erosion. There was a man in the TVA in the '30s that offered cash money for the best honey locust and other trees out of five or six states, so when they found the best then they'd go to that tree, whether it was in Georgia or Alabama or wherever it was, they'd go and take a graft off of that and they started breeding them. That's the kind of thing I'm talking about. They found good varieties of oak and all kinds of trees. Every which one was the best. You could spend a lifetime doing that.

You do that, and you've got something to pass on to other people, too. If you do it the other way you destroy the land so it can't be used by the next generation. But if you use the trees right, nature will take care of everything. You don't have to cultivate anything, and I like that. It's like holding copyright to a song: No more work and you get royalties forever.

But the chestnuts were pretty much gone by the time the TVA men were working. I remember my uncles going out in the woods already in the 1940s and cutting up what they called acid wood. Chestnut wood is high in tannic acid which is used to tan leather, then the pulp was made into paper. They sold the chestnut wood to the Champion Paper and Fibre plant in North Carolina.

Losing the chestnuts was a disaster. Hogs couldn't root for nuts anymore, and animals starved to death. Chestnuts were one of the things that mountain folks lived off of and they didn't know what to do. It was like saying that all the corn crops have a disease, and you'll never have corn again. Chestnuts were basic to the life of mountain people. They'd take and sell them as well as eat them.

I've been hearing chestnut stories all my life. Not many of us remember back that far, but everybody's family has told them about chestnuts. One story that stands out in my mind is something my daddy told me. When he was fourteen years old, that would have been in 1914 because he was born in 1900, he and his younger brother, who was twelve, went out when their daddy told them to go cut up a chestnut tree and split it up into rails. That's how they made their fences, with split chestnut rails. They did a lot of that and they used a six-foot crosscut saw. They found a big chestnut broken off up top that had a hollow space and they said, "Well, here's a good 'un. Let's saw this 'un." And they started but the saw would not go across because the tree was wider than the six-foot saw. So they chopped a hole into it, one of them got up on top of the log and chopped a hole in it. Then they took the handle off of one end of the saw—you could take the handles off to carry them—and stuck it down through the hole and my daddy got inside and put the handle back on and his brother stayed on the outside and that's how they sawed that tree.

It was Dolly's daddy that told me this other chestnut story. I was talking to him about the chestnut trees and he said, "I remember when them trees was really big, but they were already dying out." He was living up in the Greenbrier area, which is part of the Great Smoky Mountains National Park now, before the government got it and got all the people out. Back then these big families would live in one little cabin. His uncle got married and the house was too crowded for him, he wanted somewhere to be alone with his wife. There was this big chestnut tree a little bit from the house that had rotted inside and had a lot of room in there. He and his family went out there and they fixed that tree up with a roof over the top and they put a bed in there and that's where he and his wife spent their honeymoon. So it had to be at least six feet across the inside. The largest chestnut tree ever was in Haywood County where my daddy came from in North Carolina. It was seventeen feet across.

I've been hearing chestnut stories all my life.

I'm not really sure how I found out about The American Chestnut Foundation. I read a lot, mostly health books and tree books, and I study about trees. Some years ago I called up Dr. Hill Craddock [on the TACF board of directors] at the University of Tennessee at Chattanooga, and it didn't take me long to get the idea that this group really might be able to help the chestnut. I went up to Meadowview [Virginia, where the main TACF orchard is located] as soon as I found out about TACF, and saw the chestnut plantations there. The foundation is really getting close now, from what I understand they'll soon have fifteen-sixteenths of an American chestnut tree. That'll just be something for people to argue about, but if it's 99 percent American and it's got one other gene to keep it from dying of the blight, then that's close enough for me! The main thing is survival.

And they're getting to where they can survive, it's happening in my lifetime. The idea that TACF can bring the chestnut back really fascinates me. I could see that it could be done and I read the books and talked to the professors and they said, "Yeah, we're going to do it." When I found out about that I wanted to be a part of it. I'm a dreamer, you know, a big dreamer. If I hadn't been, Dolly and I would never have been in Nashville to start with. We had to dream big, and live through setbacks and disappointments to even get started.

So I got involved with the people at TACF, and then I got Dollywood involved. I'd already been planting 5,000 trees at Dollywood every winter since 1988, about 70,000 so far. I asked Hill to come up and we made a presentation, and we persuaded the management to support starting a chestnut orchard on four acres above the amusement park, where nobody goes. Jack Herschend, Dollywood's operating partner, was real supportive because he loves trees too and plants a lot of them himself. So I got a twenty-five-year lease to make sure the trees stay if the park changes hands or anything like that.

The view from the chestnut plantation at Dollywood, in Pigeon Forge, Tennessee, in the foothills of the Great Smoky Mountains. (Photo by Chris Bolgiano.)

I'm glad we're getting them back. I hope I live long enough to see them out there in the woods. I'll never see any big 'uns, of course, but I'll see them growing.

Right down in the park, we put up signs and a collection box. More than two million people go through Dollywood every year. We're making people aware and they leave little donations and actually we make some money once in a while for TACF. I knew very little that I could do personally, and I feel like my job is not to find the answers to the disease but to help promote the effort with the public. I'm out in the public a lot. Every time I'm sitting in Dollywood by the signs and talking to people, when they see the signs at least one or two out of every ten people says, "my grandpa was telling me about this," or "my daddy said his grandpa said this." They're very much aware of it, especially in this part of the country. Somewhere down the line someone's got a house that was built out of chestnut wood, or a barn or a table or something. They know what the subject's about, because it's been handed down through the generations.

So, we've got the orchard up there now. It's on four acres of pretty steep hillside. I got the bulldozer operator to make me terraces to plant the trees on, otherwise you couldn't walk around to plant them and take care of them. Then I had the idea of hooking into the Dollywood water tank that sits right above the slope to run water to the chestnut trees. And I plan to get compost from the town of Pigeon Forge to add to the soil, it's free. We're still planting and some of the trees are going to live and some of them will not. That's why we're doing it, to see which ones are the strongest. Where the trees die, we'll just plant stronger trees next time.

I'm glad we're getting them back. I hope I live long enough to see them out there in the woods. I'll never see any big 'uns, of course, but I'll see them growing. I've got some old chestnut stumps on my place, where I live, where I was born and raised. They keep sprouting, coming up from the base. And they get about 10 feet tall and get the disease and then die back down. One theory is that when we get some trees that are disease resistant we could take cuttings off of them and go through the woods and graft them on the roots of the old ones, which means that they could grow five to ten times faster than a seedling because they've got that massive root system. The trees could grow fast and they bear nuts pretty young anyway. In less than ten years we could have the mountains full of chestnuts again and the wildlife would come back. And that's not even counting the timber. Well, I always was a big dreamer. Still am. ~

Old Chestnuts

By Barbara Kingsolver

Novelist, essayist, and poet Barbara Kingsolver was born to a strong storytelling tradition in central Kentucky, between the opulent bluegrass country and the impoverished coalfields. "I used to beg my mother to let me tell her a bedtime story," she writes. The contrast of wealth and poverty also stimulated the concern for social justice that is central to her work.

Trained in biology and ecology, she began her career as a science journalist in the mid 1980s. Her articles have appeared in dozens of newspapers and magazines in North America and abroad. But she could not get "the roar of voices" out of her head and began writing novels in a closet, the only space available in her tiny house at the time. Among her eleven published books, The Poisonwood Bible *(1998), a novel about cultural and economic imperialism in twentieth-century Africa, won the National Book Prize of South Africa, was a finalist for the Pulitzer and PEN/Faulkner awards, and was selected for Oprah's Book Club. In 2000 Kingsolver was awarded the National Humanities Medal, our nation's highest honor for service through the arts.*

Her novel Prodigal Summer, *published by HarperCollins in 2000, is set in the chestnut country of southwestern Virginia where TACF maintains a chestnut breeding plantation. In her introduction, Kingsolver promises "a tithe of my future apple crop . . . to Fred Hebard of The American Chestnut Foundation for all kinds of help and an education in trees; the foundation's chestnut breeding program—a far more systematic project than the one invented for this tale—will someday return the American chestnut to American woodlands." In the following excerpts from* Prodigal Summer, *it is the hope of restoration that keeps the character Garnett Walker alive despite all his earthly trials.*

Eight years a widower, Garnett still sometimes awoke disoriented and lost to the day. It was because of the large empty bed, he felt; a woman was an anchor. Lacking a wife, he had turned to his God for solace, but sometimes a man also needed the view out his window.

Garnett sat up slowly and bent toward the light, seeing as much with his memory as with his eyes. There was the gray fog of dawn in this wet Appalachian hollow, lifted with imperious slowness like the skirt of an old woman stepping over a puddle. There were the barn and slat-sided grain house, built by his father and grandfather in another time. The grass-covered root cellar still bulged from the hillside, the two windows in its fieldstone face staring out of the hill like eyes in the head of a man. Every morning of his life, Garnett had saluted that old man in the hillside with the ivy beard crawling out of his chin and the forelock of fescue hanging over his brow. As a boy, Garnett had never dreamed of being an old man himself, still looking at these sights and needing them as badly as a boy needs the smooth lucky chestnut in his pocket, the talisman he rubs all day just to make sure it's still there.

The birds were starting up their morning chorus. They were in full form now, this far into the spring. What was it now, the nineteenth of May? Full form and feather. He listened. The prothalamion, he had named this in his mind years ago: a song raised up to connubial union. There were meadowlarks and chats, field sparrows, indigo buntings, all with their heads raised to the dawn and their hearts pressed into clear liquid song for their mates. Garnett held his face in his hands for just a moment. As a boy he had never dreamed of an age when there was no song left, but still some heart.

Garnett could still remember, from when he was a boy, a giant hollow log way back up in the woods on Zebulon Mountain. It was of such a size that he and the other youngsters could run through it single-file without even bending their heads. The thought made him smile. They had reckoned it to be theirs, for a ten-year-old boy will happily presume ownership of a miracle of nature, and then carve on it with his knife. They'd called it by some kind of name—what was it? Something Indian. The Indian Tunnel.

A surprising fact occurred to Garnett then, for the first time in his nearly eighty years: the unfortunate fellow who'd chopped down that tree, miscalculating its size and then having to leave it, must have been his grandfather. How many times before had Garnett stood right here at the edge of his seedling field staring up at that mountainside, ruminating on the Indian Tunnel? But he'd never put the two facts together. That tree must have come down near a hundred years ago, when his grandfather owned the whole southern slope of Zebulon Mountain. It was his grandfather, the first Garnett Walker, who'd named it, modestly choosing Zebulon from the Bible, even though some still did call it Walker's Mountain. Who else could have felled that tree? He and his sons would have spent a whole day and more with their shoulders against the crosscut saw to bring down that giant for lumber. They'd have been mad as hornets, then, to find after all their work that the old chestnut was too huge to be dragged down off the mountain. Probably they took away tree-sized branches to be milled into barn siding, but that trunk was just too big of an old monster and had to be left where it lay. Left to hollow itself out from the inside till nothing was left of it but a game for the useless mischief of boys.

Mules, they had to use in those days for any kind of work that got done: mules or men. A tractor was a thing still yet undreamed of. A mule could be coaxed into many a steep and narrow place where a tractor would not go, it was true. But! Some things could be wrought with horsepower that were beyond the power of horseflesh. That was the lesson he was meant to draw here, God's purpose for these paired recollections of Grandfather Walker and the Indian Tunnel. If they'd had a logging sledge or a good John Deere, that tree would not have gone to waste as boy-tunnel and bear den. Yes, sometimes horsepower can do what horseflesh cannot.

That was just it, the very thing he had been trying to tell the Rawley woman for years. "Miss Rawley," he'd explained until he was blue in the face as she traipsed through her primitive shenanigans, "however fondly we might recall the simple times of old, they had their limits. People keep the customs of their own day and time for good reason."

Nannie Land Rawley was Garnett's nearest neighbor and the bane of his life. *Miss Rawley* it was and ever would be, not *Missus,* even though she had once borne a child and it was well known in Zebulon County that she'd never married the father. And that had been some thirty years ago or more, a far cry before the days when young girls began to wear rings in their noses and bells on their toes as they did now, and turn out illegitimate children as a matter of course. In those days, a girl went away for a decent interval to visit a so-called relative and came back sadder but wiser. But not Miss Rawley. She never appeared the least bit sad, and the woman was unwise on principle. She'd carried the child right here in front of God and everybody, and acted like she had every right to parade a bastard child through a God-fearing community.

And every one of them has forgiven her by now, he reflected bitterly, peering up the rise through the trunks of her lower apple orchard toward her house, which sat much too close to his own on the crest of a small, flat knoll just before the land rose steeply up the mountainside. Of course there was the tragic business with the child to win them over, but even so, Nannie was the sort, she could get away with anything. *Every one of them just as pleasant as the day is long when they meet her out here in the lane, Nannie all rosy-cheeked amongst her daisies with her long calico skirt and braids wrapped around her head like some storybook Gretel.* They might gossip some, for how could such an odd bird fail to attract the occasional sharp arrow let loose from Oda Black down at the Black Store? But even the vociferous Oda would put a hand beside her mouth to cut short a remark about Nannie, letting the suggestion of it hang but packaging it with deep regret. Nannie bribed Oda with apple pies; that was one of her methods. People thought she was comical and intriguing but for the most part excessively kind. They didn't suspect her little figure of harboring the devil, as Garnett Walker did. He suspected Nannie Rawley had been put on this earth to try his soul and tempt his faith into doubt.

Nannie Land Rawley was Garnett's nearest neighbor and the bane of his life.

Why else, with all the good orchard land stretching north from here to the Adirondacks, would that woman have ended up as his neighbor?

Her sign alone was enough to give him hives. For two months now, ever since she'd first crept over on his side to put up that sign, he'd lain awake nearly every night, letting it get on his nerves: Heaven knows it's one thing when a Hereford jumps a fence and gets over onto a neighbor, *that* a body can forgive and forget, but a three-foot plywood sign does not get up and walk. Last night he'd fretted till nearly the crack of dawn, and after breakfast he'd made up his mind to walk out through his front seedling field to check the road frontage. Looking for "signs and wonders," as the Bible said, though Nannie's sign was known only for bad behavior.

He could see it now through the weeds, the back side of it, poking up out of the bank above Highway 6. He squinted to make sure; his eyesight had reached the point where it required some effort. Yes, the lettered side was facing the road, but he knew what it said,

Chestnut siding on an old outbuilding on the Virginia farm where Barbara Kingsolver wrote her novel Prodigal Summer. *(Photo by Steven Hopp.)*

the whole hand-painted foolishness of it commanding the roadside—*his* roadside, two hundred feet over his property line—to be a "NO SPRAY ZONE." As if all a person had to do to rule the world was concoct a fool set of opinions and paint them on a three-by-three square of plywood. That in a nutshell was Nannie Rawley.

It had started back in April when he left this steep weed patch to the county's boys for spraying, since it was a county right-of-way. The first of May he'd done the same again. Both times she'd snuck out here in the middle of the night before road-spraying day, working in darkness like the witch she was, to move her sign over onto Garnett. Now it was the second of June, and the spray truck must be due again soon. How could she always know when it was coming? Was that witchcraft, too? Most people around here couldn't even predict when their own cows were going to calve, let alone prophesy the work habits of a bunch of county-employed teenage hoodlums wearing earplugs, jewelry, and oversized trousers.

In previous years, he had talked to her. He'd had the patience of Job, informing her it was her duty to keep her NO SPRAY ZONE, if she insisted on having such a thing, inside of her own legal property boundaries. He had pointed dramatically at their line fence and stated (for Garnett was a reader), "Miss Rawley, as the poet said, 'Good fences make good neighbors.'"

She would reply, "Oh, people just adore fences, but Nature doesn't give a hoot." She claimed the wind caused the weed killer on his side to drift over into her orchards.

If only his poisons *would* drift over onto her trees. He knew very well, and had told her so, that without his constant spraying to keep them down, the Japanese beetles would overrun her orchards completely. She'd be standing out there in her calico skirt under leafless trees, wringing her hands, wondering what'd gone wrong in her little paradise. Success without chemicals was impossible. Nannie Rawley was a deluded old harpy in pigtails.

❧ ❧ ❧

Garnett stood admiring the side of his barn. Over the course of a century the unpainted chestnut planks had weathered to a rich, mottled gray, interrupted only by the orange and lime-colored streaks of lichen that brightened the wood in long, vertical stripes where moisture drained from the galvanized tin roof.

He was haunted by the ghosts of these old chestnuts, by the great emptiness their extinction had left in the world, and so this was something Garnett did from time to time, like going to the cemetery to be with dead relatives: he admired chestnut wood. He took a moment to honor and praise its color, its grain, and its miraculous capacity to stand up to decades of weather without pressure treatment or insecticides. Why and how, exactly, no one quite knew. There was no other wood to compare with it. A man could only thank the Lord for having graced the earth with the American chestnut, that broad-crowned, majestic source of nuts and shade and durable lumber. Garnett could recall the days when chestnuts had grown so thick on the mountaintops of this county that in spring, when the canopies burst into flower, they appeared as snowcapped peaks. Families had lived through the winter on the gunnysacks of chestnuts stored in their root cellars, and hams from the hogs they'd fattened on chestnuts, and the money they'd earned sending chestnuts by the railroad car to Philadelphia and New York City, where people of other nationalities and religious persuasions roasted them for sale on street corners. He thought of cities as being populated with those sorts of people, the types to hunker over purchased coals, roasting nuts whose origins they could only guess at. Whereas Garnett liked to think of his own forebears as chestnut people. Of chestnut logs the Walkers had built their cabins, until they had sons and a sawmill to rip and plane the trees into board lumber from which they then built their houses and barns and finally an empire. It was lumber sales from Walker's Mill that had purchased the land and earned his grandfather the right to name Zebulon Mountain. Starting with nothing but their wits and strong hands, the Walkers had lived well under the sheltering arms of the American chestnut until the slow devastation began to unfold in 1904, the year that brought down the chestnut blight. The Lord giveth and the Lord taketh away.

That was not Garnett's to question, the fall of his family fortunes. He didn't begrudge the sales of land that by the year 1950, when the last chestnuts were gone, had whittled his grandfather's huge holdings down to a piece of bottomland too small to support anything but a schoolteacher. Garnett hadn't minded being a teacher; Ellen certainly hadn't minded being married to one. He hadn't needed to own an empire and did not resent the necessity of close neighbors (save for one). But neither did he ever doubt that his own dream—to restore the chestnut tree to the American landscape—was also a part of God's plan, which would lend to his family's history a beautiful symmetry. On his retirement from the Zebulon County school system a dozen years ago, Garnett had found himself blessed with these things: a farm with three level fields and no livestock; a good knowledge of plant breeding; a handful of seed sources for American chestnuts; and access to any number of mature Chinese chestnuts that people had planted in their yards in the wake of the blight. They had found the nuts far less satisfactory, and of course the tree itself had none of the American chestnut's graceful stature or its lumber qualities, but the Chinese chestnut had proven entirely resistant to blight. This lesser tree had been spared for a divine purpose, like some of the inferior animals on Noah's ark. Garnett understood that on his slow march toward his heavenly reward, he would spend as many years as possible crossing and backcrossing the American with the Chinese chestnut. He worked like a driven man, haunted by his arboreal ghosts, and had been at it for nearly a decade now. If he lived long enough he would produce a tree with all the genetic properties of the original American chestnut, except one: it would retain from its Chinese parentage the ability to stand tall before the blight. It would be called the Walker American chestnut. He would propagate this seedling and sell it by mail order that it might go forth and multiply in the mountains and forests of Virginia, West Virginia, Kentucky, and all points north to the Adirondacks and west to the Mississippi. The landscape of his father's manhood would be restored.

But neither did he ever doubt that his own dream—to restore the chestnut tree to the American landscape—was also a part of God's plan, which would lend to his family's history a beautiful symmetry.

A loud buzz near his ear made Garnett turn his head and look up too fast, causing him to experience such a bout of dizziness that he nearly had to sit down on the grass. The Japanese beetles were thick as pea soup already, and it was only June. Something to add to his list for the hardware store today: malathion. The Sevin dust wasn't killing them dead enough. Or it was washing off in all this rain.

He glanced over toward Rawley's, whence came the plague. Earlier in the week he had attempted to speak to her over the fence: "The source of Japanese beetles seems to be your brush piles, Miss Rawley."

To which she'd replied, "Mr. Walker, the source of Japanese beetles is Japan."

There was no talking to her. Why even try?

He noted that her pitiful old foreign truck was gone from its usual spot between the lilac hedge and her white clapboard house. He wondered where she might have gone on a Friday morning. Garnett stepped up onto his porch. He gathered up his ring of keys, counted the cash in his wallet, and locked the kitchen door. He stole another glance over toward Nannie's, noticing with surprise a large, roughly cow-shaped patch of darkness on her roof. He walked a bit closer and squinted through the tops of his bifocals. It was a patch of the green shingles missing; they must have blown off in the last storm. What a mess that must be, in all this rain, and what a nuisance to replace. Worse than a nuisance: those old, hand-cut shingles were impossible to find nowadays. She would have to redo the whole roof if she didn't want it to look hodgepodge. He touched the corners of his mouth, trying not to harbor pleasure at a neighbor's misfortune. She did not know that in Garnett's own garage there was a stock of those green shingles, from the original lot that Garnett's father and Old Man Rawley had ordered together and shared.

∾ ∾ ∾

The bank of Egg Creek was soaked like a sponge with rain. Garnett could only look the hillside up and down and shake his head. The ground had gotten so soft that a fifty-year-old oak growing out of it had leaned over, pulled its roots out of the mud like loose teeth, and fallen over before its time. Somebody would have to be called, some young man with a chain saw who could tame this tangle of trunk and branches into a cord of firewood. Finding a man to do it wasn't the problem. This section of Egg Creek stood as the property line dividing Garnett's land from Nannie Rawley's, *that* was the problem. It was only fair that she pay for half the cleanup—or more, really, since it was *her* tree that had fallen on *him*. But they would have to come to some agreement, and for the likes of *that* no precedent existed in the history of Garnett and Nannie.

Garnett's plan today had been to go right up and rap on her screen door, but on his way up the drive he'd spied her ladders and picking paraphernalia scattered around out here in the orchard on the west side. He'd gone almost as far as the line fence that separated their fields when he heard her humming up in the foliage and saw her legs on the ladder, sticking out below the ceiling of green leaves overhead. *This is how a duck must look to a turtle underwater*, he thought wickedly. Then he took a deep breath. He wasn't going to dally around here.

"Hello! I have some news," he called. "One of your trees came down on me."

Her dirty white tennis shoes descended two rungs on the ladder, and her face peered down at him through the branches. "Well, you don't look that much the worse for it, Mr. Walker."

He shook his head. "There's no need to behave like a child."

"It wouldn't hurt you, though," she said. "Now and then."

"I have a piece of business to discuss with you," he said sternly. "I would appreciate talking with you down here on solid ground."

She climbed down her ladder with a full apple basket over her arm, muttering about having to work for a living instead of collecting a retirement pension. She set her basket on the ground and put her hands on her hips. "All right. If you're going to be sanctimonious about it, *I* have a piece of business to discuss with *you*!"

He felt his heart stutter a little. It aggravated him no end that she could scare him this way. "What is it, then?"

"That god-awful Sevin you've been spraying on your trees every blooming day of the week! You think you've got troubles, a *tree* came over on you? Well your poison has been coming down on me, and I don't just mean my property, my apples, I mean *me*. I have to breathe it. If I get lung cancer, it will be on your conscience."

Her hail of words stopped; their gazes briefly met and then fell to the grass around each other's feet. Ellen had died of lung cancer, metastasized to the brain. People always remarked on the fact that she never had smoked.

"I'm sorry, you're thinking about Ellen," Nannie said. "I'm not saying your poisons caused her to get sick."

She had thought it, though, Garnett realized with a shock. Thought it and put it about so other people were thinking it, too. It dawned on him with a deeper dread that it might possibly be true. He'd never read the fine print on the Sevin dust package, but he knew it got into your lungs like something evil. Oh, Ellen.

"I've just been festering about it too long," Nannie said. "Just now I was up there stewing over a whole slew of things at once: your poison, the bills I need to pay, the shingles off my roof I can't replace. Dink Little claims they don't make that kind anymore, can you imagine?"

Garnett felt a pang of guilt about the shingles but let it pass. "It's the middle of July," he said. "The caterpillars are on my seedlings like the plague. If I didn't spray I'd lose all this year's new crosses."

"See, but you're killing all my beneficials. You're killing my pollinators. You're killing the songbirds that eat the bugs. You're just a regular death angel, Mr. Walker."

"I have to take care of my chestnuts," he replied firmly.

"No, now, I haven't explained it to you right. There are two main kinds of bugs, your plant eaters and your bug eaters. So out in your field you have predators and herbivores. You with me so far?"

He waved a hand in the air. "I taught vocational agriculture for half as long as you've been alive. You have to get up early in the morning to surprise an old man like me."

"Well, all right. Your herbivores have certain characteristics."

"They eat plants."

"Yes. You'd call them pests. And they reproduce fast."

"Don't I know it!" Garnett declared.

"Predator bugs don't reproduce so fast, as a rule. But see, that works out right in nature because one predator eats a world of pest bugs in its life. The plant eaters have to go faster just to hold their ground. They're in balance with each other. So far, so good?"

Garnett nodded. He found himself listening more carefully than he'd expected.

"All right. When you spray a field with a broad-spectrum insecticide like Sevin, you kill the pest bugs *and* the predator bugs, bang. If the predators and prey are balanced out to start with, and they both get knocked back the same amount, then the pests that survive will *increase* after the spraying, fast, because most of their enemies have just disappeared. And the predators will *decrease* because they've lost most of their food supply. So in the lag between sprayings, you end up boosting the numbers of the bugs you don't want and wiping out the ones you need. And every time you spray, it gets worse."

"The agricultural chemical industry would be surprised to hear your theory."

"Oh, fiddle, they know all about it. They just hope *you* don't. The more money you spend on that stuff, the more you need. It's like getting hooked on hooch."

"Times change," Garnett said. "That's all."

"*Time* doesn't change; *ideas* change. Prices and markets and laws. Chemical companies change, and turn your head along with them, looks like."

Garnett brushed invisible dirt off the knees of his trousers. Why did Nannie Rawley bother him so? Dear Lord, if he had world enough and time, he still couldn't answer. He stopped pacing and looked at her there all wide-eyed, waiting for judgment. She didn't look old-fashioned, exactly, but like a visitor to this day from an earlier time—like a girl, with her wide, dark eyes and her crown of braided hair. Even the way she was dressed, in denim dungarees and a sleeveless white shirt, gave her the carefree air of a child out of school for summer, Garnett thought. Just a girl. And he felt tongue-tied and humiliated, like a boy.

"Why does everything make you so mad?" she asked finally. "I only wish you could see the beauty in it. A field of plants and bugs working out a balance in their own way. Eating and reproducing, that's the most of what God's creation is all about."

"I'm going to have to take exception to that."

She tilted her head, looking up at him. He could never tell if she was coy or just a little hard of hearing. "You want to make everything so simple," she said. "You told me the other day that only an intelligent, beautiful creator could create beauty and intelligence. But I'll tell you what. See that basket of June Transparents there? You know what I put on my trees to make those delicious apples? Poop, mister. Horse poop and cow poop."

"Are you likening the Creator to manure?"

"I'm saying your logic is weak."

"I'm a man of science."

"Well, then, you're a poor one! Don't tell me I can't understand the laws of thermodynamics. I went to college once upon a time, and it was *after* they discovered the world was round. I'm not scared of big words."

"I didn't say you were."

"You did, too! 'I realize you're no scientist, Miss Rawley,'" she mocked, in an unnecessarily prissy version of his voice.

"No, now, I just meant to set you straight on a few points."

"You self-righteous old man. Do you ever wonder why you don't have a friend in the world since Ellen died?"

He blinked. He may have even allowed his jaw to go a little slack.

"Well, I'm sorry to be the one to break it to you. But just listen to yourself talk!" she cried. " 'How could random chance—i.e. evolution—create complex life-forms?' How can you be so self-satisfied and so ignorant at the same time?"

"Well, then," he said, crossing his arms, "how *does* random chance create complex life-forms?"

"This just seems ridiculous, a man who does what you do claiming not to believe in the very thing he's doing."

"What I do has nothing to do with apes' turning helter-skelter into thinking men."

"Evolution isn't helter-skelter! It's a business of choosing things out, just like how you do with your chestnuts." She nodded toward his seedling field and then frowned, looking at it more thoughtfully. "In every generation, all the trees are a little different, right? And which ones do you choose to save out for crossing?"

"The ones that survive the blight best, obviously. I inoculate the trees with blight fungus and then measure the size of the chancres. Some of them hardly get sick at all."

"All right. So you pick out the best survivors, you cross their flowers with one another and plant their seeds, and then you do it all over again with the next generation. Over time you're, what, making a whole new kind of chestnut plant?"

"That's right. One that can resist the blight."

"A whole new species, really."

"No, now, only God can do that. I can't make a chestnut into an oak."

"You could if you had as much time as God does."

Oh, if only I did, Garnett thought with the deep despair of a man running out of time. Just enough years to make a good chestnut, that was all he wanted, but in his heart he knew he couldn't expect them. He had thought sometimes of praying for this but trembled to think what God would make of his request.

"Evolution isn't helter-skelter! It's a business of choosing things out, just like how you do with your chestnuts."

But he was drifting. "I don't know what you're talking about," he said irritably.

"What you're doing is artificial selection," she replied calmly. "Nature does the same thing, just slower. This 'evolution' business is just a name scientists put on the most obvious truth in the world, that every kind of living thing adjusts to changes in the place where it lives. Not during its own life, but you know, down through the generations. Whether you believe in it or not, it's going on right under your nose over there in your chestnuts."

"You're saying that what I do with chestnut trees, God does with the world."

"It's a way to look at it. Except you have a goal, you know what you want. In nature it's predators, I guess, a bad snap of weather, things like that, that cull out the weaker genes and leave the strong ones to pass on. It's not so organized as you are, but it's just as dependable. It's just the thing that always happens."

"I'm sorry, but I can't liken God's will to a thing that just *happens.*"

"All right, then, don't. I don't care." She sounded upset. She sat down on her bushel and put her face in her hands.

"Well, *I can't.*" He tried to hold still instead of pacing around, but his knees hurt. "That's just a godless darkness, to think there's no divine goal. Mankind can't be expected to function in a world like that. The Lord God is good and just."

When she looked up at him, there were tears in her eyes. "Mankind functions with whatever it has to. When you've had a child born with her chromosomes mixed up and spent fifteen years watching her die, you come back and tell me what's good and just."

"Oh, goodness," Garnett said nervously. The sight of a woman's tears in broad daylight should be against the law.

She fished in her pocket for a handkerchief and blew her nose loudly. "I'm all right," she said after a minute. "I didn't say what I meant to, there." She blew her nose again, like nobody's business. It was a little shocking. She rubbed her eyes and stuffed the red bandanna back in her pocket. "I'm not a godless woman," she said. "I see things my own way, and most of it makes me want to get up in the morning and praise glory. I don't see you doing that, Mr. Walker. So I don't appreciate your getting all high and mighty about the darkness in my soul."

He turned his back on her and looked out over his own land. The narrow, bronze-tipped leaves of the young chestnuts waved like so many flags, each tree its own small nation of genetic promise.

"We've both had our griefs to bear, Miss Rawley. You and I."

❧ ❧ ❧

Garnett paused halfway up the hill to take a rest. His heart was beating harder than seemed entirely necessary. He could hear the grumble and whine of the boy's chain saw already at

Seedlings at Meadowview.

work up there. She would be there, too, by now. They'd agreed to meet at noon to work out dividing the firewood and so on, and it was fourteen after, if his watch could be trusted. Well, she could wait. He was her elder; she could have a little respect. He sat down on a log next to the creek, just for a minute. A damselfly lit on the tip of a horsetail reed very close to his head, near enough for him to see it well. Its wings were black, not quite opaque but sheer like lace, with a pearly white dot at each wingtip. It reminded Garnett somehow of the underthings of women he'd known long ago, back when women wore garter belts and other contrivances that took some time and trouble to remove.

Now, why on earth was he sitting here in the woods thinking about women's underthings? He felt deeply embarrassed and prayed hastily to the Lord to forgive the unpredictable frailties of an old man's mind. He found his feet and headed on up the hill.

She was there, all right, having some kind of jolly conversation with the boy. They both turned to greet him.

"Mr. Walker! Now, you remember Oda's son Jarondell, don't you?"

"Of course. My regards to your mother." Remember *Jarondell*, he thought. That was a name for you. He was more likely to remember the expiration date on his can of Sevin dust. When the chain saw roared up again, Nannie held her hands over her ears and motioned that they should go down the path. He followed her around a bend where the roar receded to a whine, but she kept walking, all the way down to the log where he had rested earlier.

"Don't mind me," she said. "I'm in a tizzy today."

Today, he thought. "Over what, now?" He tried to sound like a father indulging a child, but the effect was lost on her. She launched eagerly onto her soapbox, leaning forward and clasping her hands on her knees and looking him straight in the face.

"It's *bees*," she said. "Down at the Full Gospel church they've got themselves in a pickle from killing their bees. *Killing* them—they fumigated! Now they've got honey two inches deep on the floor of the whole church, oozing out of the walls, and they're blaming the poor dead bees. And it's the bees that need to vibrate their wings over it night and day to keep it cool in July. Without workers in there to cool the hive, that comb's going to melt, and all the honey will come pouring out." She shook her head sadly. "Don't people *know* these things? Are we old folks the only ones left that think twice about the future? You'd think young people would be more careful. They're the ones that are going to be around in fifty years. Not *us*."

"No, not us," Garnett agreed mournfully. He tried not to think of his chestnut fields overgrown with weeds, waving their untended, carefully crossbred leaves like flags of surrender in a world that did not even remember what was at stake. Who would care about his project when he was gone? Nobody. That was the answer: not one living soul. He had kept this truth at a distance for so long, it nearly made him weep with relief to embrace the simple, honest grief of it. He rested his hands on his knees, breathed in and out. So what did it all matter, then?

They sat silent for a while, listening to the wood thrushes. Nannie pulled a handful of cockleburs from her skirt and then, without really appearing to give it much thought, reached over and plucked half a dozen from the knees of Garnett's trousers. He felt strangely moved by this fussy little bit of female care. He realized vaguely that as a mortal man, he was starved. He cleared his throat. "Did it ever cross your mind that God—or whatever you want to call him, with your balance of nature and so forth—that he got carried away with the cockleburs?"

"There's too many of them. I'll have to agree with you on that."

Garnett felt faintly cheered: she agreed. He gazed up into the dimness of her woods and was surprised to notice a sapling waggling its leaves in the breeze, uphill from the creek. "Why, look, that's a chestnut, isn't it?" He pointed.

"It is. A young one," she said.

"My eyes aren't good, but I can spy a chestnut from a hundred paces."

"That one's come up from an old stump where a big one was cut down years ago," she said. "I've noticed they always do that. As long as the roots keep living, the sprouts will keep coming out around the stump. But before they get big enough to flower, they always die. Why is that?"

"The blight chancre has to get up a head of steam before it sets off other little chancres and kills the tree. It takes eight or nine years out in the open, or longer in the woods, where a tree grows slower. The fungus inside there is more or less proportional to the size of the trunk. But you're right, they're just about sure to die before they get up enough size to set any seeds. So biologically speaking, the species is dead."

"Biologically dead. Like us," she said with no particular emotion.

"That's right," he said uncomfortably. "If we consider ourselves as having no offspring."

"And unlikely to produce any more at this point." She let out an odd little laugh.

He didn't need to comment on that.

"Now, tell me something," she said. "I've always wondered this. Your hybrids are American chestnut stock crossed with Chinese chestnut, right?"

"That's right. And backcrossed with American again. If I can keep at it long enough I'll get a cross that has all the genes of an American chestnut except for the one that makes it susceptible to blight."

"And the gene for the resistance comes from the Chinese side?"

"That's right."

"But where did you get the American chestnut seed stock to begin with?"

"That's a good question. I had to look high and low," Garnett said, pleased as punch. No one had asked him a question about his project in many a year. Once Ellen had talked her niece into bringing her third-grade class out to see it, but those children had acted like it was a sporting event.

"Well, such as where?" she asked, truly interested.

"As long as the roots keep living, the sprouts will keep coming out around the stump. But before they get big enough to flower, they always die. Why is that?"

"I wrote letters and made calls to Forest Service men and what all. Finally I located two standing American chestnuts that were still flowering, about as sick and old as a tree can get but not dead yet. I paid a boy to climb up and cut me down some flowers, and I put them in a bag and brought them back here and pollinated a Chinese tree I had in my yard, and from the nuts I grew out my first field of seedlings. That gave me my first generation, the half-Americans."

"Where were the old trees? I'm just curious."

"One was in Hardcastle County, and one was over in West Virginia. Lonely old things, flowering but not setting any seeds because they had no neighbors to cross with. There are still a few around. Not many, but a few."

"Oh, I know it."

"There were probably plenty, back in the forties," Garnett went on. "Do you remember when the CCC was telling us to cut every last one down? We thought they were all going anyway. But now, if you think about it, that wasn't so good. Some of them could have made it through. Enough to make a comeback."

"Oh, they would have," she agreed. "Daddy was adamant about that. Those two up here in our woodlot, he was determined not to let anybody get. One night he stopped a man that was up here aiming to cut them down and haul them off with a mule before the sun came up!"

"You had chestnut trees in your woodlot?" Garnett asked.

She cocked her head. "Don't you know the ones I mean? There's the one about a quarter mile up this hill, just awful-looking because of all the dead limbs it's dropped. But it still sets a few seeds every year, which the squirrels eat up. And the other one is way on top of the ridge, in about the same shape."

"You have two reproductive American chestnuts in your woodlot?"

"Are you fooling with me? You didn't know?"

"How would I have known that?"

She started to speak, then paused, touched her lip, then spoke. "I never really think of the woods as *belonging* to us, exactly. I walk all over your hills when I feel like it. I just assumed you did the same with mine."

"I haven't trespassed on your land since the day your father bought it from mine."

"Well," she said cheerfully. "You should have."

He wondered if this was really possible, what she was telling him. Certainly she knew apples, but did she honestly know a chestnut from a cherry?

"Would you like to walk up on the hill with me and see those two chestnuts? Would it do you any good to have two more seed sources for your breeding program?"

"Do you have any idea?" he asked, amazed and excited. "It would double the amount of genetic variation I have now. I would have a faster, healthier project by a mile, Miss Rawley. If I had flowers from those two trees."

"Consider them yours, Mr. Walker. Anytime."

"Thank you," he said. "That's very kind of you."

"Not at all." She folded her hands on her lap.

Garnett could picture the two old chestnuts up there, anomalous survivors of their century, gnarled with age and disease but still standing, solitary and persistent for all these years. Just a stone's throw from his property. It was almost too much to believe. He dared to hope they still had a few flowers clinging on, this late in the summer. What that infusion of fresh genetic material would do for his program! It was a miracle. In fact, now that he thought about it, if those trees had been shedding pollen all along they might already have helped him out, infusing his fields with a little bit of extra diversity. He thought he'd been working alone. You just never knew.

An hour and ten minutes later, Garnett returned to Nannie's backyard with one asphalt shingle in his hand. She was carrying a bushel of Gravensteins to her pickup truck, starting to load up for the Amish market tomorrow, and was so startled to see Garnett Walker that she stumbled and almost dropped her basket.

He held up the shingle, showing her the peculiar heart shaped profile that matched the ones on her roof, and then he threw it at her feet. It lay there in the grass next to a puddle, this thing she needed, like a valentine. A bright crowd of butterflies rose from the puddle in trembling applause.

"There are two hundred of those in my garage. You can have them all."

She looked from the shingle to Garnett Walker and back to the shingle. "Lord have mercy," she said quietly. "A miracle." ∾

We *Can* Restore the American Chestnut

By Philip A. Rutter

This essay first appeared as an editorial in the newsletter of the Natural Resources Council of America in January 1989 and was reprinted in the fall/winter 1991 issue of the Journal of The American Chestnut Foundation. *If anything, its message is more timely now than it was almost twenty years ago, and much more urgent.*

Imagine the furor if an explorer, poking into a sheltered but remote bay in southern Greenland, discovered a small but healthy population of the long-extinct great auk. International headlines would surely result, and dozens of meetings of government commissions and conservation organizations, as the world mobilized to protect, preserve, and eventually restore this fascinating bird. It is hard to conceive any other response—we could never ignore such a species in need. How is it, then, that the American chestnut tree, once the most productive component of the eastern hardwood forests, has been an orphan for decades, and projects to restore it are still unacknowledged and desperately underfunded?

The American Chestnut Foundation is a new organization created to deal with an old disaster. The great chestnut blight of the 1920s and '30s was possibly the most destructive forest disease episode in history, and was certainly one of the formative influences for the entire conservation movement. But much of the story has now been forgotten, and the species has long been considered beyond all hope of saving. It is always dangerous to forget history, and doubly so in this case: not only is there a real danger of repeating past mistakes, but an opportunity to remedy old problems with new solutions could all too easily be ignored. The chestnut, however, was simply too important a species for us to miss any chance that it might be restored. Our foundation intends to see that the full restoration of the tree to its place in the forest communities becomes a reality.

The American chestnut tree was destroyed by a human-imported fungus disease. Prior to the epidemic this tree was probably the single most important tree in the eastern hardwood forests, both from the standpoint of human economics, and in regard to its keystone role in the hardwood ecosystem. Its natural range covered some 200 million acres, and in the Appalachian regions from New England to northern Georgia it is estimated that a full quarter of all the hardwood trees in those vast forests were chestnuts.

Its unique importance to the ecosystem, including humans, lay both in the fact that it grew desirable wood 30 to 50 percent faster than oaks (to which it is related), and in that it alone of the forest trees produced generally reliable crops of nuts. Virtually everything in the forests ate those nuts, and the availability of a large, dependable food source in late fall may have accounted for much of the abundance of game reported by early explorers and settlers. Imagine a forest where a quarter of the trees could he counted on to produce one to three bushels of nuts every fall; and then imagine the impact on the entire ecosystem.

Biologically the loss of those trees was staggering, and there is evidence that the chestnut tree is not ecologically replaceable by the many species which now grow in its place. Economically, a similar loss might be felt if Douglas fir were to suddenly disappear. The extent of the damage was realized at the time, and disasters of this magnitude do not go unaddressed. The eager young men recruited into the infant Forest Service by Gifford Pinchot tackled the problem vigorously, but without effect. The fungus killed more than 99.99 percent of the chestnut population; an extraordinarily efficient pathogen. Billions of trees died; the blight was far more destructive than the currently familiar Dutch elm disease.

By the 1950s, American chestnut was reduced from a dominant species of giant forest trees to a residual population of understory shrubs, sprouting from the stumps of trees killed by the blight. At about the same time, government research on the species was halted as a waste of money. The chestnut joined the list of species exterminated by human folly—it has now long been considered an issue as dead as the passenger pigeons that once fed on it.

The chestnut, however, is far from extinct.

The stump sprouts, as a part of the unusual biology of the tree, continue to survive. They now go through cycles of growth and renewed epidemic, and since the blight has now so much less to feed on, and the spore population is consequently so much less than it was during the pandemic, it is common for trees to survive for as many as 25 years before the blight knocks them down once more. Only rarely do new seedlings get started, however, and the natural attrition of the years continues to erode the remaining sprout populations. Extinction is not here, but is a definite possibility in the foreseeable future.

The great hope stems from the fact that in the past few years several new approaches to the possible restoration of the species have been suggested, ranging from biological control of the fungus to breeding resistant trees using modern techniques to biotechnological manipulation. Virtually all scientists intimate with the tree and the fungus are highly optimistic that one or a combination of these methods could actually result in a complete recovery of the chestnut, restoring one of this continent's most productive natural resources. Governmental and business interest in funding the necessary research, however, has been slight.

The great hope stems from the fact that in the past few years several new approaches to the possible restoration of the species have been suggested.

It is not hard to understand why. Government funding of forest research has been decreasing recently, and with a shrinking pie, it is easy to see that administrators would not be eager to try to cut yet another piece from it, particularly not for a project with a history of failure. Business has perhaps less excuse, and yet it is not difficult to guess that a project with no probable payback for at least thirty years would not be very attractive in the absence of compelling reasons to undertake it.

Perhaps it is just as well. The history of governmental research on the chestnut has been one of repeated fits and starts: individual researchers have maintained their research programs by force of personality, but when they retired, years of work were lost when a successor's true interests lay elsewhere. In the worst cases, research plantings have actually been destroyed to make way for other projects. Realistically, research on forest trees must be able to count on expanses of time well in excess of the average scientist's career. Given the predictable changes of priorities the political process generates, we must consider the possibility that research on forests and forest trees, in institutions which rely on the contemporary political administration for their funding, will always be in some jeopardy.

The American Chestnut Foundation was created with these thoughts in mind. In order to supply the continuity of research necessary to work with a species with a 400-year life span, we have as our sole task the pursuit of projects that can lead or contribute to the restoration of the chestnut. We will not be sidetracked, nor will we quit. No forest disease problem is insolvable, unless abandoned.

We have the support of the national scientific community involved in chestnut research. We also seek public members from the entire nation, since the problem is one that does not respect state lines.

So far, however, we are badly underfunded by the standards of most national organizations. Our consultants tell us that the reason, in part, is that our project is slightly "different." It covers too large a region to immediately catch the eye of local philanthropists. The effects of the restoration would also be so large that they are not easily categorized as conservation, preservation of biological diversity, or economic development, a situation that can leave potential donors uncertain about whether we fit within their "guidelines."

We have as our sole task the pursuit of projects that can lead or contribute to the restoration of the chestnut. We will not be sidetracked, nor will we quit.

The sweeping impact of restoring such a key species, however, is precisely why we are determined to succeed. This is not, and was never conceived as, a "single species" project. What makes the restoration worth attempting is the very fact that the health of the entire ecosystem, humans included, could be strongly bolstered by this uniquely productive component.

There are several reasons why our project should be of special interest to the conservation community.

First, there is the fact that the tree is a "nature," "conservation," "preservation," and human "economic" project. The tree was a mainstay for game species; it also supported several specialized insect species, some of which have not been seen since the blight. And it was the economic backbone of the Appalachians. This one tree brings all these concerns together in a particularly clear fashion—it can help make it plain, to those who still do not understand, that these concerns which sometimes seem to be at odds with one another are deeply interconnected. When the forests die, it isn't just the wildlife that suffers, nor just the tender-hearted. We humans have a cold, hard, cash interest in seeing that our ecosystems stay healthy. When the tree was hurt, so were we; and badly. As a tool to teach that lesson, the American chestnut is unexcelled.

Second, the chestnut focuses many high-visibility environmental concerns in one species. Reforestation to counteract the greenhouse effect is an idea that has captured the public interest—what better species to plant than this biological powerhouse? But forests everywhere are declining; could trees withstand the already degraded environment well enough to make a real impact on atmospheric CO_2? While the proper answer to acid rain is to make the rain less acid, not find species that will tolerate poor conditions, in the meantime chestnut does tolerate highly acid soils much better than many other species. Also, chestnut trees appear to be among the survivors of the gypsy moth infestations. Perhaps this tree stands some chance of withstanding these threats to forests, when others are failing.

Third, what possible better justification for the environmental community's concern for the preservation of biological diversity could there be than the restoration to productivity of such a key species? Until recently we have not appreciated the unique roles the chestnut played in the Appalachian forests. Only now, sixty years after the blight, can we see clearly that the productivity and health of the entire ecosystem have suffered irremediable harm. Luckily, with this species, restoration is still a possibility; but for thousands of other species there will be no restoration from extinction, and no chance to reverse unrecognized damage.

Fourth, there is the hope that with the success of a project like restoring the American chestnut, we may begin to form a new habit—one of planning for the long term. Even in national policy making, habits are crucial. The first action of any administrator faced with a new problem is to see how similar difficulties have been handled in the past. As we are all well aware, far too often these days temporary patches are put on problems crying for real, long-term resolutions. If temporary patches are the only examples available, then we are likely to see the pattern repeated. Restoring the American chestnut cannot be accomplished in our own lifetimes. We hope and expect to make recovery inevitable, but the forests cannot resemble the originals in less than 300 years. We are no less determined to do it. Perhaps this may make it ever so slightly easier in the future to plan in terms of 150 and 200 years. With practice, maybe we could make it a habit.

And lastly, it looks like this is one we can win. The disease is not incurable, and the tree is a fast grower and vigorous colonizer of existing forests. If we can provide a leg up, the tree may carry out the restoration on its own. As rain forests and species continue to disappear; while groundwaters grow more foul; when even the once limitless oceans and atmosphere show unmistakable signs of damage, the chestnut blight may be a disaster that can be put right. That may be critical.

Hopelessness is one of our greatest enemies. If the majority of mankind comes to the conclusion that we are powerless to alter the apparent downward spiral of our biosphere, support for the difficult and endless tasks necessary to preserve the health of the world may waver. There is no substitute for the will to put things right, and to keep them that way. And there is no better brace for our collective will than a big win; something to demonstrate that we can, really can, make a difference. Just possibly, restoring the American chestnut might be that big win. But it is clear that we are going to need the support of the conservation community to make the restoration, and the win, a reality.

Eighteen Years On: An Icon of Hope

I've never met anyone who wasn't absolutely astonished when they woke up one day and discovered themselves to be twenty years older than when they last looked.

It's only been eighteen years since I wrote this—so I guess I don't have to wake up yet. That may be just as well. Like most of us, I'd prefer to believe that some of those eighteen years have only been a bad dream.

Ah, if only. Not everything that has happened has been horrible, though. They never found my great auks (though with Greenland melting, it could still happen), but somebody *did* find an ivory-billed woodpecker—even more astonishing, to my mind. And yes, I did recall the worldwide media explosion as I thought about this essay. Was that really an ivory-bill on that video? They're still fussing about it, of course; and it was no surprise to me when the Doubters spoke up. I don't know. I was fascinated and downloaded the available video clip here in my house in the woods, over my slow phone line. Not the world's greatest quality. The Doubters say that bird could be just a pileated woodpecker, nothing particularly special. I have pileateds here—they've been eating ants out of a black cherry tree right outside my window for . . . hmm, thirty years; so I've watched them plenty. I'll say this: if that bird in the video turns out to be a pileated, I'll eat a chestnut bur. Raw. No ketchup. There's no way; no pileated ever moved like that—wing strokes are all wrong.

From one standpoint, it doesn't matter whether that was really an ivory-bill or not. The significant thing was the vast—that's the only word—upwelling of *hope*. That grainy video is a very slender straw to grasp at, but the world not only grasped—it positively *lunged*. Everyone wanted it to be true. To me it was more than a little encouraging to see the extent of the interest, and the simple caring. People still care. We can see it.

The same message can be taken from the worldwide response to Al Gore's movie, and the current uproar over global warming, the noise about "biofuels." Tremendous enthusiasm—broadly based, and hopefully more than a flash in the pan. Though I'll bet another raw chestnut bur the noise and enthusiasm will die down again in a bit, people being what we are. Even so, people today still hope—just give them a straw. People *want* to hope. The world can work; the world can go on, and be healthy.

American Chestnut—A Gift, *1987, by Glen McCune. (Courtesy of the artist.)*

Amid all the corruptions and hatreds—which, incidentally, have been with us since Babylon was a village of five mud huts—the fact that people everywhere still hope, still care, is incredibly heartening. It's also something we can show our children—look: others care too. Don't give up, just yet.

And our tree is clearly going to be another icon of hope for our children to look to. Oh, I know—those Doubters are still there. They always are; a few even inside our fortifications! But listen—I can't tell you how *many* times someone involved in our Chestnut Foundation has come up to me and quietly admitted, "You know, I *never* thought this was going to get so far, so fast." Actually it would be easier to number the staunch believers; how many have said "I always knew this was going to work"? Well, none, actually. And yet—here we are.

From where we stand today, the chestnut restoration is working. The labor is far from over, of course, and in many ways will never be "over," life being what it is. But we have thousands of living chestnut trees, and many thousands more coming, and all with the hope that they will withstand the world and grow into forests once more.

When it happens—

Now there is a lovely phrase.

When it happens, it will not be *this* scrap of science, or that, that brought it about. It will be the hope—and the heart—of the people who wouldn't quit. Our Foundation.

Two hearts, actually—ours, and the chestnut's. ~

Philip A. Rutter, July 2007

An American chestnut sprout biding its time in the understory is made visible by the autumn gold of its leaves. (Photo by Frederick Paillet.)

Chestnuts in November

By Trumbull Stickney

Not all the trees are done, the branches mean,
The trunks begrimed and sodden, no, not all.
How fresh and, tho' a few, how prodigal
On yonder chestnut here and there are seen
White wisps, and, frilled about them, bits of green!
They colour on the deadness of the Fall,
They spring and with the 'lated swallows call
Happy next year into the year that's been.
O call not Nature spendthrift, and of these
Say not they bloom in error for the frost!
The sweetness of all things are promises
That sing our souls a little further on
Toward that which may be found in what is lost,
Which may come back again of what is gone.

Illustration by Susan Bull Reilly.

AFTERWORD

Chestnut Inspiration. The "magic" that has been the glue, the inspiration for growth, and what has sustained The American Chestnut Foundation.

Four years ago, looking ahead to the twenty-fifth anniversary to be celebrated in 2008, Ray Hornback, then vice president for development at TACF, and I had a discussion about telling the chestnut story to the public, a budding scheme that soon grew to considering a "coffee table book."

When Ray asked me who the editor might be, I responded that Chris Bolgiano would be a good choice—being a member, a donor of chestnut property in West Virginia, and an award-winning writer and author of books, including *The Appalachian Forest.* Chris already knew much about American chestnut and its story through her extensive research and her publications.

Shortly after that conversation, I called Chris from the airport while on a chestnut mission to the South. I asked her if she would be interested in editing such a book, and she responded, "Busy now but I am very interested once current obligations are complete. . . . I suggest you consider an anthology—a collection of essays. . . . You already have a wealth of information in your *Journal* and other publications." That sounded like a good approach.

Months later, at Penn State University/State College, Chris was our keynote speaker at the annual meeting, and Ray and I sat down with her later that evening to pose the question. She accepted the assignment as editor shortly after.

The next step was putting together a small committee of dedicated chestnut people and discussing details of potential content and possible next steps with publishers. I reached out to a couple of university publishers, through personal contacts. At first the reactions were quite promising. However, as a year wore on, it was clear that this wasn't going to work. One famous press said they didn't publish anthologies, even though their science editor was most interested in our project. Another (from Pennsylvania) asked what connection there was to their state (the answer being that Pennsylvania, historically, had more American chestnut than any other state).

Mary Belle Price and TACF president Marshal Case at the Price Farm inauguration, June 6, 1998.

After losing a year trying to get the publication off the ground, while pulling materials together, I woke up one morning and said to myself, "We can do this ourselves. We don't need a big university press. We simply need a publisher who shares our ideas." The very next morning, at my local Catamount

Rotary breakfast meeting, Tordis Ilg Isselhardt was the speaker, as president of a publishing company, Images from the Past. We at TACF wanted a book that could be part of the twenty-fifth anniversary (2008) celebration, and we wanted to work with a company that holds a single mission focus, like TACF. Tordis and I met two days later at the Foundation office and, as the saying goes, the rest is history.

The American Chestnut Foundation and Images from the Past were very quickly on the same path—reaching for the impossible dream—to publish an anthology and have it in print by the October 2007 TACF annual meeting, to gain some early, widespread publicity as we approached our twenty-fifth year. If we were good enough to produce the science that will restore American chestnut to eastern forests, then we were capable of doing all that was necessary to publish our own anthology.

Good, positive thinking—but how were we to pay for our grand plans on an already extremely limited operations budget? Again, the answer was to look to our own network. I phoned Mary Belle Price, long-term member and supporter, carrying the chestnut baton for her deceased husband. To be fair, and because I had wanted to dedicate the anthology to Glenn C. Price, I talked to her about the idea and what it could mean for visibility for TACF as it neared its twenty-fifth anniversary. I asked if she would be willing to allow us to borrow from the fund she had established to build a laboratory/office complex/volunteer facility. She liked the idea and immediately said yes. I suggested that we could replenish the fund with sales of the anthology. She liked that very much. Only then did I tell her of the idea to dedicate the book to her late husband. Silent and speechless, on the other end of the phone, Mary Belle was moved to tears.

Next step: get on with it and make it happen within a very tight deadline. Our chestnut publications team was in place, we had the talent and drive, but could we possibly do this within less than seven months?

Mary Belle Price and Glenn Price, 1992.

Again we turned to the extensive network that had been built up since 1998. We reached out to our honorary directors—two Nobel Peace Prize recipients—Jimmy Carter and Dr. Norman Borlaug. They both said they would contribute essays. Connect with Barbara Kingsolver, who used our Meadowview Research Farms in Virginia as a platform for her best-selling novel *Prodigal Summer.* She said yes. Get songwriter Bill Owens, Dolly Parton's uncle who put her on her career path, to tell the family story of the chestnut tree honeymoon suite. Use the connections that Ray Hornback had to civil rights author John Egerton and to Wendell Berry, the distinguished agrarian author and poet. Ask twenty-five-year editor of *Audubon,* Les Line, to write about trains and chestnut. Look up the connections of chestnut to famous people in American history—Presidents Washington, Jefferson, Lincoln, Franklin Roosevelt, and more recently Carter and George W. Bush. Go for the gold. Reach for the limits! We can do this

From left: *Bradford and Shelli-Lodge Stanback, with TACF's Fred Hebard, October 1994 at Meadowview Research Farm.*

and tell our story and engage the public. Everyone is welcome to restore a lost American icon, a keystone species. There are no political or economic barriers.

Famous-name recognition—not only presidents, but artists and environmentalists who connected with American chestnut: Thoreau, Frost, Winslow Homer, Andrew Wyeth, Gifford Pinchot: they wrote about or were inspired by chestnut, they understood the value to the American economy and the lifestyles of people of Appalachia.

Legions of generous, caring individuals from every walk of life connected to American chestnut: Glenn C. and Mary Belle Price, Bradford and Shelli-Lodge Stanback, the three generations of Weaver Family of Tennessee, the mountain man from Kentucky, the geophysicist from Maine, the politician from North Carolina, the librarian from Massachusetts, the musician from Connecticut, the philanthropist from Vermont, the innkeeper from Virginia, the orthopedic surgeon from South Carolina, the artist from New York, the financial guru from Texas, and the wildlife biologist from Pennsylvania.

The Prices pass the chestnut baton to the Stanbacks, but they make certain there is significant overlap and that not a step is missed. Mary Belle Price, working in honor of her deceased husband, Glenn, then cheers the Stanbacks on. The momentum builds, more individuals and families join the race to victory—to overcome the chestnut blight and restore an icon to its rightful place in American history.

The future looks bright. There is so much positive energy collectively working to restore American chestnut to eastern forests. It is good for wildlife, good for people, and good for the economy. Long live American chestnut, and may we pass 120-foot-high, 14-foot-diameter, blight-tolerant trees along to future generations.

The future! It is in the hands of the reader of this anthology. Are you up to helping? Will you commit to a leg of the race to, literally, save a species from extinction? Contact us, let us know what your connections/suggestions are and how you can help. Collectively, we can and will make a difference! ~

Marshal T. Case

In Memory Of

Henry I. Baldwin

John Barger

Wallace C. and Grace P. Barrett

Robert L. Bishop (Lucille S. Bishop)

Frank R. Capper (R. Alan Walter)

G. Harry Case

Helen and Melville Cornell Case

Major Marshal Rogers Case and Marshal Case Haggard

Dr. Richard B. Fischer, Professor of Nature Education

Philip J. Gensheimer, Jr.

Esther M. Johnson (Austin and Norma Jones)

Kevin Drew Kilgore

Dr. Gordon L. Kirkland, Jr.

Harold A. Knapp, Jr. (Emilie and Monty Crown)

G. John Lehrer (Kalista S. Lehrer)

Douglas John Lewis

William T. Lytle and Clara S. Lytle (Jack Lytle Bufton)

Curtis D. Ours (Jean W. Ours and the Ours family)

Henry and Rita Rydjeski

Cmdr. Francis Joseph Suhre, USN

Price M. Summerville (K.O. Summerville)

John Ellington Thompson III (Daphne Van Schaick)

Taylor Westbrook Wilcox

Honoraria and Donors

Warren J. Beaver

Karen Johnson Boyd

Dr. and Mrs. Gary Carver

Emilie and Monty Crown, in honor of Barbara B. Knapp

Ceree R. Dalton (Joel R. Hitt)

Andrew M. DeShane

Linda and Michael Doochin, in honor of our children, Jonathan, Arielle, and Jeremy

Francis Fenton

Dale Travis and Sigrid Freundorfer

Norman and Virginia Hochella

Eugene Hall Lewis

Anne & Lael Meixsell, Mntn Bay Fndn

Lee D. Miller

Moore State Park, Paxton, Massachusetts

Diana Rowan Rockefeller, in honor of her parents, Stanley S. and Arlene B. Wirsig

In honor of Mr. & Mrs. R. C. Weddle, Jr. (Dr. & Mrs. Ronald D. Weddle)

Robert and Sylvia Weiss, in honor of their children, Amy, Elizabeth, and Marian

Notes and Permissions

vi "Chestnuts in November" excerpt from *The Poems of Trumbull Stickney*. Boston: Houghton, Mifflin & Co., 1905.

Chapter 1

5 Ruby Hemenway and Albert Fritsch quotes from memories of the American chestnut collected over the years by The American Chestnut Foundation (TACF memoirs).

18, 19 "Majestic Sentinels to Bygone Years" from TACF memoirs.

19 Wendell Berry poem excerpt from *A Timbered Choir: The Sabbath Poems 1979–1997*. Published by Counterpoint, 1998, Washington, DC. Copyright Wendell Berry. Poems in the book are arranged by year, then by Roman numeral.

Chapter 2

21 Donald Culross Peattie quote from his *Natural History of Trees of Eastern and Central North America.* Boston: Houghton Mifflin Co., 1948.

22 "Where there be Mountaines" quote from *A Narrative of the Expedition of Hernando de Soto into Florida,* by a Gentleman of Elvas. First published at Evora 1557. Translated from the Portuguese by Richard Hackluyt, London, 1609. Many editions have been published since this first English translation.

Adriaen van der Donck quote from translation by Jeremiah Johnson, New York Historical Society, 1841.

William Byrd quote from *William Byrd's Natural History of Virginia, or the Newly Discovered Eden*, Richmond Croom Beatty and William J. Mulloy, eds. Richmond: Dietz Press, 1940.

William Bartram quote from his *Travels through North & South Carolina, Georgia, East & West Florida* . . . Philadelphia: James and Johnson, 1791. Bartram's *Travels* has since appeared in numerous editions, many of them abridged.

24 *The North American Sylva* of François André Michaux, plate 104, V. III, p. 10. Special Collections, University of Delaware Library, Newark, DE.

25 Passage is from P. L. Buttrick's "Commercial Uses of Chestnut," which first appeared in the October 1915 issue of the journal *American Forestry*. Reprinted by permission of *American Forests* magazine.

Cherokee Plants and Their Uses, a 400 Year History, copyright 1975 by Paul B. Hamel and Mary U. Chiltoskey.

26 "This Darling Old Fellow": Henry Ward Beecher "Chestnuts" article courtesy of the Berkshire Athenaeum, Pittsfield, MA.

34 "Bountiful Giants": Material originally published, in slightly different form, as "Memories of the American Chestnut," in *Foxfire 6*, Eliot Wigginton, ed. Garden City, NY: Anchor Press/Doubleday, 1980. Reprinted by permission of the publisher.

36 Harold Barber and William Banks quotes from TACF memoirs.

Chapter 3

39 "Moon of the Chestnuts": "The Bear Man Myth" from *James Mooney's History, Myths, and Sacred Formulas of the Cherokees.* One of the fundamental historical documents on Cherokee culture, Mooney's work was first published in two parts, *Myths of the Cherokee* (1900) and *The Sacred Formulas of the Cherokees* (1891), by the Bureau of American Ethnology.

40 Le Page Du Pratz quote from *Histoire de La Louisiane*, published in 3 vols., Paris, 1758, vol. II, p. 354–83. In John R. Swanton, *Indian Tribes of the Lower Mississippi Valley and Adjacent Coast of the Gulf of Mexico.* Smithsonian Institution, Bureau of American Ethnology Bulletin 43. Washington: Government Printing Office, 1911.

42, 43 "Fell from a Chestnut Tree": Newspaper articles from Early American Newspapers, an Archive of Americana Collection, published by Readex (Readex.com) a division of NewsBank Inc.

48 "No Chestnuts": Newspaper article from Early American Newspapers, an Archive of Americana Collection, published by Readex (Readex.com) a division of NewsBank Inc.

49 "Chestnuts are Plentiful": Newspaper article from Early American Newspapers, an Archive of Americana Collection, published by Readex (Readex.com) a division of NewsBank Inc.

P. L. Buttrick quote reprinted by permission of *American Forests* magazine.

56 "A Sight on Earth." Excerpted from "Memories of the American Chestnut," in *Foxfire 6*, Eliot Wigginton, ed. Garden City, NY: Anchor Press/Doubleday, 1980. Reprinted by permission of the publisher.

58, 59 Quotes from TACF memoirs.

60, 61 "A Painful Experience": Quotes from TACF memoirs.

65 Dr. John Brown quote from "Memories of the American Chestnut," in *Foxfire 6*, Eliot Wigginton, ed. Garden City, NY: Anchor Press/Doubleday, 1980. Reprinted by permission of the publisher.

Chapter 4

67 P. L. Buttrick article reprinted by permission of *American Forests* magazine.

70 "Gaining in Popularity": Excerpt from *New York Times* article made available from the ProQuest Historical Newspapers data base.

86 "Memories of a Noble Timber . . ." Excerpted from "Memories of the American Chestnut," in *Foxfire 6*, Eliot Wigginton, ed. Garden City, NY: Anchor Press/Doubleday, 1980. Reprinted by permission of the publisher.

92, 93 Quotes from TACF memoirs.

Chapter 5

105 "Chestnut of a hundred horses" photograph by Lucio Bertoloti, from *Gli alberi monumentali d'Italia*, Edizioni Abete, Roma, 1989, and reprinted in *El Castaño*, by Ernesto Vieitez Cortizo, edition Edilesa, Leon, Spain, 1996.

118 "A False but Famous Relative": Newspaper articles from Early American Newspapers, an Archive of Americana Collection, published by Readex (Readex.com) a division of NewsBank Inc.

Chapter 6

124 "Journey of a Chestnut Log": Copyright 2007 by John Egerton. The article was written specifically for use by The American Chestnut Foundation; printed with permission of the author.

Chapter 7

145–48 "Practical Extermination of the Chestnut Tree": Articles from the *New York Times* made available through ProQuest Historical Newspapers data base.

149 "Pennsylvania Takes the Lead": The Pennsylvania Chestnut Tree Blight Commission final report, together with other commission publications and photographs, is available on the Internet, courtesy of the Pennsylvania State University Libraries, at http://chestnut.cas.psu.edu/pabc.htm.

154 "Chestnut Trees Doomed": Article from the *New York Times* made available through ProQuest Historical Newspapers data base.

155 "Memories of a Fallen Giant." Excerpted from "Memories of the American Chestnut," in *Foxfire 6*, Eliot Wigginton, ed. Garden City, NY: Anchor Press/Doubleday, 1980. Reprinted by permission of the publisher.

Chapter 9

229 "Man with a Chestnut Mission": "Chestnuts as Slow Food" article by Corby Kummer reprinted by permission of *Atlantic Monthly* magazine.

Chapter 10

235 Wendell Berry excerpt from *A Timbered Choir: The Sabbath Poems 1979–1997*. Published by Counterpoint, 1998, Washington, DC. Copyright Wendell Berry. Poems in this book are arranged by year, then by Roman numeral.

236 "No More Work and Royalties Forever" based on an interview at Dollywood in May 2006. Printed with permission of Mr. Owens.

241 "Old Chestnuts": Excerpts from *Prodigal Summer* by Barbara Kingsolver, copyright 2000; published by permission of the author.

263 "Chestnuts in November" from *The Poems of Trumbull Stickney*. Boston: Houghton, Mifflin & Co., 1905.

Bibliography

Books

Berry, Wendell. *A Timbered Choir: The Sabbath Poems 1979–1997.* Washington, DC: Counterpoint, 1998.

Carter, Jimmy. *An Hour Before Daylight: Memoirs of a Rural Boyhood.* New York: Simon & Schuster, 2001.

Clarkson, Roy B. *Tumult on the Mountains: Lumbering in West Virginia 1770–1920.* Parsons, WV: McClain Printing Co., 1997.

Conservation Diaries of Gifford Pinchot. Harold Steen, ed. Durham, NC: Forest History Society, 2001.

Cunningham, Isabel Shipley. *Frank N. Meyer: Plant Hunter in Asia.* Ames: Iowa State University Press, 1984.

Foxfire 6. Eliot Wigginton, ed. New York: Anchor Press/Doubleday, 1980.

Kingsolver, Barbara. *Prodigal Summer.* New York: HarperCollins, 2000.

Labbe, John T., and Vernon Goe. *Railroads in the Woods.* Hamilton, MT: Oso Publishing, 1996.

Smith, J. Russell. *Tree Crops: A Permanent Agriculture.* Greenwich, CT: Devin Adair Co., 1953.

Thoreau, Henry David. *The Writings of Henry David Thoreau*, Sanborn, F. B., and Bradford Torrey, eds. Houghton Mifflin, 1906. Thoreau's writing are available in many editions.

Periodicals

The anthology draws extensively from issues of the *Journal of The American Chestnut Foundation*, Bennington, VT. Most issues of the Journal are available online at www.acf.org/Journal.htm.

CONTRIBUTORS

Sandra L. Anagnostakis is a preeminent plant pathologist who has dedicated much of her life to studying chestnut species and chestnut blight disease at the Connecticut Agricultural Experiment Station.

Don Barger and his wife, Marie, have lived their lives on the broad slopes of Chestnut Ridge at the western edge of the Alleghenies in Fayette County, Pennsylvania, where their forefathers settled as veterans of the Revolution.

Chris Bolgiano is an accomplished and award-winning author and editor. She lives on one hundred wooded acres in the mountains of Virginia.

Norman Borlaug is a recipient of the Nobel Peace Prize who is credited with saving over a billion people from starvation through his research on high-yield wheat and other food crops. Dr. Borlaug has also been awarded the Presidential Medal of Freedom and the Congressional Gold Medal.

Jimmy Carter, the thirty-ninth president of the United States and winner of the 2002 Nobel Peace Prize, is a long-term and active honorary director of TACF. He and his wife, Rosalynn, have a passion for chestnut. They enjoy their quiet life in Plains, Georgia, while continuing to travel extensively in support of many worthwhile causes.

Marshal T. Case, president of The American Chestnut Foundation, has spent his career building networks that protect wildlife and wildlife habitat and provide nature education opportunities for children and teachers. Among his many awards is the gold medal from the Natural Science for Youth Foundation.

J. Hill Craddock holds the "chestnut chair" at University of Tennessee, Chattanooga, where he teaches and has done extensive research with American chestnut.

Chris Ditlow creates custom-designed kitchen cabinets for architects and builders. His interest in American chestnut was sparked by his earlier work in the antiques business, repairing hundreds of pieces of furniture.

Mark L. Double has been a research associate in the Division of Plant and Soil Sciences at West Virginia University for more than thirty years. He served as TACF assistant treasurer for many years.

John Egerton, a Georgia-born writer, is author of the award-winning book on civil rights *Speak Now Against the Day: The Generation Before the Civil Rights Movement in the South.*

Dennis Fulbright holds a PhD from the University of California, Riverside, in plant pathology. He currently is a professor at Michigan State University, where one of his general areas of expertise is diseases of trees, including chestnut blight and *Phytophthora* root rot of conifers.

Doris Armstrong Goldman, who holds a PhD in biology from the University of Illinois, has been reintroducing native plants to the grounds at Renfrew Park in Waynesboro, Pennsylvania, for more than ten years. She researched, designed, and installed a historical reproduction of the park's circa-1800 Pennsylvania German four-square garden.

Frederick V. Hebard is a plant pathologist and senior scientist for TACF. He is also a first-rate farmer and mechanic.

Barbara Kingsolver, born in Kentucky, is an award-winning novelist, essayist, and poet. Among her many best-selling books are *Prodigal Summer*, set in the chestnut country of southwestern Virginia, *The Poisonwood Bible*, and *Animal, Vegetable, Miracle: A Year of Food Life*.

Corby Kummer, senior editor at the *Atlantic Monthly*, is one of the most widely read, authoritative, and creative food writers in the United States. He is the recipient of three James Beard Journalism Awards, including the M.F.K. Fisher Distinguished Writing Award.

Les Line, editor of *Audubon* magazine for twenty-five years, is an author and has collaborated with Hal Borland on several nature publications. He is a jazz and train buff.

William Lord, a retired veterinarian, is a naturalist and author who spends much of his time in libraries, researching material with a focus on chestnut.

Ralph H. Lutts is a faculty member at Goddard College, where he coordinates an M.A. concentration in interdisciplinary environmental studies. He is author of *The Nature Fakers: Wildlife, Science & Sentiment* (University Press of Virginia, 2001) and editor of *The Wild Animal Story* (Temple University Press, 1998).

William L. MacDonald is a forest pathologist and a professor of plant and soil sciences at West Virginia University. He is currently doing research with diseases that kill the chestnut blight fungus and may provide biological control. He has volunteered his services to The American Chestnut Foundation for many years, including serving as treasurer for more than eighteen years.

Bill McKibben is an internationally prominent environmentalist and author. His first book, *The End of Nature*, is considered to be the first work about climate change aimed at a general audience. He resides with his wife, writer Sue Halpern, in Ripton, Vermont, and is scholar in residence at Middlebury College.

Demarron Leif Meadows, a forester who lives in Kentucky, is an accomplished musician and writer who knows the mountains and mountain people.

Bill Owens is a man who plants trees, including chestnut. He is a musician and accomplished songwriter who was Dolly Parton's first manager and co-wrote her first hit songs.

Frederick Paillet is a retired senior research scientist with the U.S. Geological Survey who pursues many interests, including paleoecology and paleoclimate studies.

Philip A. Rutter, founding president of TACF, pursues his interests and research with nut-producing trees at Badgersett Research Corporation in Minnesota. He established an early chestnut network with his gift for inspiring others through hard work and example.

James Ulring, a resident of Iowa, has many interests, with a focus on land and trees. He has a passion for American chestnut and helped secure two of TACF's research farms.

Gregory Weaver is a radiologist who resides in Tennessee and involves his father and sons in the family's extensive chestnut orchard. He also has a passion for amphibians.

Donald C. Willeke is a founding director of TACF and serves, pro bono, as general legal counsel and secretary. He has a passion for chestnut that has been a driving force behind TACF and has also been a national leader in urban forestry.

Index

American Chestnut Seeds & Seedlings

Purchasing American chestnut seeds and seedlings from TACF is a member benefit. We offer a special introductory membership rate if you place an order when you join. All information needed is on our Web site at www.acf.org, or you can call or send for an order form at

The American Chestnut Foundation
P.O. Box 4044
Bennington, VT 05201
(802) 447-0110

Seeds and seedlings are pure American chestnut, grown from surviving trees. They are not blight-resistant, and are likely to become infected if exposed to blight. Should the trees you grow survive, you can help maintain a supply of pure American chestnuts, which may benefit TACF's research to develop blight-resistant hybrids. Since 2006 TACF has had limited quantities of highly blight-resistant backcross chestnuts for initial testing and research only (not yet available to the general public). Seeds are expected to be available for wider distribution to our members in the following 7 to 15 years.

Why should you plant these plants? There are several reasons to plant American chestnuts now:

1. To preserve native germplasm

2. To get accustomed to the care and maintenance that chestnut trees require

3. To benefit from the side effects of planting and growing chestnuts:

- Nut crops—yummy!
- Wood for making stuff
- A place where people can learn about the tree and, unfortunately, learn about how quickly the fungus can attack and kill a tree with no intervention

Proceeds from sales of seeds and seedlings to TACF members support our research to breed a blight-resistant American chestnut tree and to restore the tree to its native forests in the eastern United States.

Planting Tips

Once established, American chestnuts grow quickly and vigorously: well-grown trees can flower in eight years or less. But how does a would-be chestnut horticulturist grow chestnut seedlings well? The four steps are simple ones:

1. Choose the best possible permanent site for them.
2. Space them correctly.
3. Protect them from herbivores.
4. Nurture them.

Nothing ensures success as well as the correct planting site.

1. Avoid windy sites and frost pockets. Hillsides or well-drained bottomlands are best.
2. Chestnuts thrive in well-drained but moist soils. Avoid chronically wet sites. Sandy, gravelly, or loamy soils are best.
3. Heavy clays are less desirable but as long as they aren't wet will usually be tolerated.
4. Plant in acid soils of a pH of 4.5 to 6.5. (Chestnuts are unusual among most trees in their preference for highly acidic soils.)
5. Plant in full sun for most vigorous growth and nut production. Chestnut is shade-tolerant but attains full stature only where its canopy is exposed to full sunlight.